Barnett, Samuel Anthony

The human species

Date Due

MAY 6 '77			
NOV 7 1986			
DEC 1 4 1990			
FEB 19 92			
NOV 2 8 2003			

The Human Species

A BIOLOGY OF MAN

S. A. BARNETT
Australian National University

HARPER & ROW, PUBLISHERS
New York, Evanston, San Francisco, London

THE HUMAN SPECIES

STANDARD BOOK NUMBERS: 06-040501-5 (Paperback Edition)
06-010214-4 (Clothbound Edition)
LIBRARY OF CONGRESS CATALOG CARD NUMBER: 74-176293

CONTENTS

PART ONE: REPRODUCTION AND HEREDITY

PART THREE: LIFE AND DEATH

LIST OF PLATES

LIST OF DRAWINGS AND DIAGRAMS

PREFACE

IN DECEMBER 1968 a man circumnavigated the moon for the first time. With a group of colleagues, I listened to the broadcast of the splashdown. We were dining in a house on the edge of the Rajasthan Desert. Our host, a zoologist, is a specialist in the desert fauna, especially the species of economic importance. The explorations of the moon represent a marvellous technical achievement; but on that occasion in Jodhpur my appreciation was marred by the thought of what my host and his colleagues could do, if a small fraction of the cost of the space programme were available for their work. Their researches, however well endowed, would probably never hit the headlines of the world's press; but they would contribute directly to human welfare, and also to our knowledge of earthly biology.

I thought of this incident when a preface was required for the twenty-first birthday edition of *The Human Species*. This book had an origin in the 1930s. At that time large numbers of people, even in the richest countries, were shown, more clearly than ever before, to be grossly malnourished. This finding, and the improvements that eventually resulted, represent one of the major achievements of our century. This was also the period of the debate on racism provoked by the German fascists. The Nazis told lies about Jews, Negroes and others. In response scholars tried to communicate authentic scientific findings on human differences to the public.

Both to make full use of nutritional science and also to combat racism an informed public is essential. The same need holds for much else, from the pill to pollution. Hence in this book I try above all to give reliable information; but I also have a point of view, and I try to make this clear.

Concern with what ought to be known and could be done can lead to overstatement of the depressing features of current events. The problem is to strike a balance between present achievements, on the one hand, and dangers and depravity, on the other. This balance is certainly not achieved by the news media of the West. The newspaper editors, especially, prefer headlines of crisis, disaster or horror – sometimes real, sometimes invented – to any others. There are countries in which success is given more of its due. The Indian press presents triumphs, such as that of the green revolution, at length; it would be well if this example were imitated in some technically more advanced countries.

The scientific understanding we have of ourselves and our environment we owe to a rather small number of men and women who have made original contributions to knowledge. The application of this knowledge depends on a larger corps of people, most of whom are unknown even to their own public. To these agronomists, engineers, geneticists, physicians and others, I dedicate this book.

S.A.B.

ACKNOWLEDGEMENTS

Among the many people who have helped with advice about this book at some stage are: Professor M. Abercrombie, F.R.S., Sir Wilfrid Le Gros Clark, F.R.S., Dr A. R. Hill, Dr M. L. Johnson, Dr Charles Lack, Professor L. S. Penrose, F.R.S., Professor G. Pontecorvo, F.R.S., Dr G. I. M. Swyer, Dr J. C. Trevor and Dr J. S. Weiner. I am very grateful to all of them.

S.A.B.

Acknowledgement is due also as follows for permission to use illustrations either in the original or in a modified form:
Text-figures. Pp. 22, 23, 24, 45, 47, 48: *Reproduction and Sex* by G. I. M. Swyer (Routledge, London). Pp. 98, 99, 103, 104–5, 109: *Mankind So Far* by W. Howells (Sigma, London; Doubleday, New York). Pp. 111, 113: *Human Biology* by G. A. Harrison *et al.* (Clarendon, Oxford). Pp. 115, 117: *Penguin Science Survey B* 1963. P. 171: *Outline of Human Genetics* by L. S. Penrose (Heinemann, London). P. 180: *New Horizons in Psychology* edited by B. Foss (Penguin, Harmondsworth). P. 198: *Man the Tool-Maker* by K. P. Oakley (British Museum, London). Pp. 227, 288: *The World's Food* by M. K. Bennett (Harper, New York). P. 256: *The White Plague* by R. and J. Dubos (Gollancz, London). Pp. 264, 274: *J. Hyg. Camb.* 1945, B. Woolf and M. Waterhouse. Pp. 289, 290: *The Growth of World Population* (National Academy of Sciences, Washington). P. 295: *Population Dynamics* by R. Thomlinson (Random House, New York).

Plates. 1, 2, 3, 5, 6, 8, 10, 11, 12, 13: Pitt Rivers Museum, Oxford. S. K. Roy. 9: Alexander Lipschutz. 7, 14, 17–30: World Health Organization. 15: Aerofilms Library.

PART ONE

REPRODUCTION AND HEREDITY

Sexual reproduction entails a complex development from a minute fertilized egg. A human being spends the first forty weeks of life as a parasite within the mother. The control of reproduction is a major and revolutionary feature of modern society.

The differences between individual human beings depend partly on what they inherit from their parents, partly on differences of environment: heredity and environment interact in complex ways to produce the end-product of the adult individual. Neither heredity nor environment can properly be said to have the greater influence on variation among individuals; but we can influence environment (for instance, nutrition or working conditions), whereas heredity has generally to be accepted.

The great variety of inherited differences is maintained by the mixing of the inherited factors, or genes, in sexual reproduction. The genes are transmitted from parent to offspring in microscopic structures, the chromosomes, which are present in the sperm and egg and also in every cell of the adult body. The regular behaviour of the chromosomes determines laws of heredity which apply to man as to other organisms.

1

FROM EGG TO ADULT

O why did God,
Creator wise, that peopl'd highest Heav'n
With Spirits Masculine, create at last
This noveltie on Earth, this fair defect
Of Nature, and not fill the World at once
With Men as Angels without Feminine,
Or find some other way to generate
Mankind?

MILTON

A HUMAN being starts life as a single cell about one-tenth of a millimetre in diameter. The cell is an ovum, or egg. It is stimulated to begin development when it is penetrated by a sperm. The ovum, contributed by the mother, is vast by comparison with the sperm contributed by the father. Moreover, only part of the sperm unites with the egg: this essential part is the nucleus.

The difference in size between egg and sperm suggests that the mother must have more effect on her child's characteristics than the father. This is not the case: in general, inherited effects are equally contributed by the two parents. This is because (as we shall see later) the nuclei of the two cells play the crucial part in genetical transmission. The essential first step in development is the fusion of the sperm nucleus with that of the egg. This event sets in motion the whole complex of processes by which a speck of jelly becomes, in a few months, a being recognizably human.

SPERM AND EGG

The semen of some mammals is produced during only one part of the year, the rutting season, and only at this time does the male display interest in the female; but in an adult man the production of sperm is continuous, and if there is seasonal variation it is not of practical significance.

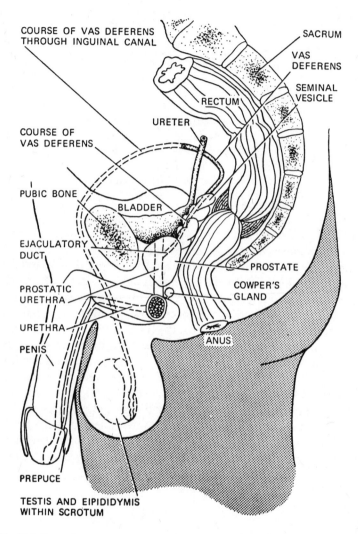

The Male Reproductive Organs. The end of the vertebral column and of the intestine are also shown

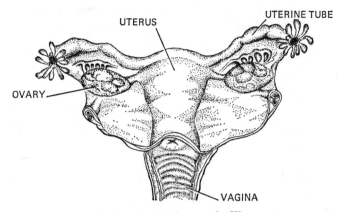

The Reproductive Organs of a Woman

A special feature of the testes of most mammals is their presence in a sac of skin, the scrotum, outside the cavity of the abdomen. In some species with a breeding season they descend into the scrotum from the abdomen only during this period. In this position the testes are kept at a temperature several degrees lower than that of the inside of the body, since they have only a thin skin, with no fatty layer, such as occurs elsewhere, between them and the air. If the temperature of the scrotum is experimentally raised the sperm produced are ineffective, and temporary sterility may result. In man

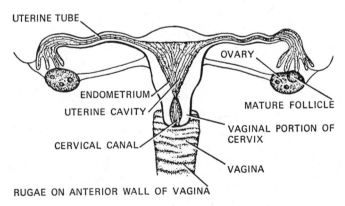

The Reproductive Organs of a Woman from behind, with the uterus, tubes and vagina drawn as if cut to show the inside

the application of hot water to the scrotum can have this effect, and it has been suggested that taking hot baths at night can reduce fertility; fortunately, there is no evidence that this possibility is actually realized to any important extent, though the continuous wearing of a suspensory belt has caused sterility.

Egg-production, however, is carried on successfully within the abdomen, in the two ovaries. Eggs are released intermittently: some mammals produce them only in spring, others at regular intervals throughout most or all of the year. In those that have litters

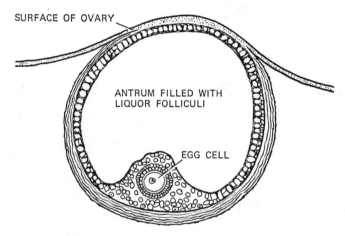

A Ripe Follicle in an Ovary, containing an egg cell

several eggs ripen at once, some in each ovary. A woman is usually fertile between the ages of fifteen and forty-five, though exceptionally the fertile period is much longer. During this period one egg develops at intervals of about twenty-eight days, in alternate ovaries, except during pregnancy (and to some extent lactation) when no eggs ripen. A few women produce more than one egg at a time and so give birth to two or more children at once. An advantage in producing only one child at each birth is that a human child has a long period of slow development, during which parental care is vitally important, and parental care would be less effective if several young were born together.

THE MENSTRUAL CYCLE

The childbearing period in a woman is marked by the 'monthly period'; at fairly regular intervals there is a loss of blood and other matter from the vagina, lasting for about four days; the commonest interval between the beginning of one period and the beginning of the next is twenty-eight days. What is the connexion between this *menstruation* and the monthly ripening of an egg-cell?

A cell destined to become an egg first becomes conspicuously different from the others by enlarging; it also comes to be surrounded by a mass of smaller cells, in the midst of which appears a space full of liquid into which the egg projects. The space, with its surrounding cells, is called a follicle, and the follicle enlarges and protrudes on the surface of the ovary. Eventually it bursts and discharges the egg, which enters the tube leading from the ovary to the uterus (or womb).

While this ripening has been going on a change has been taking place in the uterus. The inner lining grows thicker, and its blood supply is increased by enlargement of the blood vessels. By the time the egg is liberated the growth is completed and the wall of the uterus is now in a state in which it can receive a fertilized egg and allow it to develop. It remains in this state for about fourteen days and then, if the egg is not fertilized, quite suddenly it breaks down: much of the thickened tissue of the inner lining comes away in fragments and, since this tissue contains enlarged blood vessels, some blood is lost too. This is the material lost in menstruation. After menstruation the whole cycle begins again: there are a few days of inactivity and then the lining of the uterus again begins to thicken; meanwhile another egg (usually in the ovary of the opposite side) is ripening.

Menstruation therefore occurs roughly half-way between the liberation of one egg and the next. If the cycle always lasted exactly twenty-eight days, its most usual length, it would be possible to date the time of egg production with some accuracy: it would probably be fourteen days after the first day of menstruation. But many women have cycles of average length as low as twenty-five days or as high as thirty. Moreover it is not usual for a woman to have consistently the same interval from one period to the next. So although the ovary, with its regular production of eggs, has been called a time-piece, it is not a reliable one.

This is of practical importance, both to couples who wish to make sure of having a child and to those who wish to avoid one. Coitus can lead to pregnancy only if a ripe egg-cell is present. We do not know exactly how long the unfertilized human egg survives, but a rabbit's egg lasts about six hours. Rabbit sperms last about thirty hours. The figures for human eggs and sperms may well be

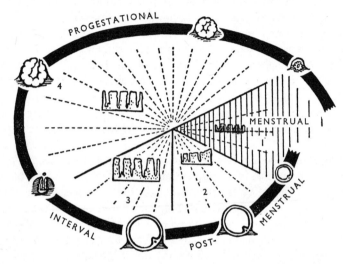

Menstrual Cycle. The stages through which the ovary and uterus go during the menstrual cycle. The outer rim shows the changes in an egg follicle in the ovary: at the beginning of stage 4 the egg is discharged, and if the egg is fertilized the uterine wall (shown within) is ready to receive it. If pregnancy does not begin, the uterine wall breaks down and produces the menstrual flow (stage 1)

different, but coitus is most likely to cause pregnancy if it takes place about half-way between menstruations. This fact is the basis of the 'safe-period' method of contraception. Some people, especially Catholics, are adjured on religious grounds not to use any of the efficient contraceptive methods, but are not prevented from avoiding coitus at the time when the woman is presumed to be most fertile. Unfortunately the 'safe' periods are by no means wholly safe, since coitus just before or just after menstruation can be followed by conception. However, if only the two periods of seven days immediately before and after menstruation are used, the chances of conception are reduced, and so this is a real, though unreliable, method of family limitation.

What is the function of the menstrual cycle? All mammals have a cycle of some sort: what use is it? A partial answer to this can be given for most mammals. Eggs are produced only intermittently, sometimes seasonally, and the uterus must be enlarged to receive them; at the time when eggs and uterus are ready the behaviour of the female changes: she is said to be *on heat*, or *in oestrus*, and she is

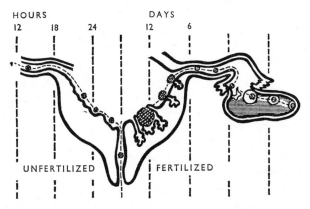

HOURS   DAYS
12   18   24   12   6

UNFERTILIZED   FERTILIZED

The Ovum and the Menstrual Cycle. On the left the egg-cell is shown in successive positions after its discharge from the ovary, when fertilization does not take place. On the right successive stages of implantation are shown, after fertilization in the tube which leads from the ovary to the uterus

willing to receive the male. At other times the male is repulsed, and coitus is impossible. It is said that the only animals in which rape, or coitus with an unwilling female, is known, are human beings and white mice. (Heat, or oestrus, in other animals does *not* correspond to menstruation in a woman, but to the time when an egg is liberated.) Evidently the oestrous cycle synchronizes the activities of the male with the internal changes in the female, but in the human species it has lost this function. Nevertheless the cycle remains, though in altered form.

While most mammals have an oestrous cycle, only a few menstruate: they are certain monkeys, the apes, and ourselves. A few others, including the bitch, have a show of blood at certain times, but this is not due to breakdown of the inner lining of the uterus.

question: what happens to the unfertilized egg - does it leave the body with the menstrual material? when does it start deteriorating?

THE SEX HORMONES

The cyclical changes so far described are structural. In laboratory animals they can be observed by dissection, and by microscopic examination of the various organs; in human beings they have to be studied for the most part in post mortem material, for instance in the organs of people killed in accidents. This sort of study does not tell us how the changes are brought about: how, for instance, the uterus becomes ready for the early embryo at just the time of the liberation of an egg from the ovary.

The menstrual cycle, and other features of our reproductive physiology, depend on the endocrine, or ductless, glands. The most familiar glands secrete a liquid with a special function and pass it out through fine tubes, or ducts; the tubes of the sweat glands end on the skin surface, those of the salivary glands (which produce spittle) in the mouth. There are many other such glands, for instance those which discharge digestive juices into the stomach and intestines. The endocrine glands, on the other hand, pass their secretions directly into the blood, and have no ducts to lead the secretion away.

One endocrine gland is the *pituitary*, a small organ lying in a pit in the bone below the brain and above the roof of the mouth. Removal of this gland, or of the anterior part of it, from a male rat stops sperm production in the testes; but extracts can be made which, injected into the animal, restore sperm production to normal. These extracts evidently contain a substance – a *hormone* – which the intact gland passes into the blood and which stimulates the sperm-producing tissues of the testes. In mammals in which sexual activity is seasonal, sperms ripen only in the breeding season; this ripening depends on the pituitary, which produces the testis-stimulating hormone only at this time. Probably, the pituitary is in turn stimulated by the brain, and in particular by the hypothalamus, which lies just above the pituitary and is connected to it. (What stimulates the hypothalamus is for most species not known; but in some it is the increase in the amount of daylight in spring.)

The pituitary has many functions besides stimulating the testes, and it produces several hormones; but here we are concerned only with the part it plays in reproduction. That of a woman has a function similar to that of a man: it stimulates the ovaries to go through their regular cycle of changes, and the menstrual cycle depends on it. The primary action of the pituitary on the ovaries is to stimulate egg-production; but it has other actions, and to understand these we must go further into the way in which the ovaries work. We have seen how the cycle of egg-production in the ovaries is paralleled by a series of changes in the uterus; if both ovaries are experimentally removed, say, from a rat, the changes in the uterus stop. Clearly the ovaries in some way control the uterine changes; how they do it has been shown by further experiment. Extracts of ovary can be made (just as with the pituitary) which induce growth of the inner wall of the uterus; this is the same as the growth which occurs in the normal cycle before an egg ripens. The ovary is, in fact, an endocrine organ as well as a source of eggs. The hormone which brings about growth of the uterus is called the *oestrogenic hormone*, or oestrogen.

But it is not the only hormone produced by the ovary. When a ripe egg is discharged it leaves, in the ovary, the tissues of the follicle in which it has developed. These tissues grow, to form what is called a *yellow body* (or, more usually, a *corpus luteum*). This structure secretes a hormone, *progesterone*, which is necessary for the further development of the lining of the uterus. The production of this too is stimulated by a pituitary hormone. After about fourteen days, if there is no pregnancy, the yellow body collapses, and so does the inner lining of the uterus. The changes of the menstrual cycle therefore depend on hormones from the pituitary and from the ovary.

If, however, the egg is fertilized, and burrows into the wall of the uterus to begin development, the yellow body remains, and grows still further. And if, early in pregnancy, the yellow body is removed, abortion takes place: the uterine wall collapses and the embryo dies. (This has been observed mainly in experimental animals which have litters: they have several yellow bodies in each ovary, one for each egg liberated; and all the yellow bodies have to be cut out for abortion to occur.)

The reproductive hormones are therefore the means by which the changes in the reproductive organs are synchronized. In particular, in a woman, they accurately dovetail events in the ovaries and the uterus. This is the practical significance of the menstrual cycle in women.

This is not, however, the only function of these hormones: they play an essential part also in the control of the *development* of the reproductive organs. Consider first the development of the male at the time of puberty, usually between the ages of thirteen and sixteen: not only does sperm production begin, but the penis enlarges; hair appears on various parts of the body; and growth of the larynx causes the voice to deepen. If the testes are removed before puberty, these changes do not take place. This operation, castration, is commonly practised on domestic animals: male cattle become bullocks, horses become geldings, and so on. It has also

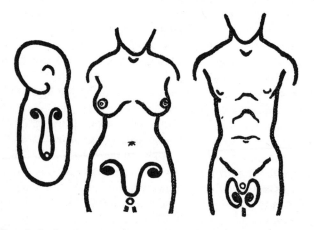

The Gonads in Development. In the embryo the gonads (ovaries or testes) develop far forward in the abdominal cavity. In both sexes they descend during development, and in the male they eventually pass through the abdominal wall into the scrotum. The differences in physique between male and female (further mentioned in chapter 9) depend on the secretion of hormones by the gonads

been extensively used in the past on human beings: eunuchs were castrated slaves who could be trusted with a man's wives; and to provide cathedral choirs with trebles and altos promising choirboys were emasculated so that their voices should remain high.

The effects of castration on general development can be prevented by the use of a hormone found in the testes: the testes, in fact, like the ovaries, are endocrine organs, and secrete a hormone which plays an essential part in sexual development. Descent of the testes themselves into the scrotum, like sperm production, depends on the pituitary; occasionally a young man has testes which fail to descend, and preparations which have an action like that of one of the pituitary hormones can sometimes remedy the defect. During the development of a woman the oestrogenic hormone of the ovary does work similar to that of the testis hormone in a man. The initial stimulus comes again from the pituitary, which, generally between the ages of twelve and fifteen, stimulates the ovaries to begin the secretion of oestrogen. This evokes a general growth of the accessory reproductive organs, the uterus, vagina and the breasts; the menstrual cycle is set going; and hair appears in the arm-pits and in the pubic region.

The reproductive hormones, then, by their many actions in the body, ensure that the organs of reproduction both *develop* and *function* in unison. Our knowledge of the way in which they work is far from complete, but the chemical nature of some of them is known, and some use has been made of them in medicine. The example of undescended testes has already been mentioned. As another we may take the common complaint of dysmenorrhoea, or pain during menstruation. The origin of this pain is far from fully known, but it is sometimes at least an accompaniment of cramps or contractions of the uterine muscles – the muscles which are largely responsible for expulsion of a child when it is born. It is sometimes possible to treat this complaint successfully with hormone preparations.

This example has been taken because it illustrates very well the state of our knowledge of reproductive physiology. The hormonal treatment of dysmenorrhoea was based on the experimental study, often on laboratory animals, of the effects on a number of organs of administering a variety of substances in various dosages. It was, in fact, an application of knowledge carefully and laboriously acquired. It contrasts with some other treatments that at one time had a good deal of notoriety but which lacked sound physiological foundation. The most publicized was the operation in which monkey testes (called 'monkey glands', evidently to preserve the proprieties) were grafted into old men to rejuvenate them. Leaving other objections on one side, this operation is unsound because such grafts cannot survive: the grafted tissues rapidly degenerate and disappear.

CONTRACEPTION AND 'THE PILL'

The most notable practical application of hormone physiology belongs entirely to the period since 1950. This is the use of substances which, when taken daily by the mouth, prevent the release of eggs by the ovaries; or, in other words, 'the pill'. At present, the most widely used oral contraceptive is similar in its action to progesterone. This hormone does more than keep the uterus in a state to support pregnancy. It also acts on the pituitary: as more progesterone passes into the blood, the pituitary secretes less of the hormones that act on the ovaries. Without pituitary hormones to provoke them, the ovaries do not produce eggs. This is what happens in a normal pregnancy: ovulation ceases throughout the nine months of gestation, and indeed does not begin again, as a rule, until some months after the child has been born.

Since pituitary hormones act on the ovaries, it may seem anomalous that the ovaries in turn should influence the pituitary. But in fact this is typical of the way in which bodily processes are regulated. Any change tends to bring about some counter-action. This is the sort of self-regulating system which we say works by negative feedback.

Regular administration of progesterone would prevent pregnancy. Unfortunately, it cannot be used for this purpose, because taken by mouth it is ineffective. This difficulty has been overcome by the manufacture, after much effort, of substances with effects similar to those of progesterone, and active when swallowed. These are the 'oral progestagens'. A woman takes her first pill five days after the beginning of a menstruation, and continues to do so for twenty days – or now, more usually, twenty-one days. She then stops for seven days, during which there is bleeding, but not as much as that of ordinary menstruation.

The first question is whether this method is reliable. As the Chinese say, it is no good going to bed to save light, if the result is twins. The pill has now been tested on a vast scale. It is indisputably the most certain contraceptive method, short of surgery to block the tubes or remove the ovaries or uterus. When, very rarely, there seems to have been a failure, enquiry usually – perhaps always – reveals that the pill has been forgotten at the crucial time. For many people in wealthy countries, the cost is small relative to the family budget. Hence the pill is becoming the method of choice for millions of women in countries, such as the United States and Britain, in which the chemical industries can meet the demand. Five million American women were, it is calculated, taking the pill by 1965.

Unlike surgical interference, oral progestagens have no permanent effect on fertility. Many women have conceived after deliberately ceasing to take them. Indeed, a kind of 'rebound' is thought to take place: pregnancy is probably more likely when a woman discontinues oral contraception. In one investigation, out of eighty-five women who stopped, sixty-nine conceived within two months. Hence, surprisingly, progestagens have been used (successfully) in the treatment of infertility. In fact, these or similar substances have been used in the treatment of various disorders since 1938.

Various minor effects are attributed to taking progestagens. Some women are said to experience nausea, like that of early pregnancy. Some report tender breasts. There may be a change in weight – in either direction. Occasionally there is loss of sexual responsiveness. Usually, if any of these does appear, it lasts for only two or three months. But there is some difficulty in deciding on the significance of these reports. Some women have breast discomfort without taking the pill (or becoming pregnant); the same applies to intermittent depression, and to headache. It is therefore desirable to find out whether women who suspect that progestagens are responsible for any of these have experienced them *before* taking the pill. Often, they have, and so their causes must lie elsewhere. However, if any disagreeable effects do persist, this method of contraception may have to be given up. Perhaps soon there will be a greater variety of progestagens and, if a woman is ill-affected by one, another will serve.

Side-effects are not all adverse. The most important is increased enjoyment of the pleasures of sex, for both parties. This no doubt results partly from freedom from the disagreeable features of using mechanical methods, such as a vaginal diaphragm or a condom; but it may also reflect the disappearance of anxiety about pregnancy. There is also a series of minor complaints, which wax and wane with the menstrual cycle, all of which can be reduced by progestagens. Pain at the time of the period (dysmenorrhoea) is the most serious; a phase of melancholy just before the period (pre-menstrual depression) is another. Even the tendency to come out in spots (acne) at this time may be diminished.

At first it seems surprising that such an apparently 'unnatural' procedure should be beneficial. This raises the question of what is 'natural'. There is a sense in which 'natural' means 'primitive'. Until recently, virtually all healthy women, from the age of about fifteen until near the menopause after the age of forty, were pregnant or nursing a baby. Hence, the near-barren condition of many women of these ages in advanced countries is quite abnormal, that is, unusual. They are certainly not in the condition to which the bodies of their ancestors were adapted during millions of years of natural selection. This by no means signifies that they *ought* to return to bearing from twelve to twenty children (and losing most of them); but it does suggest that what is now accepted as natural, namely, bearing only two or three children in a lifetime, is biologically just as extraordinary as taking the pill. Moreover, progestagens induce a state akin to that of pregnancy and lactation, in which ovaries do not produce eggs.

A last and crucial question is, then, whether progestagens are indeed harmless. If several million women are taking the pill, some will inevitably become severely ill just as some will be involved in motor accidents. Unfortunately, a few examples of, say, cancer or thrombosis among such women may lead to scares in the newspapers and even in the medical press. Even a single case of thrombosis can be used as an excuse for alarming headlines. The fact that some stories about the pill are irrational and irresponsible does not, of course, prove that it is safe. The stories merely make it more difficult for the public to discover the true facts.

The only way to deal with this sort of question rationally is to investigate not single individuals but large numbers. The method is to record, over several years, the health of many thousands of women who take the pill, and compare them with thousands of similar women who do not. If one group then has a much higher percentage of some disease, something useful has been learnt. When enquiries have been made on these lines, no clear evidence has emerged that progestagens increase the danger of disease. The only ill-effect that seemed at all probable, on the evidence published up to the end of 1966, was on milk-production by women feeding a baby. Some women have experienced a decrease in the flow of milk, evidently owing to their use of progestagens.

The most recent important studies have been on thrombo-embolism. In advanced countries this is the commonest cause of death among women of child-bearing age (fifteen to forty-five). It is, however, still not a common disease, among all those that afflict us: in Britain just over two in every thousand women develop some form of thrombo-embolism; and only a minority of them dies. The trouble arises from the formation of a blood clot, usually in a vein: the clot may be carried to the heart, and thence into a lung artery. This can obstruct the blood flow to the lung, with consequent death of the lung (or part of a lung) from which the blood supply has been cut off. This condition is commoner among pregnant women than those not pregnant – though among them it is still rare. Most investigations have failed to find any effects of progestagens; but some have brought evidence that they slightly raise the chances of thrombo-embolism, though still not to the extent that pregnancy does. The increased chance of death may be about three in 100,000.

There is then still much to be learnt. There has not yet been time to find out the effects of taking progestagens regularly for many years. Hence, although there have been authoritative medical pronouncements in support of this method, they are always accompanied by some cautious qualification. Each individual faced with this problem has still to make up her own mind on what to do. In doing so, it is essential to ignore anything written in the popular press.

There are (apart from surgery) two kinds of method alternative to the pill, both of which have been practised for much longer. One is coitus interruptus, in which the semen is not discharged until the penis is withdrawn. This much-used method is not only unsafe but also unsatisfying; and it is liable to induce anxiety in both parties. The other involves some mechanical obstruction. A man achieves this by wearing a sheath. This is the most reliable method after the pill, but disagreeable to use. Also disagreeable for a woman is the method of the vaginal or cervical cap, in which, before coitus, a hemisphere of rubber, with a stiffened rim, is placed in the vagina to prevent entry of semen into the uterus. The cap is left in place for eight to twelve hours. Subsidiary methods include the use of a foam containing a sperm-killing substance; this too has to be inserted in the vagina shortly before coitus.

The way in which these devices work is obvious. Another mechanical method, ancient but recently revived, certainly works, but how is not known. This is the 'intra-uterine contraceptive device', or IUCD. A plastic object, usually loop-shaped, chosen to be of suitable size, is inserted, not in the vagina, but in the uterus itself, and left there indefinitely. IUCDs have to be fitted by a physician or other trained person. They are coming into use in advanced countries, especially for women who cannot afford oral contraceptives or who would be liable to forget to take them; but their major

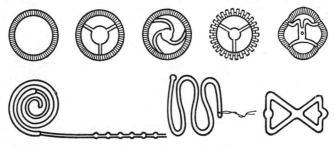

Intra-uterine Contraceptive Devices

use is perhaps destined to be in poor countries where no other effective method will be practicable for many decades. They do not give total protection: the best reduce the annual rate of pregnancy to about two women in every hundred. Further, they are liable to be passed out of the uterus, and the woman may not know that this has happened. In view of their possible world-wide use, we need much more information about them.

SEXUAL BEHAVIOUR

The need for more facts has recently become obvious also for sexual *behaviour*. Most people know what they themselves, and perhaps a few friends, do; many assume that theirs is the 'normal' and 'natural' way of behaving, and that any other sorts of behaviour should be despised or condemned. Others, in ignorance of what their fellows do, believe themselves abnormal, sometimes because they have been taught to look on sexual functions as disgusting or frightening.

The various possible attitudes are all products of the particular teachings of some section of their own society. Studies of other societies, and of the different strata within a society, have revealed an immense variety in accepted codes and practices. In many communities sexual relationships between young children are taken for granted; in others, extra-marital relationships are part of the conventional pattern of behaviour; in yet others, open homosexual behaviour has been usual. These facts exemplify the general plasticity of human behaviour which we discuss further in chapter 5.

Recently, scientific scrutiny has been applied, not only to groups remote from Western civilization, but to the populations of countries such as Britain and the United States. Research on the sexual behaviour of people in advanced societies has generally been inspired by the known frequency of sexual difficulties within marriage – often, it is believed, due to ignorance – and by the need for a sound basis for advice to the married or to the young.

Small children are capable of sexual behaviour. All go through an early phase of touching and exploring their genitals and should be allowed to do so. It is doubtful whether there is any period in childhood in which sexual responsiveness is wholly absent, but it is, of course, at puberty, when a new hormonal balance develops, that the need for sexual activity becomes strong.

In the male such activity reaches its maximum very early, around the ages sixteen to twenty; thereafter it declines, at first very gradually and always slowly, without any sudden change in later life. There is great variety of habits among healthy men. Some regularly enjoy coitus several times a day, others only once a week or less often. The form of sexual activity varies a great deal between individuals: masturbation, nocturnal emissions (in which ejaculation takes place during sleep), and homosexual relationships are all common, as well as the biologically 'normal' heterosexual coitus. Masturbation is, indeed, almost universal. Accepted custom in our society, to say nothing of the law, is ill-adapted to our needs or our actual behaviour. No physiological harm need arise from any of these types of sexual behaviour; harm can, and often does, arise if feelings of shame or guilt are engendered in children or adolescents. One obvious conclusion which might be drawn is the desirability of early marriage.

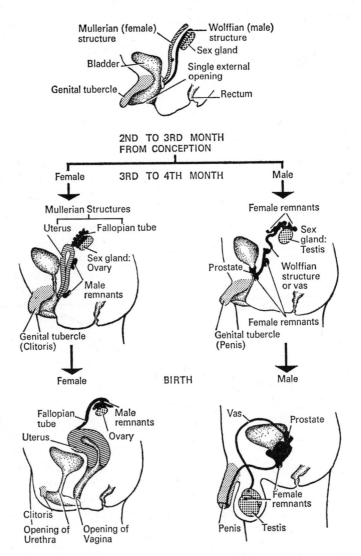

Differentiation of the Reproductive Organs. At two months after the beginning of development, the sexes are alike

The female pattern is different. Young girls, like boys, are capable of erotic arousal at an early age, but far fewer have much sexual experience before maturity. Sexual activity includes masturbation and homosexual relationships; in women, unlike men, the latter do not come under the condemnation of the law in Western countries. Early sexual experience probably helps to ensure the attainment of sexual satisfaction in marriage. These statements are based on the reports made by large numbers of people about their own experiences. In modern Western countries, especially among the middle class, the sexuality of children and youths has often been refused acknowledgement; when it has emerged, it has been punished. This has led to much misery. In most communities sexual maturity at around fifteen is, and has been, taken for granted. Today, in the 1970s, it is again coming to be almost universally accepted.

The two sexes are alike in the early development of sexual capacity, but women do not reach their highest level of sexual activity until much later than men – commonly, it seems, in the thirties; later in life they are potentially more active than men. On the other hand, some women, but few men, seem able to live contentedly for long periods with little or no sexual outlet. Another difference is that most men are easily stimulated by sexual associations – hence the pin-up girl and the leg show; while women, on the whole, tend to be less aroused by associations, and more by direct contact. This difference is often not known to married couples, and may lead to mutual misunderstanding.

It is commonly said that, among the differences between the sexes, is a profound contrast in the nature of the orgasm attained at the climax of coitus. In a man orgasm is marked by the ejaculation of semen, and this, of course, has no counterpart in a woman. However, in other respects orgasm in the two sexes is less unlike than has been thought. In both there are rhythmic movements, accompanied by raised pulse and respiratory rates and blood pressure; and in both there is tumescence, or swelling of certain tissues due to increase in the blood supply; in a man the principal tissues concerned are those of the penis, in which the swelling causes erection; in a woman the clitoris (which is the small analogue of the penis) and the labia minora similarly swell; in both, the breast nipples and the internal tissues of the nose also become engorged. After orgasm, there is a rapid decline in tumescence, and a general and pleasurable relaxation throughout the body. Apart from ejaculation, the main difference is that a man rarely enters coitus without reaching orgasm, while women often do so. There is great variation in the ability of women to attain a climax; the explanation of this is not clear, but the inhibition of sexual responses in childhood no doubt plays a part.

FERTILIZATION

After surveying the organs of reproduction and their mode of functioning, we come to the *raison d'être* of the whole complex system. We are all forty weeks older than we acknowledge, and it is the events of this neglected period that now concern us.

The egg, on discharge from the ovary, enters the mouth of the tube which leads to the uterus. Fertilization usually takes place in the tube: sperms, discharged into the vagina, make their way into the uterus and so into the tubes, and if an egg has recently ripened one of the sperms fertilizes it. Sometimes a fertilized egg remains in the tube instead of moving down into the uterus. After a few weeks of development, internal bleeding results from rupture of the tube, and an operation becomes necessary. Fortunately this happens only in about one in three hundred pregnancies.

Although only one sperm fertilizes each egg, a vast number are present in each ejaculation. About a teaspoonful of semen is discharged in each coitus; this contains perhaps 240m.* sperms. The presence of many sperms is evidently needed to ensure fertilization, and they probably help to create the necessary chemical conditions in vagina, uterus, and tubes. When infertility in a married couple is investigated the husband's emissions are often found to contain a much smaller number of active sperms than the normal; and, although many millions of sperms are present, they are evidently not enough for normal fertility.

The study of the chemistry of seminal fluid, and of the numbers and behaviour of sperms, has been stimulated by the use of *artificial insemination* in stockbreeding. By collecting the semen of a selected male a breeder can use the male to serve many more females than would otherwise be possible, and so can more rapidly improve the genetical qualities of his herd. In man artificial insemination is now being used for a different purpose. It is sometimes impossible for a

---

* Throughout the book 'm.' stands for 'million'.

married couple to have children, even though the woman is normal. If the difficulty is due to the husband's impotence, but his semen is normal, the semen can be collected artificially and injected into the wife's vagina. When the defect is in the husband's semen a physician may use that of an anonymous donor.

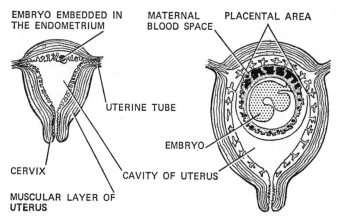

The Uterus in Early Pregnancy. On the left the embryo has just become implanted. On the right the placenta has become distinct

The controversy over this practice illustrates how social problems spring from human applications of biology. Artificial insemination has been attacked on religious and moral grounds, and complaints have been made that it raises grave legal difficulties. The use of a donor's semen has been called adultery, and is further condemned (absurdly) because producing donor semen involves masturbation; and a child of artificial insemination has been said to be legally 'illegitimate', which leads to various difficulties, especially over the inheritance of property. Despite these complaints, which perhaps conceal an irrational repugnance, artificial insemination, like modern contraception, is yet another example of technical advance giving us further control over nature: if it is applied with the consent of both man and wife it can give, and has given, the greatest satisfaction to both; and, although it does raise moral and legal problems, they can be solved. The religious objections are in much the same terms as those in which the churches opposed the use of anaesthesia in childbirth a century ago.

The history of other advances in human biology and medicine suggests that artificial insemination will continue to cause controversy, but that it will nevertheless be used, and that its use will increase.

OURSELVES UNBORN

The timetable of pregnancy, and of the growth of the unborn child, is conveniently reckoned not from fertilization but from the beginning of the last menstrual period. On this scheme the most probable time of fertilization is the end of the second week. The fertilized egg then spends about a week travelling down the tube and floating in the uterus. During this time development begins: the egg-cell divides, and successive cell-divisions give rise to a ball of cells. The earliest stages of human development are not known, owing to the difficulty of getting material, but those of other mammals, including one species of monkey, have been fully studied. The embryo becomes implanted in the inner wall of the uterus (already, as we have seen, prepared to receive it) after several divisions of the cells have taken place. Soon after implantation it becomes completely embedded in the uterine tissues. The presence of the embryo prevents menstruation when it is next due, and this is usually the first indication to a woman that she is pregnant. Rarely, a loss of blood resembling that of menstruation occurs, sometimes more than once, at the times when the monthly period would have been expected.

When implantation has taken place the uterus continues to grow and to increase its blood supply. On the average the uterus increases in weight thirty times during a first pregnancy.

During its early weeks the embryo undergoes rapid development and a number of striking anatomical changes, of which some are listed opposite. In this early phase the embryo's hold on life is rather precarious, and spontaneous abortion is common: the embryo dies, becomes detached from the uterus and passes out of the vagina, probably with blood and other debris. Very early unplanned abortion (in the first six weeks or so) is often painless and harmless, and probably occurs in at least one out of five pregnancies; the proportion has been estimated to be even as high as one in three. Other mammals, such as the rabbit and the sow, also suffer a similar proportion

WEEK *after* *last* *men-* *struation*	TIMETABLE OF DEVELOPMENT
2 (end)	Fertilization
3	Egg travels down tube into uterus; begins to divide
4	Implantation in wall of uterus
5	Early stages of skeleton and nervous system
6	Head, heart and tail visible; gill pouch rudiments present; rudiments of arms and legs. Length about 6 mm ($\frac{1}{4}$ in.)
7	Chest and abdomen formed; fingers and toes appear; eyes developing. About 12 mm ($\frac{1}{2}$ in.)
8	Face, features and external ears developing; gill rudiments disappearing. About 21 mm ($\frac{7}{8}$ in.), weight 1 g ($\frac{1}{28}$ oz.)
9	Face completely developed; now resembles a human child. Length 30 mm (1·2 in.), weight 2 g ($\frac{1}{14}$ oz.). From now on embryo usually called a *foetus*
14	Limbs, including fingers and toes and nails, fully formed; external genital organs developed. Sex can be determined by trained person without microscopic examination. 77 mm (3 in.), 30 g (1 oz.)
18	Movements (quickening) begin; heart can be heard; hair all over body; eyebrows and eyelashes. 190 mm ($8\frac{1}{2}$ in.), 180 g ($6\frac{1}{2}$ oz.)
23	Head hair appears. 300 mm (12 in.), 450 g (16 oz.)
27	Eyes open. 350 mm (14 in.), 875 g (31 oz.)
32	400 mm (16 in.), 1425 g (3 lb. 2 oz.). If born now can survive, given special care
36	450 mm (18 in.), 2375 g (5 lb. 4 oz.). Better chance of survival now, in eighth month, than in seventh (contrary to commonly held belief)
40	Full term. Skin covered with cheese-like material. Head hair typically 25 mm long; may be other hair on shoulders, but soon disappears. Head still very large relative to body. 500 mm (20 in.), 3250 g (7 lb. 4 oz.) *All measurements are averages, and there are many wide departures from them, especially in the later months*

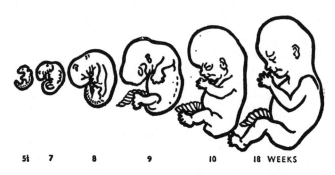

5½   7   8   9   10   18   WEEKS

Human Embryos. The umbilical cord is shown in the three largest

of early harmless abortions. In the human species the majority occur in the period from the eighth to the twelfth week. Perhaps many of the aborted embryos are defective, and could never have become normal individuals. If so, their early elimination can be regarded as a natural economy, but the mother may feel very ill for some time after it has happened.

RECAPITULATION OF ANCESTRAL CHARACTERS

A feature of early development, much discussed but not always well understood, is the so-called recapitulation of ancestral stages. It is sometimes thought that we go through a fish stage representing the fish stage of our evolution, and it is even said that we 'climb our family tree' during our embryonic existence. Neither of these statements is quite true.

About 300m. years ago our ancestors were certainly some kind of primitive fish, and on land the stages in our ancestry included a cold-blooded reptilian phase and, later, warm-blooded primitive mammals with hair instead of scales and young which were born in an active state instead of hatched from eggs.

What traces of this evolutionary history can we find in individual development? The most obvious are found about four weeks after fertilization (week six in the table on page 43). Externally the embryo seems to have rudimentary gills (though they never fully develop); it has a tail, of considerable length relative to the whole body; and in general it resembles, not a fish, but a *fish embryo*.

Internally the resemblance is carried further: the arrangement of the blood vessels is fish-like, and the principal muscles of the body are divided into segments which in a fish become those we can easily see when we eat, say, cod or salmon.

All these structures undergo a rapid and complex transformation, and within a few weeks leave little obvious trace. This transformation is, on the whole, directly into the structural arrangement typical of the human being: it is not possible to discern a phase in embryonic development corresponding to the reptilian stage in evolution. Some traces of our pre-human ancestry may be found at every stage in development, including the adult: there are, for instance, the much commented-on muscles which a few gifted people can use

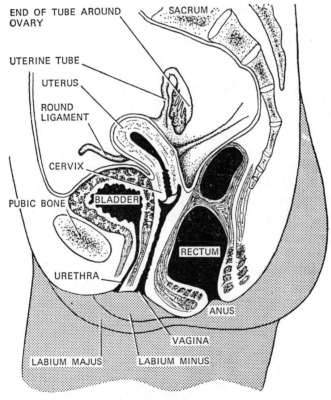

The Pelvic Organs of a Woman

to waggle their ears, but which in most of us are ineffective; most mammals can move their ears, and in us these muscles are a vestige reminding us of a mobile-eared ancestry.

We can see, then, traces of our evolutionary history in our development, but the study of embryology does not save us the trouble of using other methods to work out how we evolved. There are further examples of the ways in which development fails to reflect evolution. Take, for example, the shape of the face. Most mammals have a prominent snout, but a man's face is flat. If there were a straightforward recapitulation of ancestral characters, the human embryo should develop a snout and then lose it. In fact, no snout ever appears in human development. In mammals which have snouts, the forward growth of the face occurs late: all early mammalian embryos are flat-faced. Hence the shape of the face in man is an embryonic character retained in the adult. This is the opposite of what would be expected if the simple idea of recapitulation were true. Even more obvious is the *placenta*, or after-birth, the structure which enables us to draw nourishment from the maternal blood stream. This large organ develops partly from embryonic tissues, but it does not represent any stage in our evolutionary history. It is an embryonic modification characteristic of mammals.

To sum up, we can find indications of our ancestry at every stage of our development, including the adult, but there is no simple recapitulation. It is not only the adult structure that undergoes evolutionary change: the whole of our life-history has been subject to change; at some stages, however, the difference from the ancestral arrangement is rather less than at others.

PREGNANCY AND THE PLACENTA

The most obvious of the evolutionary changes undergone by mammalian embryos are those connected with development in the mother's uterus, instead of outside the body. The egg of a reptile, like that of a bird, has a large yolk which provides the food on which the embryo lives until it hatches. A mammal has no yolk at all: all food is supplied by the mother, and the structure of the embryo is adapted to this parasitic life. At implantation the egg, as we have seen, is already divided into a number of cells. Not all these cells are destined to form the child: some of them form *extra-embryonic* tissues – outside the embryo. The embryo is surrounded by these tissues and, once implantation is complete, the tissues in turn are surrounded by those of the uterine wall.

The extra-embryonic tissues thrust minute, finger-like processes into the uterine wall, and so greatly increase the area over which food material can diffuse into the embryo. This is the beginning of the formation of the placenta. It is constituted partly by embryonic and partly by maternal tissues, and is eventually shed as the *after-birth* soon after the child is born. The placenta grows rapidly in the

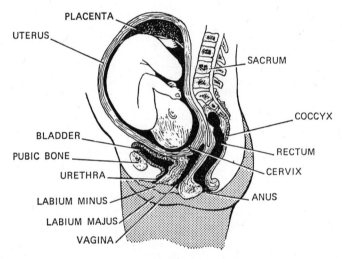

The Pelvis of a Woman with a Foetus just before Birth

early stages, and by full term it weighs about 450 g (1 lb.). After the first few weeks it becomes localized on one side of the embryo, and connected to the embryo only by the umbilical cord. The cord contains blood vessels which carry blood in both directions between the placenta and the child, and it has to be cut when the child is born. The navel is the scar marking the junction of the cord with the belly.

The blood and blood vessels in the umbilical cord are all part of the embryonic system: the mother's blood does not mingle with that of the child, though in the placenta they are separated only by exceedingly fine membranes. Across these membranes pass the substances exchanged: oxygen and food from mother to child, carbon dioxide and other waste products in the opposite direction.

The demands of the embryo for certain foodstuffs put a strain on the mother which may injure her if she is inadequately fed or otherwise in poor health. It is not the general demand for food that is important: it is a fallacy that a pregnant woman needs a great deal of extra food. The average net gain in weight during a first pregnancy is about 11 kg (23 lb.), and during later pregnancies about 9·5 kg. The child accounts for about one-third of the gain; the rest is due to

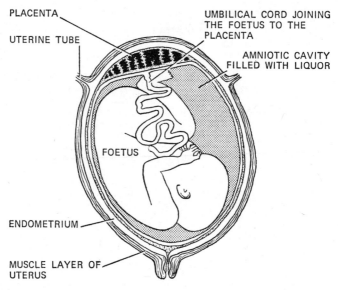

A Late Foetus with the Placenta in the Much-enlarged Uterus

the enlarged uterus, increase in body fat, the placenta, and the 'bag of waters' which surrounds the embryo and protects it from injury. The whole of the gain in weight takes place after the sixteenth week; before then there may even be a loss. But a gain of 11 kg in thirty-four weeks is not very much, and the extra daily intake of food required is small.

In Western countries, where there is little gross under-nutrition or malnutrition, the nutritional difficulties of pregnancy are due to special shortages. The old maxim 'a tooth for every child' reflects the calcium deficiency that is common in mothers. A pregnant woman who gets too little calcium in her food transfers calcium from her bones and teeth to the embryo; as a result, her skeleton and teeth may be weakened; the effect on the child is thus reduced. Similarly, according to one investigation, anaemia due to iron shortage occurs in at least one American woman in three in the last three months of pregnancy, owing to the demands of the embryo for iron. Deficiency of calcium, iron, and other dietary essentials, notably vitamins, can be avoided by giving pregnant women a good diet, as we shall see in chapter 12.

Some other problems of pregnancy are less easily solved. Predicting its duration is one. The birth of a child is predicted on the assumption that it will take place 280 days, or forty weeks, after the first day of the last menstruation. This is not far from the mean duration of pregnancy, found from studies of large numbers of normal births; but, as most parents know, there are many wide departures from it. In one study of 537 white American women, all of whom bore living children, the results were as follows:

	per cent
before 266th day	12·7
2nd week before (days 266–272)	12·3
1st week before (days 273–279)	22·0
on 280th day	3·7
1st week after (days 281–287)	24·2
2nd week after (days 288–294)	15·6
after 294th day	9·4

If the percentage for each day is taken it is found to be highest for the 280th day, and to fall away slowly both before and after; hence 280 days is the mode as well as the mean length of pregnancy; but it will be seen how impossible it is to predict accurately in any one case.

It is easy to make statistical studies such as the above, given secretarial help and a punched-card system; but other problems of pregnancy require more elaborate study. The most obvious are the so-called *toxaemias* of pregnancy – an expression based on an old belief that they are due to 'poisons in the blood'. The toxaemia of early pregnancy is pernicious vomiting, an exaggeration of the common morning sickness. Some nausea or vomiting is exceedingly common early in pregnancy: in North America it is said to be severe in about one-third of all cases and mild in a third; the rest are entirely free. When mild, it disappears about the twelfth week, but the most severe cases, which are rare, require special treatment. The toxaemias of late pregnancy are all accompanied by high blood pressure, and usually by a disturbance of the chemistry of the body which causes an excessive retention of water. In an extreme case, now very rare when there is good ante-natal care, convulsions develop.

General ante-natal care is the most effective counter to these dangers, and where it is practised it has already greatly reduced the incidence of serious cases. But the causes of the toxaemias of pregnancy are still unknown, and since about one pregnancy in fifteen, even in an advanced country such as the United States, is complicated by one of them, they would repay extensive research.

Much the same applies to childbirth itself, the aspect of pregnancy which probably looms largest in most minds. The pangs of childbirth seem to have been taken for granted throughout history, and when, a century ago, anaesthesia was invented, its use in childbirth was condemned as 'unnatural' and 'immoral'. But the most obvious objection to anaesthesia (which causes unconsciousness) is that it is not safe; it also deprives the mother of the unique pleasure felt on holding her child immediately after delivery. Today the emphasis is rather on analgesia, which is the relief of pain without loss of consciousness. Quite recently new and better analgesics have been found, and they are coming to be widely applied. It is, however, said that pain can be largely prevented without the use of drugs, by instruction of the mother in the nature of pregnancy and in what is required of her during the actual birth. This instruction includes lessons in the technique of muscular relaxation – a means of reducing harmful tension, due to fear. Fear of pregnancy, largely due to ignorance, is common, and is considered to contribute a great deal to the discomfort of childbirth. Once again, therefore, the importance of ante-natal care and instruction is evident.

Another probable source of difficulty in labour, among women who live a sedentary, urban existence, is lack of muscle power. The habit of taking plenty of regular exercise, from childhood onwards, can help to prevent this.

More research, and wider application of what is known, by means of improved health services, are needed along all these lines: improvement of ante-natal care, psychological preparation of the mother, and analgesia. Meanwhile important facts have been brought out by an entirely different approach. In a primitive community nearly all women begin to bear children soon after puberty: the average age of the mother at the first birth is perhaps seventeen. In advanced communities, especially today, the age is sometimes much greater. Maternal and infant mortality both tend to rise in proportion to the age of the mother, as does the incidence of abnormal babies; probably, the best age for having a first child is twenty-two. Subsequent children should be born at intervals of about twenty-four months.

It is important to be clear on exactly what this signifies. It is not that a married couple should despair of bringing up a family if the woman has, say, reached her thirties without having a child. Antenatal and obstetric care has advanced so far that, even when the mother is over forty, the successful birth of a first child is no longer a matter for astonishment. Certainly, if early child-bearing is practicable, it should be encouraged, but the figures just quoted are important for society as whole, rather than for the individual. The reasons for late marriage and delayed maternity are mostly economic. (We have already seen that there are good psychological grounds for supporting early marriages.) If social organization obliges women to delay child-bearing to the detriment of their health and that of their children, the obvious conclusion is that the social organization should be changed.

GROWTH

A healthy child usually weighs 3·4 kg (between seven and eight pounds) at birth, and doubles this weight in twenty weeks or less. This growth rate, though lower than that before birth, is not maintained. A child aged twelve months, and about 10 kg in weight, takes about another four years to double that weight. (As always, there is much variation around these averages.) The main features of growth from birth to puberty are first that it is steady, and second that the rate declines. Regular, careful measurement of weight or height, of the same children as they grow up, show that there are, with one exception, no sharp fluctuations in growth at any age (in the absence of severe illness). For the greatest accuracy, the weighing or measuring should be done at the same time of day, by the same person and with the same equipment. Any parent with a reliable balance or scale can attempt this.

While total growth is steady, the growth rates of parts of the body are not all the same. Some differences are obvious. A newborn child's head is enormous, relative to the rest of it, compared with that of an adult. The brain and head have reached about eighty per cent of their adult size by the age of four, when the whole body is less than forty per cent of its final weight. At the other extreme, the organs of reproduction are still around only ten per cent of their final weight just before puberty at, say, twelve years.

The strangest pattern of growth is that of lymphoid tissues: these include the 'glands' in armpit and groin, which palpably swell when there is local infection, and the thymus which lies in front of the heart. These tissues grow rapidly from birth to puberty; at about twelve years they are nearly twice their adult size, but thereafter they decline. Among the lymphoid structures are the tonsils, visibly much larger in the throat of a young child than that of an adult, and the neighbouring adenoids. Minor trouble from these structures, when they are excessively large but otherwise normal, often clears up spontaneously in adolescence, because the tissues shrink.

The exception to the steady but declining growth rate is at adolescence, when there is a sudden spurt of growth. A girl usually shoots up when she is between ten and a half and thirteen, a boy about two years later. At the peak, a boy grows at the rate of about 10 cm (four inches) a year, a girl rather less; this is also the growth rate of a two-year-old.

Not only are the sexes quite out of step at this time, but there is much individual variation. As J. M. Tanner has remarked, 'The statement that a boy is fourteen is in most contexts hopelessly vague.' From a group of that age in years one may pick some who are still children, others who are grown men already with adult sexual needs and experience. The same applies to girls. For research it is possible to use developmental age, calculated from the growth of the skeleton – which parallels fairly well the growth of other organs and of the intellect and emotions. This requires an X-ray of the wrist joint. But we are a long way from the day when a parent,

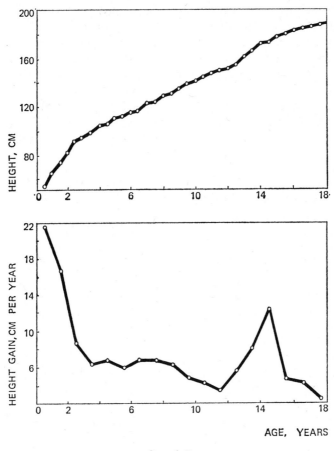

Growth Rate

asked the age of a child, replies proudly that his skeletal age is 11·5, although he was born only 10·7 years ago.

These facts have disconcerting implications for policy in the schools. (Still more disconcerting is the *earlier* age of maturity of mid-century children; a class of young women requires different management from that of a giggle of schoolgirls.) A fixed school leaving age fails to match the variety we find among school children. A rigid system favours early developers. Boys, especially, are handicapped if they mature late.

In a well-fed, healthy population, individual differences in maturity have been smoothed out by the age of eighteen. All are now adult men and women, capable of becoming parents and potentially near their peak of physical achievement; they have also reached their maximum 'mental' age, as measured by 'intelligence tests'. Though they have, no doubt, much to learn (and plenty of capacity to learn more, given the opportunity), the man or woman of eighteen should be ready to face the challenge of twentieth-century life, including the problems discussed in the rest of this book.

NATURE AND NURTURE

*I can trace my ancestry back to a protoplasmic primordial atomic globule.
Consequently, my family pride is something inconceivable. I can't help it.*

W. S. GILBERT

IT IS sometimes said by Europeans that all Chinese look alike. Doubtless few take this statement seriously; certainly, it is very far from the truth. In every human group individuals differ from each other both physically and in behaviour. There are two sources of this variation: in the first place individuals differ in what has been handed on to them from their parents, that is, in their *heredity*; second, the influences that act on the individual from outside, and make up his *environment*, vary greatly. The study of variation and heredity, is *genetics*.

If a child has insufficient iodine in his food he fails to grow normally and becomes a dwarf, of the type known as a cretin. This was formerly common in Switzerland. It is an example of environment influencing growth: a simple alteration in the environment, the addition of iodine to table salt, prevents the effect. But similar dwarfs occasionally appear in communities in which there is no lack of iodine: no known alteration in the amount of iodine in the food, or in any other environmental agency, can then affect their occurrence. In this case the condition is said to be due to heredity. These two examples show that variation in stature can be affected by both 'nurture' and 'nature'.

The word 'heredity' is used here in a slightly unfamiliar way. If a tall father has a tall son, it is sometimes said that the son inherits his tallness from his father. But the case of the dwarfism due to heredity is different, since the parents of the dwarf are themselves normal: there is no question of the dwarfism being inherited from one of the parents in the usual sense. This sort of thing is quite familiar from our experience of normal features. Two brown-eyed parents may have a blue-eyed child: when this happens the parents may say the child 'inherits his eyes from his grandfather', or something of that sort.

But there is no direct handing on of *characteristics* from generation to generation, since all are developed anew in each individual. If one inherits a house, the house itself is actually handed over. We may recall the Wodehouse young man who, asked if he believed in

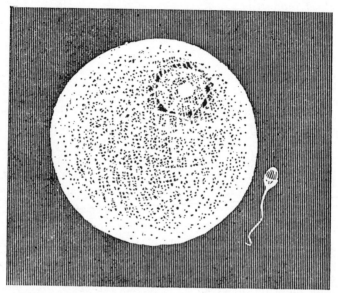

Egg and Sperm. Human egg-cell, with sperm-cell drawn to scale. The egg is about 0·13 mm in diameter ($\frac{1}{250}$ in.); the sperm is about 0·055 mm in length

heredity, replied, 'Of course, that's how I got my money.' This, legal inheritance, must be distinguished from biological inheritance. The material passed to us from our parents, and responsible for biological inheritance, is microscopic: it is contained in the egg and sperm.

THE CHROMOSOMES AND HEREDITY

Each egg and sperm has a complete set of the structures called chromosomes, and the chromosomes carry the genetical factors, or *genes*. This confers an equal role in heredity on the two kinds of cell. To appreciate the role of chromosomes we must understand something of the microscopic structure of the body tissues. If small fragments, or very thin slices, of animal or plant tissues are examined under a microscope, they are seen to be divided into exceedingly small compartments, the cells. Tissues grow by increase in the size of the cells, followed by division of each cell into two. Cells vary a great deal in shape and function, but nearly all have a nucleus. Ordinarily a nucleus is a nearly spherical object without any obvious internal structure, but when a cell divides most of the nuclear material condenses, to form objects resembling rods or threads. These are *chromosomes*, and their number varies with the species of animal or plant; man has forty-six, or twenty-three pairs. Each chromosome can be seen, soon after it appears, to be already split along its length; later, the halves of each chromosome separate, and two complete sets, each of forty-six chromosomes, are formed. The cell then divides into two, and each newly-formed cell takes one set. However many times cell division takes place, each cell has a nucleus made up of the full complement of twenty-three pairs of chromosomes. This process is illustrated on page 58.

An important exception is provided by the germ cells – the egg-cells of the female and the sperm-cells of the male. When the germ cells are produced, in the ovaries and testes respectively, the chromosomes behave differently: each egg or sperm receives only twenty-three chromosomes, or one of each pair present in an ordinary cell, as shown on page 59. When an egg is fertilized by a sperm the two half-sets of chromosomes come together; hence in the fertilized egg the full number of 46 is restored.

This is the means by which each parent contributes equally, on the average, to a child's constitution. The expression 'on the average' has to be put in, because, if a single person is studied, it often seems that resemblance to one parent is much more marked than to the other. This is not because there has been any abnormality in the chromosome mechanism: it may be because some of the genes of one parent mask the effects of the corresponding ones on the other set of chromosomes.

The chromosome mechanism ensures that the genetical factors are distributed throughout the body. The fertilized egg is itself a cell, and all the cells are derived from it by a series of repeated divisions. And we have already seen that, after division, each cell has a full complement of chromosomes.

If, then, a child has hair similar to that of its parents, it is not because the hair is handed on in any material sense, like a wig, but because the parents' chromosomes, carrying genetical factors which bring about the development of that particular kind of hair, are passed on, and are present in the cells of the skin from which the hair grows. (The example of hair is taken because hair characters are relatively little affected by environment. In general, of course, part of our resemblance to our parents is due to sharing a common

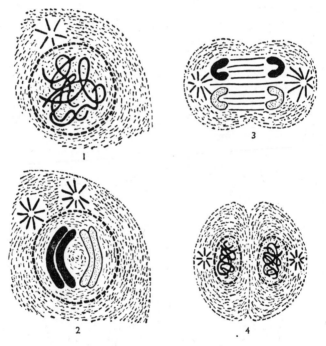

Division of the Nucleus of an Egg-cell (Mitosis). The nucleus, when not dividing, appears as a structureless, roughly spherical object. When division begins the chromosomes become visible as double threads; the members of each pair separate, and two daughter-nuclei are formed, each with the same number of chromosomes as the parent nucleus. The whole cell then divides, and each daughter cell gets one nucleus. This happens throughout the body in the cells of growing tissues. The number of chromosomes is here shown as only one pair, for simplicity: man has twenty-three pairs. The star-like structures are called asters; they take part in the orderly separation of the chromosomes

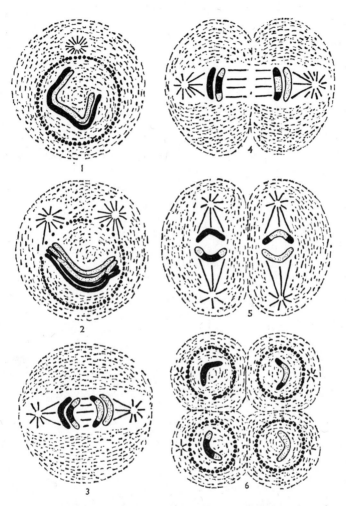

Chromosomes of Egg or Sperm. When egg and sperm-cells (gametes) are formed, in the ovaries and testes respectively, a special type of nuclear division (meiosis) takes place: the result is that, in man, the nucleus of an egg or sperm has only twenty-three chromosomes, instead of twenty-three pairs. At fertilization the full number of forty-six is restored. Here only one pair is drawn, and a single parent cell is shown giving rise to four sperm cells, each with the half-number of chromosomes (haploid). After each chromosome has split (figure 2) there is an exchange of material between them: hence figure 3

environment with them: for example, we grow up in the same country, and so learn the same language.)

It can now be seen why in biology the words 'heredity' and 'inherited' are often avoided. As Helen Spurway has said: 'Everyday speech perpetuates archaic concepts. It is still literate to say I inherit my father's nose, his surname, and his watch.' Often, therefore, a difference between two individuals is said to be 'genetically determined': this means that it is due to differences in the genes carried by the chromosomes and transmitted in the way described. One of the pioneers of genetics, Francis Galton, preferred to speak of *nature* and *nurture*, instead of heredity and environment.

It is now possible to be clear about what the often misused words *familial, congenital, constitutional,* and *idiopathic* signify. A disease is sometimes said to be familial when it occurs in several members of the same family or group of related families. By itself, this tells us nothing about its causes. A familial disease may be largely due to the transmission of a particular gene, or it may be caused by some environmental influence that acts on many members of the family. Tuberculosis, for example, is particularly common among people, such as those of the mining communities of South Wales, who do exhausting work in conditions that encourage its appearance. If several members of the same family get tuberculosis it is often because they all suffer these conditions, or because one infects others. However, there may be a genetical factor *as well*. People vary a great deal in their resistance to tuberculosis, and part of the variation is genetically determined. Hence there are families of persons all with a lower resistance than the average, because they all possess a particular set of genes.

This is far from saying that tuberculosis is an 'inherited disease'. The immediate cause of tuberculosis is infection with a particular kind of microbe, the tubercle bacillus, or TB, together with a certain degree of susceptibility in the infected person. The infection itself is an environmental effect, arising usually from the presence of the microbe in the air or in milk. But susceptibility is affected both by other environmental influences, such as housing, and also by genetical factors.

Hence the word familial covers a complex set of possibilities. The same applies to the word congenital. A congenital condition is, strictly speaking, one evident in the new-born child. The word

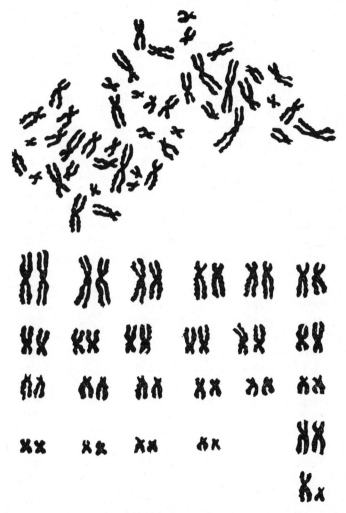

Human Chromosomes. Above, the chromosomes of a woman, in a dividing cell (drawn from a photograph). The cell outline is not shown. Below, the same chromosomes arranged in a standard order. The last pair are the sex chromosomes (see pages 73 and following). For comparison, below the two X chromosomes of the female are the X and Y sex chromosomes of a man. X chromosomes are not so-called because they are X-shaped, nor are Y chromosomes Y-shaped

refers to the time of appearance of the condition, and not to its cause. The cause may be genetical, at least in part, but sometimes it is wholly environmental. For instance, congenital syphilis is due to infection of the child by the mother shortly before birth – a purely environmental effect. By contrast, 'lobster claw', an abnormality of the hands and feet (illustrated on page 171), appears, as far as we know, in all individuals with a particular rare gene, and it is always evident at birth.

The other two words, constitutional and idiopathic, are used principally by medical writers. Like the first two, they are often employed loosely, with a meaning (if any can be discerned) rather like that of congenital. They tend to imply that the condition described is 'inborn' or genetically determined, but often they signify little more than that the causes of the condition are obscure. It would be an aid to clear thinking if both terms were discarded.

One further expression, of a rather different kind, should certainly be given up. This is the word 'blood', used in the sense of 'heredity'. Expressions such as 'royal blood' are firmly rooted in our language, but obviously have no literal validity. They are part of the excellent public-relations system run by or for monarchies and aristocracies. There is also an erroneous belief that the mother's blood flows directly into the blood vessels of the embryo. But the notion that a person is of 'noble stock' or has 'good blood' involves also the confusion of legal with biological inheritance which has already been mentioned. Royalty, nobility, 'family' in general, depend on the inheritance of name, title or estates or other property. Commonly, the inheritance is in the male line, and takes no account of the many ancestors not in that line. Some personage may be able, perhaps, to trace his ancestry back to William the Conqueror. So, probably, could every English person living today, if the records had been preserved. If we do not allow for the marriage of relatives, the number of our ancestors living in the eleventh century works out at many millions more than the total population of England at that time. Hence we are, not only all descended from William the Conqueror, but also from all of his contemporaries who have left descendants. This is a general consequence of sexual reproduction in the absence of rigid restrictions on mating.

ENVIRONMENT (OR 'NURTURE')

In the discussion above the term environment, like heredity, is used in a sense rather different from the usual. Environment in this book refers to every influence that acts on the individual from outside, from fertilization of the egg onwards.

The environmental influences that first act on a human being are those of the womb, or uterus. The nutrition of the unborn child depends on the food materials carried in the mother's blood. As we saw in the previous chapter, this blood circulates in the tissues of the womb, and some of the materials dissolved in it diffuse into the blood stream of the embryo, which is separated from it only by very thin membranes. If the mother herself is receiving a poor diet, the child too will suffer: deficiency of calcium in the mother's food may be responsible for defective bones or teeth in the child.

Evidence is beginning to be found of an effect of the emotional state of the mother on her unborn young. Possibly, if a pregnant woman undergoes severe mental stress, there is more danger of abnormal development for her child. If so, the state of the mother must influence the child through a change in the mother's blood. There is nothing here in common with the belief that what a mother sees or thinks during pregnancy directly affects the appearance or thoughts of the child after it is born. There is no support for the belief that, if a pregnant woman sees strawberries, her child will have a 'strawberry mark'. In a novel published shortly before the First World War a child is described as being born 'hating his father', as a result of the feelings of his mother towards her husband. A new-born infant could not hate in this fashion, because it lacks a sufficiently developed nervous system. Only later can a child be induced to hate. The influence of the thoughts of a pregnant mother on her child is through such prosaic matters as the blood supply to the womb. She cannot ensure that her child will have a placid temperament by being calm herself, or that he will appreciate the arts as a result of her visits to picture galleries and concerts during pregnancy.

Once a child is born the environmental influences acting on him become much more complex. His parents form a most important part of the environment, but there are also other people, the climate, food, disease germs in the air and elsewhere, and many more subtle influences.

'LAMARCKISM'

The importance of environmental influences is indeed obvious, and there are plenty of further examples in later chapters. There is, however, one supposed action of the environment which has caused violent controversy. It is commonly thought that if, let us say, a man becomes by training skilled in a particular trade, his children are likely to inherit some of this acquired skill. (Of course, many children learn their father's trade as they grow up, but *learning* from one's father is for our present purpose not different from learning from a school teacher: heredity is not involved in a biological sense.)

This doctrine, misleadingly called 'the inheritance of acquired characters', is associated with the name of Lamarck, an eighteenth-century biologist. And so we sometimes speak of *Lamarckism*.

According to Lamarck, and to many other biologists of his time and later, various effects operating during the life of an individual influence the character of the individual's offspring: the most important are use and disuse, but Lamarck considered that the will or desire of an organism to perform an act was also important. Lamarck was unusual for his time in being an evolutionist: he was convinced that (as is now generally agreed) species are not immutable, but undergo a slow process of change; change, he thought, was brought about by the influence of the environment on successive generations, and their efforts to adapt themselves to it.

One of the reasons for doubting the Lamarckian theory is our knowledge of the chromosomes and genes, and of the part they play in heredity. If the theory were true, we should have to suppose that a process, such as learning to be a good pianist, caused changes in a person's genes, or other transmitted material, so that children subsequently conceived would be capable of becoming pianists without training, or with less training. There is no known way in which this could occur, and what we know of the ways in which genes change is against it.

Nevertheless, many experiments have been devised to test the theory. Most of these experiments have failed to give acceptable evidence of a Lamarckian effect: the genes seem for the most part to be remarkably stable, and unaffected by ordinary environmental changes. For example, the effect of disuse was tested when flies were bred in the dark for sixty-nine generations; at the end their eyes were unaffected, and they reacted normally to light.

It is possible to breed a strain of animals (or plants) in which genetical variation has been almost, or quite, eliminated. Such a strain is called a *pure line*. In animals, something very close to a pure line can be got by brother and sister mating for thirty or more generations, and this has often been done with quickly breeding species such as certain flies, and even with rats and mice. Such lines cannot be quickly altered by selection, as can those in which there is much genetical variation. If several successive generations are, for example, bred in a cold environment, this does not give them an hereditary ability to withstand cold.

Pure lines are, however, of great value for some types of research. If, for instance, the effects on growth of two diets are to be compared, it is desirable to give the diets to two groups of animals, each as nearly as possible genetically identical: any differences observed between the groups are then probably not genetically determined, and a possible source of error is avoided. Inbred stocks are also of great importance in agriculture and stockbreeding.

These principles are important also for human biology. If two human groups, such as the inhabitants of Japan and of Scotland, are compared in respect of a character such as height or fertility, both of which can be measured, the averages may be found to differ. The two groups certainly have different environments, and doubtless also differ genetically. The difficulty is to find out the extent to which environmental and genetical differences influence the observed variation in height or fertility. In later chapters we shall see that it is possible to reach some conclusions on problems of this kind. It is however essential to realize that the difficulties exist.

To sum up, Lamarckism is without experimental foundation, and contrary to everything we know of the mechanism of heredity.

TWINS AND HEREDITY

One of the problems that remains is to determine *how much* variation in a given character, such as stature, is due to heredity, and how

3

much to environment. Certain human beings provide us with a special opportunity for answering such questions. They are the so-called identical twins.

Human twins are of two kinds. About two pairs in every three are the result of the presence, when insemination occurs, of two egg-cells instead of only one. (This ratio applies to Europeans but not to all other groups.) Both are fertilized, and they grow side-by-side in the womb. Small mammals such as cats, dogs, rats, and rabbits, and some larger ones such as pigs, lions, and tigers, produce several young at a birth in this way. Binovular, or two-egg, twins can be and often are very different from each other; they may of course differ in sex. Twins of the other type develop from a single fertilized egg which gives rise to two separate individuals. They are genetically identical: since they both originate from the same fertilized egg-cell, the chromosomes in the nuclei of the cells in all parts of their bodies are derived from the single set of chromosomes originally present in the egg. Such twins are often remarkably alike, not only in appearance but also in personality. They are always of the same sex.

But they are never quite identical. Most are brought up together, and so have very similar environments as well as identical heredity. Nevertheless, even then, differences can be detected, though they are much less, on the average, than those between ordinary brothers or sisters, or between binovular twins. For example, uniovular twins differ in their scores in intelligence tests, on the average, by about nine points. Ordinary brothers and sisters differ by sixteen points.

The ways in which marked differences can arise between uniovular twins are very complex. An example concerns a woman who suffered from high blood pressure (arterial hypertension) for eight years. This woman was lighter at birth than her twin, grew more slowly, and was always behind her twin in physical and intellectual development; she also had more infectious illness. The healthy twin never developed high blood pressure, but tests showed that she was *potentially* hypertensive; possibly, had she suffered severe stress at any time, she would have developed hypertension, like her sister. In this instance, evidently, the initial poor start, presumably resulting from conditions in the uterus, led to an accumulation of disadvantages for the weaker twin: as a result, her development in *every* respect – intellectual and emotional as well as 'physical' – was influenced.

Important studies have been made of twin pairs that have been parted early and brought up in different conditions. It is common to hear of such pairs that they remain remarkably similar. Often, this is true: there are instances of separated pairs being reunited as adults, as a result of one being mistaken for the other. Similarity between uniovular twins, whether separated or not, extends to the most extraordinary details: for instance, the distribution of decay in the teeth is often the same. Sometimes the similarity is of medical importance. One of a pair of uniovular twins living in Oxford died of an inoperable cancer of the stomach. The survivor was X-rayed, but no trouble could be detected. X-raying was repeated at three-monthly intervals, and after a year there appeared a slight indication of a growth in the stomach wall. The surgeon consulted held that the X-ray evidence alone was insufficient to justify operation, but he operated nevertheless, and duly removed a very early cancer of the type of which the first twin had died. The patient recovered.

Members of pairs that have been separated in infancy are not always strikingly similar. One pair of boys, born in Glasgow, was separated at three years: one remained in a working-class quarter of the city, the other went to live in a village outside. At sixteen, when they were compared, both were above the average in their score in intelligence tests, but the city child scored 125 to the other's 106. Both were good at football, but the country-bred one was physically superior; in particular, he was 25 mm taller; he was also mechanically abler.

Many other examples have been recorded. They show that the difference between an environment which favours intellectual development, and one which severely restricts it, can lead to a difference of twenty points. This, as far as test scores go, is about the difference between the general average of the whole population, and the lowest score which allows entry to a university.

Environment can, then, affect both intellectual achievement and physical development. Even more marked emotional differences sometimes arise. Two American girls, uniovular twins, were separated in infancy. One lived in a comfortable middle-class family with many social contacts and a good education. The other was looked after by a poor couple, and the education she received was not so good. At twenty the first girl was a cheerful, sociable individual, clearly enjoying life and without evident difficulties. The other was moody, shy, diffident and depressed, and spoke with a lisp.

THE INTERACTION OF NATURE AND NURTURE

It is sometimes asked: which is the more important, heredity or environment? There is no simple answer. If the question means, which has the greater *effect*? no general answer is possible, but only a number of particular answers. For instance, individual differences in eye-colour are mainly determined genetically, and so for this character heredity may be said to be the more important. At the other extreme, infection with measles, for example, depends on the presence in the environment of a sufficiently heavy concentration of the germs that cause measles.

Between the two extremes come characters such as stature. Heredity certainly plays a part in determining a person's height: if you have tall parents you are *more likely* to be tall than short. On the other hand, growth is equally certainly affected by environmental influences such as nutrition. In England, before 1940, boys who went to schools at which heavy fees were charged ('public' schools) were on the average about 10 cm (4 inches) taller than the children of poorer parents who could afford to send their children only to free schools. This by itself proves nothing: the poor might conceivably be genetically incapable of growing to the stature of the rich. However, if the children of the poor receive diet and other conditions like that of the more fortunate children, they resemble them in height and weight. This effect was observed on a large scale during the Second World War, when rationing and price control made possible a great improvement in the diet of most people in Britain.

The height of any one person is, then, an expression of the combined effects of his genetical make-up and his environment. We cannot properly say that one has a greater effect than the other. This interaction of nature and nurture has often been illustrated by experiments on animals. It is possible to isolate pure strains of mice with different capacities for growth. The different strains grow best in different conditions: there is no single environment that is best for all kinds of mice. We can reasonably suspect that the same applies to man. So the adage that one man's meat is another's poison expresses an important biological principle.

Despite these facts, there are still those who attach more weight to nature than to nurture, and others who insist that nurture is all-important. Those who put the emphasis on nature, or heredity, we shall mention again, in chapter 8. Meanwhile it is as well to consider what is meant by those who lay especial emphasis on environment. So far, in answer to the question: Which is the more important? we have given only a non-committal and rather irritating response that often comes from scientists. Neither nature nor nurture, we have said, can reasonably be regarded as having a greater effect than the other.

But it is possible to improve on this. If the question is considered from a practical point of view, from the point of view of getting something useful achieved, then the emphasis must be put on environment. This, of course, applies only when man is being considered. We can, and do, improve our livestock and our culti-vated plants by breeding: in doing so we kill the young that do not please us, permit only a selected few to breed, and perhaps derive much of our stock from artificial insemination or hand pollination. Before doing so, we have to decide on the precise environment for which we are breeding: an animal bred for one set of conditions may do very badly in another. But for man selective breeding of this sort is rarely proposed. We must, with a few possible minor excep-tions, accept the genetical constitutions of existing populations, and try to adjust the environment to them. If coal-miners dislike coal-mining, and if they are also liable to serious disease as a result of their work, there is no question of breeding a strain of men that will react differently. The problem is to alter the conditions of coal-mining. Later chapters will provide much more evidence in support of this conclusion.

3

MENDELISM AND MAN

> There are many laws regulating variation, some few of which can be dimly seen and will be hereafter briefly mentioned.
>
> CHARLES DARWIN

ALTHOUGH we can do nothing to alter our own genetical constitutions, and though few of us would alter our plans for marriage on biological grounds, it is nevertheless worth while to know all we can about human genetics. The principles of genetics have mostly been worked out from experiments on plants that can be artificially pollinated, and on quickly breeding animals, such as the famous fruit fly, *Drosophila*. The first man to publish an accurate account of the way in which what we now call genes determine differences between individuals of the same species was an Austrian priest, Gregor Mendel. Mendel used sweet peas for his experiments. It is an extraordinary fact that, although the journal in which he published was available in London and other centres in 1866, it was completely ignored.

In 1900 two Germans, C. Correns and E. Tschermak, and a Netherlander, H. de Vries, independently published papers confirming Mendel's observations. Since then an enormous mass of research has been done on the subject, but Mendel's priority is still acknowledged in the name 'Mendelism'.

MENDELIAN HEREDITY AND CHROMOSOMES

It is possible to give examples of 'Mendelian heredity' from man. Let us suppose that a woman with bright red hair marries a man with black hair; and that all their offspring have black hair. In the offspring of such a cross, the black-haired state masks red hair and is referred to as *dominant* to red hair; red hair is said to be *recessive*. Let us now suppose that one of the children of this couple marries the child of a similar couple, and that they in turn have a large

70

family: say, twelve children. Although they themselves have black hair, one in four of their children, on the average, will have red hair: that is, the most probable number of red-haired children out of twelve will be three.

Characters are sometimes said to skip a generation, and this is an example. What is the explanation? In the previous chapter we saw that every individual receives one set of chromosomes from each parent; and the chromosomes are the bearers of the genes. Bright red hair depends on the presence of a gene which we may represent as r, and red hair occurs only in individuals (of either sex) who have received r from both parents. Red-haired people therefore have the constitution rr. In the case described above the woman of the first couple was of this constitution. Her husband, on the other hand, had no r gene. In him, the corresponding genes were for black hair, and his constitution may be represented as RR. Capital letters indicate dominance.

Each of the children of this couple received r from the mother and R from the father. Their constitution was thus Rr, and their hair black, since R always causes black hair even if r is present. The next step was the marriage of two persons with the constitution Rr. Their children may be RR, Rr, or rr, and the *average* proportions of black to red will be 3:1. This three-to-one ratio is observable only if large numbers are studied: it cannot be established from observation of one or two families, even if they are exceptionally large. In fact, as we have already seen, ratios of this kind were first worked out on plants, and then on insects, before they were demonstrated in man. To observe a Mendelian effect it is necessary to breed plants or animals for two generations, and to study the proportions in which the characters occur in large numbers of individuals. By no means all characteristics are inherited in this simple fashion, and the early workers had to hit on ones that are.

The new genetics showed that heredity is not a blending process. Each person had formerly been regarded as a blend of the characters of his parents, just as orange-coloured paint can be made by blending yellow and red. In the example of hair-colour red hair appears in undiluted form in the second generation. We therefore attribute its appearance to genes that are transmitted intact from parent to offspring.

Characters may therefore appear in new combinations as a result of marriage between persons carrying different sets of genes. In one extreme instance, in South Africa, a Griqua woman married a Scot, and their daughter married a 'white' man of mixed parentage. The latter couple had four sons: one was very tall, almost white, but had brown eyes and coiled hair; one was of medium height, had a darker skin, brown eyes but straight, black hair; the third was also of medium height and rather darker than the second, with brown eyes and Kaffir-type hair; the fourth, again of medium height and coloration, had brown eyes and brown-black Hottentot-type hair.

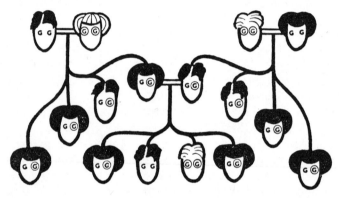

Inheritance of Red Hair in Man. Bright red hair is a recessive condition, that is, one which appears only in individuals with two genes of a particular kind. 'G' stands for 'gene'

Hence in this family various features appear in unfamiliar combination: in the first son, for instance, Negro-type hair with a light skin.

If characters are determined by genes on different chromosomes they must be expected to *segregate* in this way. Each chromosome that an individual receives from his father may have come from either of his father's parents; and each chromosome from his mother, from either of her parents. Different children of the same family will receive different combinations of chromosomes, and so may display different combinations of grandparental characteristics.

But each chromosome carries many genes. Hence there should be characters that do not segregate or separate in this way, but remain together. *Linkage* of characters is indeed well known to occur in

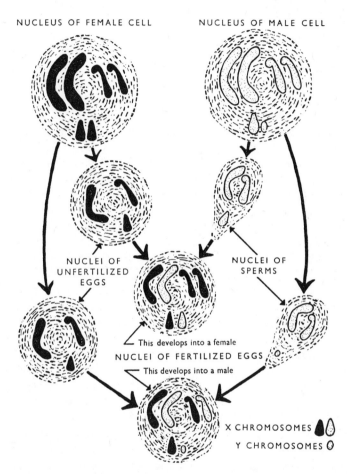

NUCLEUS OF FEMALE CELL   NUCLEUS OF MALE CELL

NUCLEI OF
UNFERTILIZED
EGGS

NUCLEI OF
SPERMS

└ This develops into a female
NUCLEI OF FERTILIZED EGGS
└ This develops into a male

X CHROMOSOMES
Y CHROMOSOMES

Sex Determination. Sex is determined at the moment of fertilization, and depends on the sperm: eggs fertilized by a sperm with an X-chromosome become females; those fertilized by one with a Y-chromosome become males. Certain genes, such as the one causing haemophilia, are on the X-chromosome and are said to be sex-linked. Only three pairs of chromosomes are shown

many animals and plants, but there are not many examples from man. For our present purpose it is not of great importance, since linkage is very rarely complete. The reason for the failure of linkage is shown in the diagram on page 59: it is an exchange of material between pairs of chromosomes during the formation of the eggs and sperm. This exchange of material inevitably breaks the linkage between genes on the chromosomes.

To sum up, genetical effects are determined by individual particles, the genes, and the genes may appear in any combination in different individuals. This recombination is the origin of many of the differences between people that we see around us. Even people living in a small community in very similar environments may vary greatly in appearance and other characteristics. Though part of the variation may be due to small environmental differences, some comes from the mixing and reshuffling of the genes in each generation.

SEX DETERMINATION

One of the most obvious of the characteristics that may be said to be inherited is sex. Granted, environmental agencies can interfere with the development of sex characters: in some mammals the presence of a twin of opposite sex in the womb can cause the development of a mixture of male and female organs; in other words, the production of an intersex. But in normal development sex is determined by the chromosomes by a simple mechanism, shown on page 73. Of the twenty-three pairs of human chromosomes, one plays a special part in sex determination. In a woman's cells the members of this pair are identical, as far as can be seen with a microscope; both are called X-chromosomes. In a man's cells there is only one X-chromosome; with it is a smaller one, the Y-chromosome. Now consider what happens when the germ-cells are produced, each with a half-set of chromosomes. Each egg-cell gets one X-chromosome, but a sperm-cell may have either an X-chromosome or a Y. There are consequently two kinds of sperm. If an egg is fertilized by a sperm with an X-chromosome, the fertilized egg (with its full set of chromosomes) will have two X-chromosomes and will develop into a female; but if a Y-bearing sperm fertilizes it there will be one X and one Y, and so development will be into a male.

Can we then control sex in man, or in other animals, by allowing only X-bearing, or only Y-bearing, sperm to reach the egg? At present, in 1971, the answer is, no: attempts have been made but so far none has been entirely successful. However, in normal conditions the Y-bearing sperm may have the better chance of fertilizing an egg. In any large population rather more boys are born than girls: in Britain about 106 boys for every 100 girls: that is, the sex ratio at birth is 106. We do not know what the sex ratio is at conception; it has been said that more male foetuses die than female, but this is doubtful. Certainly more males are conceived than females. This is not what would be expected from the sex-determining mechanism: female-producing sperm (X) and male-producing sperm (Y) develop in equal numbers and, if the two types have equal chances of successful fertilization, the sex ratio at conception should be 100. The fact that it is higher suggests that Y-bearing sperm have an advantage.

The possibility of different behaviour by the two types of sperm is important. Quite apart from the control of sex in man, it would be of great value if it could be arranged that the great majority of calves born in dairy herds were female; similarly, on poultry farms, it would be an advantage if most chicks hatched were female. Artificial insemination is already well established. Perhaps, quite soon, it will be possible to treat sperm, collected for artificial insemination, so that only one kind remains active.

In man the high initial sex ratio, combined with the higher mortality among males, gives a sex ratio of about 100 at puberty; youths of each sex are in about equal numbers. But in advanced countries the lower death rate among women continues, and at eighty-five the sex ratio is about 55: nearly two women to each man. The greater survival of women is not fully understood; occcupational hazards play some part, but it is doubtful whether they are the only cause.

Certain genes carried on the X-chromosome may take effect in males owing to the absence of any corresponding genes on the Y-chromosome. (In a female the other X-chromosome will usually carry a counterpart or *allele* of the gene concerned.) The best-known example is the gene responsible for the disease haemophilia, in which the blood clots only very slowly, if at all. Haemophilics have a very low expectation of life, since they may bleed to death from a small cut, or through internal haemorrhage. Haemophilia is,

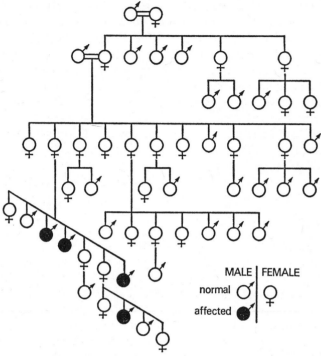

Haemophilia. Pedigree illustrating origin by mutation, or sudden change, in a normal gene, occurring in a family with no previous history of haemophilia

with perhaps one exception, known only in males. A man gets the disease as a result of receiving from his mother an X-chromosome which carries the haemophilia gene. The mother has another X-chromosome carrying an allelic gene which enables her blood to clot in the normal way, and so is not a haemophilic. Hence haemophilia is almost always transmitted by a normal woman carrying, unknown to herself, a gene that is likely to kill half of her sons. Only half the sons, on the average, will be affected: the others will have received the other, normal X-chromosome. Theoretically a woman could have two haemophilia genes, and so have the disease. Only one such case has been reported, perhaps because the possession of the two genes usually kills before birth.

One of the women known to have been carriers of haemophilia was Queen Victoria of England: one of her sons, at least three

grandsons and six great-grandsons have been haemophilics, including members of the ruling families of Spain and Tsarist Russia;
but the members of the present British royal house have escaped
the offending gene.

Genes carried on the X-chromosome are said to be *sex-linked*,
and several are known in human beings. A common sex-linked gene
is responsible for the most frequently found type of colour-blindness,
in which red and green are confused. This (recessive) condition
occurs much more frequently in men than in women, because a
woman must have two of the appropriate gene, and this combination
can occur only rarely. Of European males, about 1·4 per cent are
handicapped in this way.

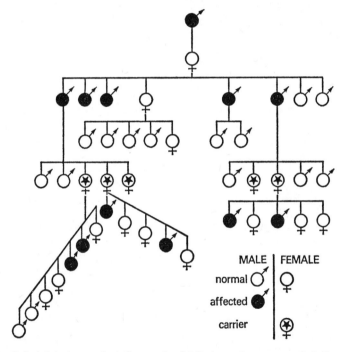

Sex-linked Inheritance. A pedigree of red blindness due to a sex-linked gene:
the effects of a sex-linked gene are shown more often by males than by females,
since in the latter a normal gene on one of the X-chromosomes usually masks the
effect of the mutant gene on the other chromosome. In a male there is no
second X-chromosome and there is no masking

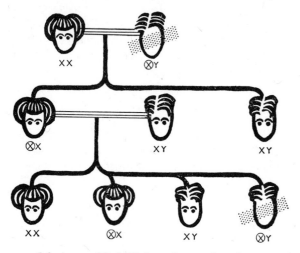

Inheritance of Red Blindness. See previous figure

There is a further, rather odd, possible type of gene, namely, one carried on the Y-chromosome. Such a gene can influence only males, and must be transmitted from father to son. The condition of hairy ears, illustrated in plate 4, is an example, and probably the only one known in man.

CHROMOSOME ABNORMALITIES AND MUTATION

The main facts given in the preceding sections have been known for several decades. They form part of genetics – the science of variation and heredity. Formal 'Mendelian' genetics entails the assumption that the genes are stable: each time the nucleus divides, its component chromosomes divide too (as shown on page 58), and so a complete set of chromosomes is present in all nuclei, except those of ripe eggs and sperms which have a half set (page 59); and for most purposes we assume that not only the chromosomes but also the many genes they bear are exactly reproduced too. Furthermore, the stability holds from generation to generation: the genes survive unchanged during their passage in the germ cells and the process of fertilization.

This view is contrary to the still widespread belief in the 'inheritance of acquired characters'; but, as we saw in the discussion of 'Lamarckism' in the preceding chapter, this belief is not tenable. What the rejection of Lamarckism implies may be restated briefly: suppose an individual develops some adaptation to his surroundings, such as greater skill at some task or resistance to disease; does this lead to changes in his genes, so that his offspring are similarly adapted but *by genetical means*? For complex many-celled organisms there is no cogent evidence of any such effect.

Nevertheless, neither the chromosomes nor the genes are wholly stable. Sometimes the nuclei of the body cells or of sperm or egg have the wrong number of chromosomes; this abnormality can be seen under the microscope. Furthermore, individual genes may change, or *mutate*; if this happens in a sperm or egg which later develops into an adult, each body cell will contain the mutant gene, and the presence of the gene may be inferred from its effects on the appearance, development, or chemistry of the adult. Sometimes, however, when the effects are recessive, the gene can be detected only when it is present in the double dose, or homozygous state: in this case its existence may be evident only after many generations.

In the 1950s new techniques for the study of human chromosomes made possible a rapid development in knowledge of chromosome abnormalities in man. As already described, human body cells proved to have a chromosome number (the diploid number) of forty-six, and not forty-eight as had been thought. There followed a series of reports in the medical journals on patients with one chromosome too few (monosomy) or one too many (trisomy).

In 'Klinefelter's syndrome' a person, apparently male, has undeveloped testes, little facial or pubic hair, a feminine distribution of fat, and often some breast development. Such people are probably always sterile. They are trisomic for the sex chromosomes: XXY, instead of XX (normal female) or XY (normal male). 'Turner's syndrome' occurs in apparent females: the ovaries are undeveloped, and body and intellect are stunted. Such people are monosomic: they have one, solitary X chromosome. Still more rarely there are two Y chromosomes: the constitution is then XYY or XXYY. These people are often over 182 cm (six feet) in height, and intellectually subnormal. XYY males are very rare indeed in any general population, but are found in appreciable numbers in prison and hospital groups among males with a tendency to violence. Evidently, an extra Y chromosome is associated with a certain type of criminality. But not all people with two Y chromosomes are criminals; and we do not yet know how anti-social behaviour develops as these individuals grow up.

Abnormalities occur also, as one would expect, in the autosomes, that is, the chromosomes other than those of sex. The best-known example involves one of the smallest pairs of chromosomes. There is a kind of idiocy, 'Down's syndrome' (misleadingly called 'Mongolism'), which can be recognized very early in life and which was for long without satisfactory explanation. A genetical effect was obviously involved, but of what kind was not clear. It is now known to be due to trisomy: all the body cells of people of this kind have forty-seven chromosomes instead of forty-six.

These and similar observations are interesting, even though the abnormalities are very rare. Perhaps one day they will help towards understanding the way in which the chromosomes and genes work. But they are much less important than 'point' or single-gene mutation, in which one sub-microscopic unit of heredity undergoes a sudden change. Once such a change has taken place the mutant gene continues to reproduce itself in its altered form; consequently, if it occurs in the nucleus of an egg or sperm it may be transmitted from generation to generation.

Gene mutation occurs in all organisms, as far as is known, from the ultramicroscopic viruses, through bacteria, up to the largest and most complex of animals and plants. Evidently the genes are inherently slightly unstable, or at least are not always copied with complete reliability when they reproduce themselves at division of the nucleus. However, if mutation were frequent many individuals would be produced with no chance of survival. Most mutant genes are disadvantageous: they reduce the efficiency of the organism if they have any appreciable effect at all. This is because (as further discussed in chapter 4) we and other organisms are products of natural selection: our existing collections of genes must approximate already to the most favourable for the conditions in which we and our ancestors have lived. Further, the complete complex of genes in an individual must form a balanced combination: if many of them are mutant genes the chances of the balance being maintained are small.

Accordingly, we find that the genes mutate only rarely. This can be illustrated from a few examples of natural mutation rates in man: that is, mutation rates which have not been raised by radiation from the products of bomb explosions or other artificial sources. The examples are of genes whose mutant forms produce severe deficiencies, but not severe enough to prevent all the people affected from breeding. Achondroplasia is a kind of dwarfism in which the head and body are of normal size but the limbs are very short. Another example is retinoblastoma, in which a malignant tumour develops in the retina of one or both eyes; this causes death unless it is removed early in life. Yet another is epiloia, in which benign tumours develop in many parts of the body and cause epilepsy and mental deficiency; this disease, however, varies a great deal in its manifestations and may be very mild. For each of these conditions there are examples of affected people having children; and each condition has been found to be dominant. To establish the mutation rate, it is necessary to discover the frequency with which the conditions occur in people whose parents are *not* affected: since the conditions are dominant, every such case may be attributed to mutation. The mutation rates, estimated in this way, are one in five per hundred thousand per generation. It is of course not at all certain that all other genes mutate at this sort of rate; but we can be sure that none mutates very much more frequently.

INJURIOUS RADIATIONS

The subject of mutation in man has recently been given added interest, because the deliberate action of some people is leading to increases in mutation rates both in ourselves and in other organisms. The most prominent cause of extra mutation is the radiation resulting from the test explosions of powerful bombs; the bombs are, of course, designed to kill large numbers of people, not to produce mutation. Radiation from other sources could also increase mutation: for instance, X-ray equipment used for the diagnosis or treatment of disease, or even the paint on luminous watches.

To be clear on this subject it is necessary to know the effects on the body of the various sorts of injurious radiations. The injuries are of two kinds: first are those which harm the person exposed to the radiation; second are the effects on the genetical material, which become manifest in later generations. The first or immediate effects include burns and cancer of the skin (both of which can arise from misuse of standard X-ray equipment); destruction of bone marrow which results in a severe form of anaemia; cancer of the blood-forming tissues, familiar under the name of leukaemia; and death from radiation sickness – a condition produced in large numbers of people as a result of the explosion of atomic bombs at Hiroshima and Nagasaki in 1945. There have recently been substantial increases in the numbers of people suffering from the hideous and fatal disease of leukaemia as a result of the testing of hydrogen bombs by the U.S.A., the U.S.S.R., Britain, and now France and China.

These direct effects can be quite easily guarded against when the radiation is not scattered indiscriminately over the earth's surface. People working in atomic power stations or with X-ray equipment can be protected against receiving a dose which would have even a mildly ill effect. *In this aspect* the radiations are analogous to a poison: provided the dosage over a given period does not exceed a certain amount, no harm is done.

The situation is quite different for the second kind of injury. *Any* additional radiation falling on the ovaries or testes of people who will later have children increases the mutation rate in the germ cells from which future generations will spring. There is no dosage of which we can say: *this* is the permissible maximum. It may be asked whether it matters if the mutation rate in man (or other organisms) is raised. The most obvious reason for objecting to damage to our hereditary material is that the number of seriously defective, deformed, or inviable infants will be increased. This is obviously undesirable in itself. There is no reason to expect a corresponding increase in the numbers of outstandingly able people: as we have already seen, most mutant genes are disadvantageous. There is also a more theoretical aspect. Mutation rates in ordinary conditions (that is, the 'natural' rates) may be regarded as products of natural selection: they represent a balance between excessive stability and consequent lack of genetical adaptability on the one hand, and instability which might lead to a great deal of defect and infertility on the other. For us to interfere with this balance, without knowing a great deal more about it, and about human genetics generally, is thoroughly irresponsible.

MENDELISM IN PRACTICE

The obvious places for trying to apply genetics usefully are the farm and the garden. In man there is less scope, but it has nevertheless some potential importance. Sometimes a man or woman about to marry wishes to know whether there is a danger that children of the marriage will display some undesirable feature. In the previous chapter we saw, for example, that both tuberculosis and at least some types of cancer are influenced by genetical constitution. But for both diseases the genetical effect is too small to be taken into account when marriage is considered. If, for instance, a near relative has died of one of these diseases there is no cause for alarm, nor any reason for avoiding marriage.

Some diseases, however, are determined genetically in a quite straightforward way. Haemophilia is one example, and others are given in chapter 8. There is, in fact, a considerable mass of knowledge on the genetics of human defects, and an authority on human genetics can occasionally give useful information to couples who wish to have children. It is, however, not possible to give this information in a short, non-technical book.

A special case is that of marriage between cousins. The effects of

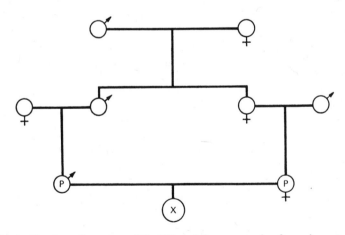

Cousin Marriage: the parents (P) of X each have one pair of grandparents in common. X has a higher probability of receiving two similar mutant genes than has the offspring of parents who are not cousins

cousin marriage can be considered from the point of view of the individual or of the community. The individual wishes to know the chance of producing defective children. It is possible to answer this for particular cases: the danger comes from recessive traits, and, as a rule, we cannot say if genes for such traits are present since a gene of this type, unless sex-linked, causes the traits to develop only in company with another, similar gene. If both cousins carry the same

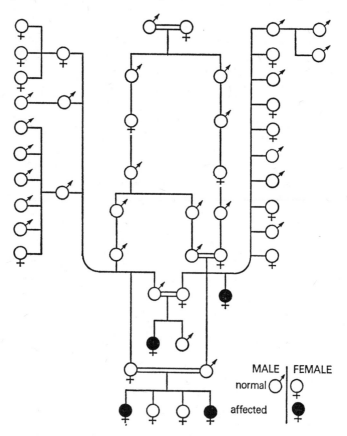

Transmission of a Recessive Character. Pedigree of blistering of the skin. In three instances the marriage of cousins led to the production of children with the condition, though the parents were normal. (This sort of thing happens in only a small proportion of cousin marriages.) By chance, only females were affected in this example

gene for a particular defect, then the most probable proportion of their children showing the defect will be one in four, or twenty-five per cent.

It must be emphasized that most cousin marriages do not produce defective children. Nevertheless, two first cousins are more likely both to carry the same harmful genes than are two individuals taken at random from the population. Hence the chance of two first cousins having defective children is higher than that of an unrelated pair.

This fact does not, and need not, deter first cousins from marrying. The exceptions are cousins with relations who have developed any known recessive defects: these include a fatal skin disease called xeroderma pigmentosum, a form of idiocy (juvenile amaurotic), and a form of deaf mutism; all are rare.

On the other hand, from the point of view of the community, cousin marriage is perhaps undesirable. If the marriage of first cousins ceased, there would be a fall in the incidence of the three conditions just mentioned: this is because, although only a small proportion of cousin marriages produce them, the number so produced is large relative to the total number of sufferers. However, the total genetical effect of forbidding cousin marriages would be quite trivial, and it would be difficult to justify the consequent interference with individual happiness.

Cousin marriage is one form of inbreeding. The most intense form possible in man is pairing between parent and offspring or between sibs (that is, brothers and sisters). Such inbreeding is of great value in plant and animal husbandry, but it is forbidden in most human communities. The danger of producing defective children is a good deal greater from 'incestuous' marriage than from marriage of first cousins. Apart from obvious defect, close inbreeding may lead to lowered fertility.

SOME LIMITATIONS OF MENDELISM

Does all heredity conform to Mendel's comparatively simple rules? Far from it. Characters such as height and weight, which show 'continuous variation' (illustrated on page 87), are influenced, not by one or two genes only, with the rest neutral in their effects, but by many. In most adult human populations every height, to the nearest millimeter, is represented, between something less than 150 cm and something more than 180 cm. A good deal of this variation (as we saw in chapter 2) reflects differences of environment. But, in so far as it is genetically determined, the genes responsible are probably to be numbered in hundreds, and each has only a small effect. The total number of genes, in one half-set of human chromosomes, is believed to be about 20,000; hence there is plenty of scope for complexity.

This sort of thing is very important when characters such as 'intelligence' are considered. Although there is a correlation between the intelligence of parents and that of their children (even when the children are separated from their parents), there is no simple transmission of intelligence, however the latter is measured or defined, as there is of red hair.

The same principles can be applied to many diseases. It is sometimes asked: is insanity inherited? Since definitions and diagnoses of 'insanity' vary, this would in any case be difficult to answer. But various inquiries have been made on the incidence of diagnosed psychosis in the families of psychotics. The sort of conclusion which has been reached, so far, is that, if a person becomes psychotic, the chance of any one of his brothers or sisters also becoming insane is about one in twenty; whereas the figure for the population as a whole is about one in a hundred. (These figures apply, approximately, to the white population of the United States.)

A psychosis, such as schizophrenia, arises when a person with a certain kind of genetical constitution is reared in a particular sort of unfavourable environment. An important aspect of a person's environment is the relatives with whom he grows up. Some people may have genetical constitutions which, in unfavourable conditions, lead them to behave so that they make *other* members of their family psychotic. The causation of these conditions is probably highly complex, and involves most intricate interactions of nature and nurture.

Studies on this kind of problem are done, where possible, on twins, and the twin method has been used in psychiatric research. It has also been employed in work on susceptibility to infectious disease. A notable example is tuberculosis. If one of a pair of uniovular twins has tuberculosis, the other nearly always has it too; for binovular twins (who are not genetically identical) the concordance

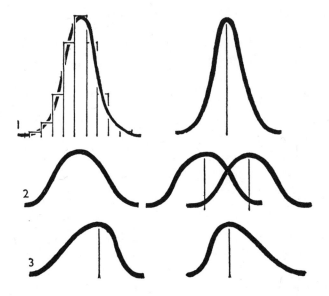

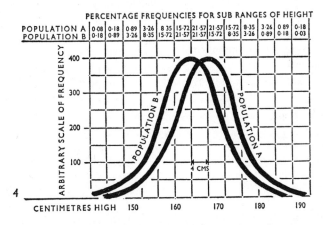

	PERCENTAGE FREQUENCIES FOR SUB RANGES OF HEIGHT													
POPULATION A	0·08	0·18	0·89	3·26	8 35	15·72	21·57	21·57	15·72	8·35	3·26	0 89	0·18	
POPULATION B	0·18	0·89	3·26	8·35	15·72	21·57	21·57	15·72	8·35	3·26	0·89	0·18	0·03	

Variation in a Measurable Character. If the height is taken of every person in, say, a large town, the number of persons at each height, to the nearest cm, can be shown in a series of rectangles, as in the first figure. The modal or most 'popular' height would perhaps be 170 cm, with the numbers falling off progressively on each side of the mode. The smooth curve in the first figure is another way of presenting the same facts. The curves shown are of the type called 'normal' or 'Gaussian'. When we study genetical variation due to differences in

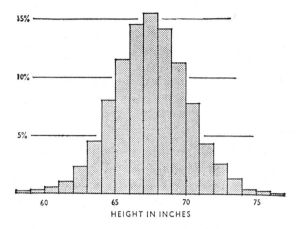

Distribution of Heights of British Men. A histogram illustrating the distribution of a measurable character influenced both by many genes and by the environment

is much lower. Here, therefore, we find clear evidence of genetical variation in susceptibility to tuberculosis. The practical implications, apart from the obvious one of avoiding infection, are that especial care is desirable for adolescents and young adults with tuberculous relatives; and that people with tuberculosis in the family should not be employed in work such as nursing, in which the incidence of the disease tends to be high. It must be emphasized that the most

---

many genes, and not just one or two, this is the sort of variation which is often found.

When two large groups of people are *compared* in regard to a measurable character, such as strength or fertility or mathematical ability, the two distribution curves may differ both in shape and in the position of the mode, as shown in the other figures. See also the actual examples above and on pages 149, 150, 151 and 182.

Comparisons of this kind illustrate that great overlaps can occur, even when averages are different. It *may* be true that women, on the average, are genetically inferior to men in mathematical ability, but it does not follow that no women can excel in mathematics, and in fact some do. Sometimes we know nothing about average differences, but only the performances of champions. For example, Negroes have often excelled at sprinting, Finns at long-distance running; nevertheless, as recent events have shown, other countries can produce champions in both

important causes of tuberculosis are environmental; the discovery that some people are genetically more susceptible than others does not alter this fact.

To sum up, most important human characteristics are influenced by many genes (as well as by the environment), and so fall outside any simple Mendelian scheme. Their incidence in the population must be described in terms of frequency distributions (as on pages 87 and 88); and predictions about *particular individuals* are of little use. It is not of much practical value to be told, for instance, that the chances are about one in seventeen that one will die of a particular disease before the age of sixty; nor is it really useful to know that about one in a hundred of one's children is likely to be mentally deficient. On the other hand, statistical facts of this sort are of great importance in such matters as the planning of health services for large populations.

PART TWO

HUMAN DIVERSITY

Man is a product of evolution. The main features which distinguish him from his nearest living relatives, the apes, are his large brain, manual dexterity, and the power of speech: these, with other special characters, make possible man's unique form of social organization. His brain, in particular, is so organized that his behaviour is free from the rigidity of the 'instinctive' activities of most animals, and is consequently highly flexible and adaptable to new conditions.

Only one human species exists today, and the physical differences, such as skin colour, by which human types are classified, are of only trivial significance, although for social or political reasons they are sometimes given a spurious importance. All human groups or 'races' include individuals of a wide range of ability and social worth; there is no justification for saying that one group is innately inferior to another, and the social achievements of each group depend largely on the natural resources and amenities available. Theories of the inferiority or criminality of particular sections often arise from the political needs of a dominant group, such as foreign conquerors or employers of cheap labour. Much ability is wasted and injustice caused by the inferior position which colonial and other backward peoples occupy. Similar waste and injustice occur wherever there are large unprivileged classes of poor people. In most countries women form an unprivileged class.

4

FROM APE TO MAN

We must, however, acknowledge, as it seems to me, that man with all his
noble qualities ... still bears in his bodily frame the indelible stamp of
his lowly origin.

CHARLES DARWIN

GENETICS is a study of differences between individuals. We come
now, in this and the next five chapters, to differences between large
groups. Today few dispute that men, like other animals and plants
and indeed the earth, the sun, and the stars, are a product of evolution.
The present chapter deals with the stages of the evolution of men
from primitive apes, and the variety of human types that have existed
in the last million years.

THE EVIDENCE OF ROCKS AND FOSSILS

For at least the past 500m. years ice, wind, and rain have been
eroding the surface of the earth, while in other parts rivers and
sea have been depositing layers of new rock made up largely of the
eroded particles. If we dig deep into the earth we find that the
rocks are arranged in layers and, where there has been no violent
disturbance, such as those due to volcanoes or earthquakes, the
older rocks are the deeper.

Each type of rock that has been laid down by sea or river water
contains its own characteristic fossils; so does the coal-bearing rock
formed from primeval forests. Fossils are the traces of plants and
animals: as a rule only the hard parts, such as bones, are preserved,
and they undergo a chemical change in which the organic material
is replaced by rock substance, without alteration of the original
structure. The skeletons of giant 'dinosaurs' that one sees in the
museums are made, not of bone, but of rock in the form of the
original bony skeleton.

Not only can the order in time of the different rocks be determined;

their ages also can be roughly calculated in various ways. The evolution both of the rocks and of living things has taken some hundreds of millions of years. The group of backboned animals (the vertebrates), to which we belong, began in the sea more than three hundred million years ago, and at first the only vertebrates were fish-like animals. Some early fish gradually developed the capacity to live on land, and so gave rise to the land vertebrates. The earliest of these were amphibians (a group now represented by frogs and newts), but for the greater part of the time after this the most prominent land vertebrates were reptiles, including the notorious dinosaurs, pterodactyls, and so forth. One branch of these reptiles developed feathers, wings and warm-bloodedness, and became birds.

Meanwhile, even before the great reptiles evolved, an entirely different branch of the reptiles specialized in a different way. The original peg-like teeth (as in a crocodile today) became more complex, as ours are: some became grinders, others came to be similar to front and eye teeth. During the period of the great reptiles some of these creatures with complex teeth developed warm blood and the capacity to bear young in an active state (instead of laying eggs); we do not yet know when, because the skeletons that remain do not tell us. They were probably all small, like shrews. But, by the time the great reptiles perished, evidently as a result of drastic climatic changes involving the whole world, there were mammals in existence ready to take their place. 'Blessed are the meek, for they shall inherit the earth.'

The mammals, the class of warm-blooded, furry vertebrates that includes our own species, have been the main land vertebrates for sixty million years. We have an enormous mass of fossil remains of some groups: we can trace every detail of the evolution of some modern hoofed mammals, and of large carnivores such as lions and tigers from small, undistinguished creatures. Other groups of mammals have left fewer fossil remains, because they did not live in surroundings which favoured fossilization. Among these less well-recorded orders is unfortunately that of the Primates, the one that includes the monkeys, apes, and men – nearly all forest-dwellers. Nevertheless it is possible to give an account of the evolution of mankind from ape-like creatures.

THE CAUSES OF EVOLUTION

But first we must see something of how evolutionary change has come about. The man whose researches finally brought scientists to accept the theory of organic evolution was Charles Darwin. Among a number of evolutionists of the eighteenth and nineteenth centuries, Darwin not only presented a mass of evidence for the fact of evolution; he also produced the first convincing theory of how it had occurred. At the same time as Alfred Russel Wallace, he put forward the theory of *natural selection* (often miscalled the 'survival of the fittest').

Natural selection depends on two things: first, inherited variation; second, either a selective mortality, so that some types tend to live longer than others, or inherited differences in fertility. *Inherited variation* has already been discussed, in chapters 2 and 3. Its agents are the genes, and mutation ensures a continuous supply of new forms. Here we discover the biological advantages of sexual reproduction. Each individual that arises from the union of sperm and egg possesses genes from two individuals – the parents. Hence each individual (apart from uniovular twins) is genetically unique, and there is always much genetical variation in any population. Potentially advantageous genes (which may have arisen separately by mutation) can become associated in one individual, and new and more effective combinations of genes can appear. This genetical variation among individuals makes a species adaptable: in particular, if the environment changes, new types, fitted to the new conditions, may arise quite quickly.

For *selective mortality* we have to assume the production of off-spring in excess in each generation. In a population of constant size this excess will not survive, and with the excess will disappear certain genes. In every plant or animal species studied, even the least fertile such as elephants, gannets and man, many more offspring are produced than are needed to maintain populations at a constant level. Many young die, and there is often a substantial mortality among young adults too. This mortality is one of the means by which natural selection occurs.

Evolutionary change has sometimes been observed while it was taking place. For example, in some species of moths black varieties, formerly very rare, have replaced paler forms in industrial areas where backgrounds are bare and dark: the black types are less conspicuous, and so better equipped to evade their enemies. The colour difference is genetically determined. This is an example of the replacement of one *variety* by another. Darwin thought that varieties were incipient species, and today we have evidence that he was right.

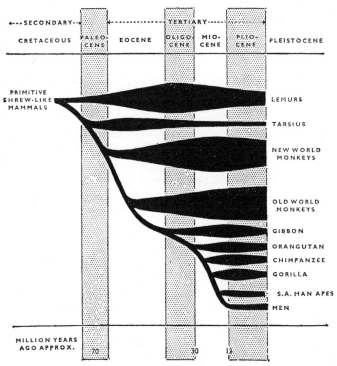

Family Tree of the Primates

One way to decide whether to call two types separate species is to find out whether they yield fertile offspring when crossed. The horse and the ass can be crossed, but the mule which results is sterile. Some crosses of this sort, between fairly widely different types, give offspring with impaired fertility. The gypsy moth, of which the Latin name is *Lymantria dispar* (indicating that only one species is involved), is found in a number of areas, including Western Europe and Japan. Each area has its own particular 'race', and these can be

1 NEGRIFORM – Two Zulu women of South Africa, photographed half a century ago.

2 EUROPIFORM – An Arab of North Africa.

3 EUROPIFORM – A bedouin woman of North Africa.

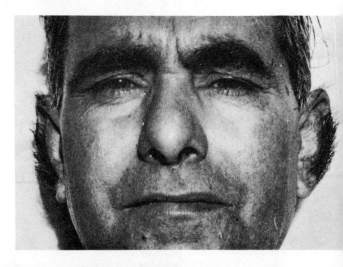

4 EUROPIFORM – An Indian. This man has hairy ears, probably as a result of an unusual gene on his Y-chromosome.

5 MONGOLIFORM – A man of Siberia.

6 MONGOLIFORM – A Chinese in traditional dress.

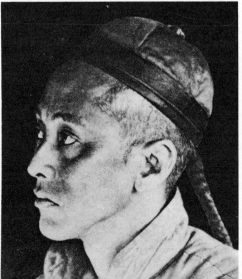

7 MONGOLIFORM – A man of Sarawak.

8 MONGOLIFORM –
Dakota of North
America in
traditional dress.

9 MONGOLIFORM –
Girl of Tierra del
Fuego. This child
is pure Fuegian.

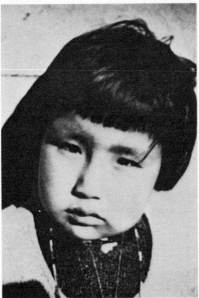

10 POLYNESIAN –
Woman of Samoa.

11 POLYNESIAN – Maori
girl of New Zealand.

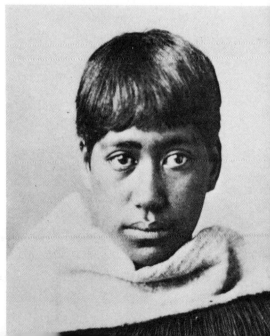

12 A PRODUCT OF RACE CROSSING – Daughter of a European and an Australiform. There is no evidence of physical disharmony, such as has sometimes been said to result from intermarriage of diverse groups.

13 AUSTRALIFORM –
Arunta girls of Central
Australia.

14 Dwellers in the
Egyptian desert.

crossed; but the resulting offspring usually breed among themselves only with difficulty, if at all. Evidently the geographical varieties of *Lymantria* are on the way to becoming distinct species, and this is another instance of evolutionary change which can be observed in progress.

PREHUMAN FOSSILS

The preliminaries to the evolution of man took place between thirty and sixty million years ago, when the tailless apes appeared as a group separate from that of the ordinary monkeys. The monkeys leap from one tree-hold to another, and use all four limbs for grasping; the apes on the other hand make first-rate trapeze artists, since their normal way of moving in trees is by swinging with their hands. Inevitably, however, the distinction becomes blurred as we go back in time, towards the common ancestor of both groups.

But we have no intimate knowledge of the life of the early apes; we have as yet only their teeth and lower jaws; these, the least destructible parts, have survived in sufficient numbers to be found. One lower jaw, from the Faiyum, near the Nile, is called *Propliopithecus*. It belonged to an ape far smaller than any we know today, perhaps not more than 46 cm (18 inches) high. It lived when the main lines of mammalian evolution had already appeared; in particular, the Primates (the order of lemurs, tarsiers, monkeys, and apes) had by this time formed the main groups, apart from man, into which we divide them today, with the monkeys of the New World and the Old World already distinct.

The figure on page 96 shows the geological epochs into which the Tertiary period, the period of mammals, is divided. *Propliopithecus* belongs to the Oligocene, when apes or their ancestors were evidently rare. But in the next epoch, the Miocene, some millions of years later, apes were comparatively widespread and common. Today, apes are found only in south-east Asia and west and central Africa, whereas the Miocene fossils have been found in north and east Africa, and widely dispersed in Europe and Asia.

These Miocene apes belong to a group called the Dryopithecinae. They include a variety of types, ranging in size from that of a small gibbon to something like that of a gorilla. *Dryopithecus*, a large European and Asian type which has been known for some time from its jaws and teeth, has grinding teeth which resemble both those of the chimpanzee and gorilla and our own. A similar form, first found in India, is assigned to the genus *Sivapithecus*.

We have only a few fragments of the rest of the skeleton of either of these, but other Dryopithecine fossils found recently, in Kenya, provide a more complete picture of the group. Among them is *Proconsul*, a large form something like a chimpanzee. The skull of *Proconsul* is lightly constructed compared with that of modern apes,

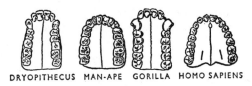

DRYOPITHECUS MAN-APE GORILLA HOMO SAPIENS

Upper Jaws and Teeth. Dryopithecus has a dental arch like that of a modern ape, that is, 'square'; '*Plesianthropus*', one of the South African man-apes, has the curved, human type. Note the massive canine in the gorilla, not found in the others

and it lacks their heavy brow ridges and very projecting muzzle; in certain respects it has more in common with monkeys than it has with modern apes. A number of limb bones, belonging to various Dryopithecine types, have also been found in Kenya. The thigh and arm bones are slender and, relative to the body, the arms are shorter and the legs longer than are those of present-day apes. Hence the proportions are half-way between those of apes and men. The structure of these bones indicates that their owners were not tree-living: they did not leap from branch to branch, like monkeys, nor swing like gibbons, but lived on the ground; probably they were active, agile creatures, able to run and jump. Hence, although our ancestry no doubt includes a tree-living phase, our Miocene predecessors evidently already lived on the ground.

As links between men and apes, another group of recently discovered African fossils are even more important. They are called collectively the Australopithecinae, but here we shall refer to them as the South African man-apes, although they were not apes. (They have nothing to do with Australia either.) These forms have been given a variety of generic names, such as *Australopithecus*, *Plesianthropus*, *Paranthropus*, *Zinjanthropus*, and so on: students of human evolution are always fertile in such inventions. It would, however, be more reasonable to put them all in one genus, *Australopithecus*: this genus might be divided into species.

These fossils are much more complete than any of those so far mentioned; they also display a remarkable patchwork of human and non-human features. The brain, skull, and teeth are of ape-like proportions, but the details of structure include a number of similarities to man. Like the gorilla and chimpanzee they had brains of less than half the size of our own, and heavy protruding jaws with large teeth. The average cranial capacity of five skulls has recently been estimated at 576 cubic centimetres – rather more than that of most gorillas. The teeth are arranged in the jaw in human fashion, to form a curved arch; the canines (or eye-

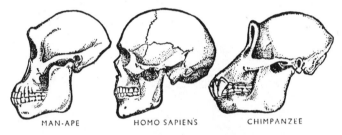

MAN-APE   HOMO SAPIENS   CHIMPANZEE

Skulls of Apes and Man. The South African man-ape has a cranium of similar size to that of the modern chimpanzee, but in other features is more human: note especially the teeth, and the absence of heavy ridges on the cranium

teeth) are not tusk-like as are those of modern apes; and the grinding teeth are human in the details of their construction: these man-apes chewed their food as we do. In the skull, the margins of the nose are formed, as in apes, by a bone called the premaxilla, but the brows lack the heavy ridges above the eyes characteristic of modern apes, and the cheek region also is human in construction.

We have limb skeletons as well as skulls. Parts of two arm bones (humerus and ulna) and a skull have been found together in one lump of rock, and may therefore be assigned with certainty all to the same animal. This is important, because bones found near each other have sometimes given rise to fierce but inconclusive arguments on whether they belonged to the same individual. The almost complete pelvic skeleton, and wrist, thigh and ankle-bone fragments have also been found. Most of the man-apes were smaller than most men, but perhaps resembled human pygmies.

There are, however, some more recently discovered forms ('*Paranthropus*') which were probably above the average height of modern man. More important, the limb bones are found to be in structure (though not in size) typically human, even in detail. The limbs of the South African man-apes certainly resembled ours, and these creatures walked erect as we do. The thumbs too were like ours, and not those of modern apes, since they were evidently efficient grasping organs, probably capable of manipulating tools and weapons. The ankle bones, however, were partly ape-like, and

Pelvic Girdles. The girdle of a chimpanzee is shaped for walking on all fours; that of *Australopithecus* is, like ours, modified for an upright gait

so allowed greater mobility. The erect posture is confirmed also by the structure of the base of the skull, where it joins the vertebral column: the skull was held erect, like ours, not poked forward like that of an ape. The ape-men lived on the ground, on grasslands, instead of being forest-dwellers.

The general picture, then, is of a small, man-like body, with a head more ape-like than human but with some human features. It is therefore natural to ask whether the ape-men had developed greater intelligence than true apes. In size of brain they were no different, and so it is, perhaps, unlikely for that reason alone. But it has been suggested that the man-apes used tools. Baboon skulls have been found near some of the remains, fractured as if they had been struck by a blunt instrument. This suggests that the man-apes were at least intelligent enough to hunt and to kill their prey with weapons. According to the most recent finds *Australopithecus* not only used pebble tools but also probably made them. We therefore ought perhaps to abandon the expression 'man-ape', and to refer to the South African fossils as men.

FOSSIL MEN

The last sentence provokes the question, where is the line drawn between man and not-man? Clearly, if we had a complete series of fossils, as we have for some other mammals, we should have to choose a quite arbitrary point in the series to mark the division. As it is, there are two possible sorts of criteria. First, we can use anatomical features: this, indeed, is the obvious thing to do, since fossils give us direct information on structure, but only indirect knowledge of anything else. So William Howells, the anthropologist, says that 'man zoologically became man when he first walked erect on the ground, or at least developed an arch to his foot'. Second, we can say that the use of specially manufactured tools is diagnostic of man, in which case *Australopithecus* was, by definition, human.

It is, of course, a matter of terminology – of nomenclature – whether we call the South African man-apes 'men' (more technically, Hominidae) or 'apes'. The important fact is that creatures existed with this curious combination of human-type limbs and ape-like skull. The fossils we possess evidently come from the beginning of the Pleistocene, and so are earlier than the earliest known other human remains. Beings of very similar structure were probably among our ancestors. Unlike apes, they were hunters capable of walking long distances as well as using tools instead of teeth.

By the middle Pleistocene, perhaps half a million years ago, several forms of men existed in Java and China, and may have existed elsewhere. The first discovered, and among the most ancient, was the famous fossil man of Java, called *Pithecanthropus erectus* by his discoverer, E. Dubois. This name was at first given to nothing more than a skull cap, a thigh bone, a lower jaw, and a few teeth. From these the existence was inferred of an exceedingly primitive man, with a brain midway in size between a man's and a

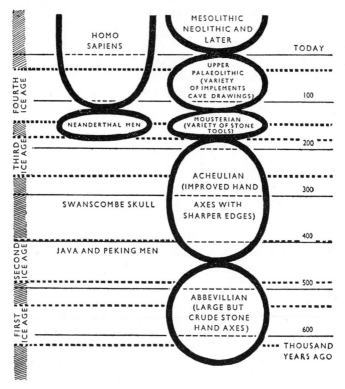

Fossil Men and their Cultures. The stone-tool cultures mentioned are those of western Europe; there are many others

gorilla's, and teeth intermediate in structure, but with erect posture. This diagnosis has been confirmed, not only by further discoveries in Java, but also by much more extensive discoveries near Peking. Peking man has been called *Sinanthropus pekinensis*, but is now treated by many as a variant of *Pithecanthropus*. Moreover, some authorities prefer to call both Java and Peking man *Homo erectus*, to indicate a close kinship with ourselves.

Today we are familiar with the fragmentary remains of about forty Peking men, women, and children, although all the original fossils were lost in the Second World War; none was anything like complete, but we can be certain, not only of the similarity to the Java men, but also that the brain size on the average was greater:

the males had an average brain capacity of about 1150 cubic centimetres, which is 250 above Java man and about 350 below us. (Adult male Europeans have a mean cranial capacity of about 1500 cubic centimetres.) They varied, however, from 900 to 1250. Limb bones are fully human in structure in both the Java and the Peking men. As for height, Java man seems to have resembled us (about

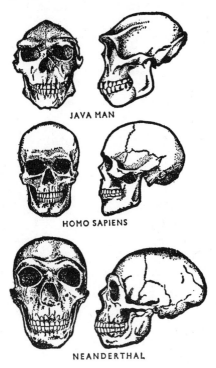

JAVA MAN

HOMO SAPIENS

NEANDERTHAL

Human Skulls. Java man (*Pithecanthropus*) has the smallest cranial capacity of the three types, and the heaviest bony ridges. Modern man has the most lightly constructed skull, no snout, and correspondingly well-developed nose and chin

168 cm, or five feet six inches), while Peking man had a height of about 150 cm.

The evidence for the use of tools by Java man is not complete: stone implements have been found in the same deposits as the skeletal remains, but that is not absolutely conclusive. But Peking man certainly used stone implements, and their structure shows that he was right-handed like us. They include heavy choppers and smaller flaked scraping tools. They belong to the old stone age, but are not the most primitive of all known stone implements. The main food was evidently venison, to judge by the bones found in the caves, but many other species were hunted. Peking man may also have killed and eaten other members of his own species: in other words, he was perhaps a cannibal. Moreover, he may have cooked his food. Certainly, there are patches of blackened earth which show that he had fire. From all this we can suspect that he also had speech, since the construction of tools and the use of language probably developed together. More information on *Homo erectus* may be available soon. In 1963 and 1964 fossils similar to those from Peking were found in southern China. So far a mandible, teeth,

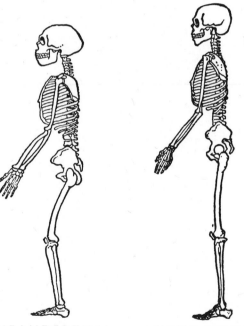

NEANDERTHAL   HOMO SAPIENS

Skeletons. In skeletal structure we (*Homo sapiens*) are fully modified for walking upright on two legs. *Gorilla* is not adapted for walking, but has long arms suitable for 'brachiation' in trees. *H. neanderthalensis* is usually described as

a skull cap and a few other bits have been dug up. Perhaps this type of man was widespread in Asia during the middle Pleistocene.

Other groups of men were in existence at about the time when the Java and Peking men lived. Perhaps the most notable is that represented by a massive jaw found in a sandpit at Mauer near Heidelberg. Heidelberg Man had no chin, but the features of his teeth and the shape of his dental arch are unmistakably human.

The men of Java and Peking probably lived about a million to 700,000 years ago, mid-way through the Pleistocene period. Human fossils assigned to the early part of the Pleistocene are fragmentary and difficult to interpret. We must therefore now come to the Upper Pleistocene. During a great part of this period most of the Old World seems to have been inhabited by men that regularly buried their dead. Like some American Indians and the Ainu today, they also left, in the graves, tools and sometimes animal skulls. Hence we have large numbers of well-preserved specimens, together with the tools they used and the remains of animals they hunted.

These men have from the first been classified as belonging to the same genus, *Homo*, as ourselves: the Latin name of the best-known form is *Homo neanderthalensis*, from the place in Germany in which

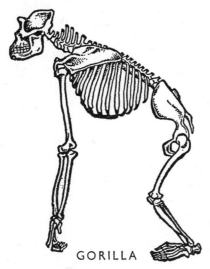

GORILLA

having a bowed posture, but this is now thought to be a misinterpretation of the fossil evidence

one of the first skeletons was discovered. Neanderthal man occupied parts of Europe and Asia and also North Africa. Remains of other, similar types have been found in central and south Africa, and in Java.

We have partial skeletons of more than twenty individuals, and the fragmentary remains of many others. It is therefore possible to see that these archaic forms of Upper Pleistocene man, like modern man, varied greatly in their skeletons.

Neanderthal men, in the form in which we know them best, are distinguished by a remarkably large brain: the average cranial capacity was 1450 cubic centimetres, without distinction of sex, while the figure for the average male European today is 1500. On the other hand, they had prominent brow-ridges, a receding forehead, and no chin. The teeth were larger than ours but of similar structure. It is uncertain whether Neanderthal man stood perfectly erect or not, but his supposed stoop has probably been exaggerated. The average height was about 150 cm (five feet).

Neanderthal man, compared with modern man, was not very enterprising in his use of stone tools. He flaked stone to make scrapers and pointed implements, and simple bone tools were also used. The stone-age culture for which he was responsible was the Mousterian. He seems to have hunted mainly by means of fall-traps. Neanderthal man is commonly believed to have lived in caves, but it is perhaps the archaeologists who have the cave-dwelling habit: caves make convenient sites for archaeological study, and are places where skeletons are likely to be preserved. Probably only a few of the Neanderthalers themselves lived in caves. There are no cave paintings associated with Neanderthal man.

It has been held that Neanderthal was no more than a cousin of modern man; that he evolved quite separately from our own immediate ancestors and was later replaced by *Homo sapiens*. The early Neanderthalers are more like ourselves than the later ones: this is evidence of evolutionary divergence from our own line. Moreover, in Europe the Neanderthal communities were quite suddenly replaced by men of modern type, evidently as a result of immigration by the latter. As we dig down we find first the comparatively recent traces of *H. sapiens*, and then, quite abruptly, an earlier deposit with Neanderthal remains. There was no gradual change from one type to the other.

To recapitulate, the nearest we have to primate forms ancestral both to ourselves and to modern apes are Miocene types such as *Proconsul*. The next stage is that of the South African man-apes, which had already acquired the type of skeleton needed for walking upright; but they had ape-like skulls and correspondingly small brains. Nevertheless, they evidently made tools. The men of Java and Peking not only walked erect, but also had larger brains and more human skulls than the man-apes. Correspondingly, their tools were more advanced. Peking man grades into Neanderthal man. The later Neanderthalers diverged from our own type, and were finally displaced by us throughout the world.

COMPLEXITIES

It would be convenient if the story of human evolution could be left like this, but other fragments fail to fit into a simple scheme.

The earliest comes from the lower Pliocene of central Italy. *Oreopithecus* is about 10m. years old. Many skull fragments are known, and also an almost complete, though flattened, skeleton. This creature had a remarkably flat face, like ours, with canine teeth less strongly developed than those of modern apes, and certainly no projecting, ape-like muzzle. But the body resembled that of a chimpanzee. *Oreopithecus* is no monkey (even though in some details its teeth are like those of monkey), and it caused some excitement among paleontologists – always rather volatile people – at one time. Nowadays it is assigned to a family on its own. It represents an extinct form of ape with some human features which were perhaps evolved independently.

Nearer the modern apes there is another, more formidable animal, *Gigantopithecus*, from the early Pleistocene. This animal was first known from massive molars bought in apothecaries' shops in Hong Kong, where they are reputed to have magical powers. Later, lower jaws were found in caves in China. If *Gigantopithecus* were alive today it would be one more big ape, but with less of a muzzle and smaller teeth than those of gorillas. A fanciful suggestion is that it does survive in the Himalayas, as the legendary yeti.

Deposits of still more recent date have yielded a miscellany of fragments, once parts of beings undoubtedly human yet with substantial differences from ourselves. The most famous is the

Swanscombe skull. This skull is known from two fragments, forming the back and base of the brain-case and part of one side. They were found in a gravel pit south of the Thames between Dartford and Gravesend. William Howells, the American anthropologist, remarks on the geological appeal of the district and refers to

the perils of any navvy who works there: the back of his neck is hot from the breath of archaeologists, and he can hardly throw a shovelful of gravel in any direction without hitting some tweedy individual from a learned society.

The Swanscombe skull belonged to a woman in her early twenties. Her skull bones were thicker than is usual in modern skulls, but her cranial capacity seems to have been 1325 to 1350 cubic centimetres. Her importance is that she was probably a near contemporary of Java and Peking man, and so provides fairly convincing evidence for the existence of men of modern appearance in the Middle Pleistocene.

There is some further fragmentary evidence of the existence of *sapiens*-like individuals in the Middle and Upper Pleistocene, *before* the appearance of Neanderthal man. The Steinheim skull is one: this is another woman, rather like the Swanscombe specimen but also with some distinct Neanderthal features. Two further fragments, found at Fontéchevade, in the Charente district of France, and of Upper Pleistocene date, are of unusually thick bones, but have otherwise modern appearance and no Neanderthal features.

Another Pleistocene skull, which has caused a good deal of trouble, is that of *Piltdown man*, also called the Sussex woman. The brain-case, found accidentally in a gravel pit, resembles that of modern man in general form, but the bones are twice as thick. It is now known, as a result of chemical tests, to be less than one hundred thousand years old. Near the brain-case a lower jaw was found, in circumstances that suggested that the two fragments belonged to the same individual. This jaw-bone has no chin and resembles that of a modern ape, and some authorities were led to believe that the Sussex woman had a skull for the most part resembling ours, but a jaw like that of a chimpanzee or orang-utan. This proved too much for some palaeontologists to swallow; and the sceptics have now at last been proved to be right: refined methods of chemical analysis have shown that the jaw is indeed that of a modern ape, skilfully faked to make it seem to belong to the brain-case (which is a genuine fossil). Irritation at a practical joke may be tempered by the reflexion that this recent discovery provides a striking vindication of the view that man is the product of an orderly, though complex, evolutionary process, from primitive Primate, through generalized human forms, to our own species.

MODERN MAN

Our own type, for which the name *Homo sapiens* is usually reserved, has spread and multiplied over the whole world, especially within the past 10,000 years. In our bony structure the distinctive features include the relative lightness of the bones, brow-ridges which

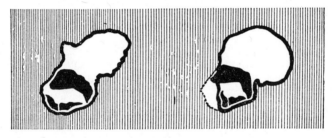

Nose and Chin. Outline of skulls of gorilla (left) and man (right), with nasal cavities and tongue muscles in black. In modern man the projecting nose allows the same amount of nasal cavity as in the gorilla; and the thickness of the front part of the lower jaw bone is on the outside in man, giving him a chin and making room for the tongue muscles

form no more than a pair of small bumps in the forehead, hollow cheeks, a well-developed chin and a prominent nose. The last two features are related to the disappearance of a projecting snout: without the development of a prominent nose this would have left rather little room for the nasal cavity; similarly the tongue muscles would have had to be very small, but for the change in the shape of the lower jaw that gives us our chins.

At this point it might be thought appropriate to introduce some of those well-known portraits of long-haired, uncouth-looking individuals, which are supposed to represent the facial appearance and even the expressions of early human types. It is, however, not possible to reconstruct accurately the features of a modern man from his skull, let alone those of long extinct forms. The portraits, entertaining though they are, have therefore been omitted.

As for our teeth, we have a better record of the modifications they have undergone than those of any other structure. There is an unbroken series of teeth, modern or fossil, from the completely ape to the human. We have lost both the canine tusk and the cheek teeth adapted for tearing flesh with a shear-like action; and our teeth are relatively small and close together. The reduction in the size of the canines, and the modification of the molars for grinding only, may have taken place during a period when our ancestors were of great size, or at least had very heavy skeletons. Men of sufficient size or weight would probably have had teeth large enough to tear flesh without special modification. We are probably now undergoing evolutionary change in the direction of fewer teeth: some people fail to develop the normal number of molars, and this is perhaps related to the overcrowding of the teeth due to reduction of the snout. Our own teeth are capable of dealing with a varied, but not a very tough diet. Man is, in fact, capable of living on a far wider range of foods than most mammals: omnivorous behaviour such as we display is hardly found elsewhere, except among the rats and mice that share our food.

Our hairlessness may be a result of large size. Large mammals lose heat from the body surface less easily than small ones, since the greater their size the smaller is the ratio of surface area to volume; they are thus less likely to require hair to keep them warm. Just as elephants and other large mammals are relatively hairless, it may be that our ancestors lost their hair, as a result of mutation, when they were of great size. Today our hairless condition, like the structure of our teeth, makes us more adaptable: by varying our clothes we can tolerate an exceptionally wide range of climates. Few, if any, other animal species are as widely spread over the earth as *Homo sapiens*.

But our adaptability is, more than anything else, related to the remarkable nature of our brains and limbs. The way we move about is very unusual. The apes are exceptional in having an 'upright' position whilst moving. This is related to the trapeze method of locomotion (brachiation), a mode which is most highly developed today in the gibbon, with its long arms and small legs. Though our arms are long for a mammal, they are shorter than those of apes, and our legs are relatively long; in us the physique of the upright apes as been adapted for walking. It is believed that the line of apes that led to man did not develop the specialized limbs needed for the tree-living as opposed to the ground-living habit.

Walking upright requires more than an enlargement of the legs.

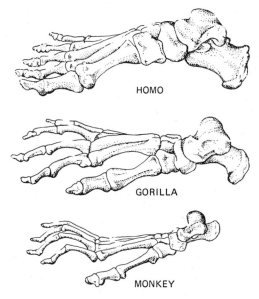

HOMO

GORILLA

MONKEY

Skeletons of the Feet of Three Primates

The curves of the vertebral column alter so that we are not bowed when walking as an ape is. There are also important changes in the foot. The human big toe is non-opposable: that is, we cannot use it in grasping objects as we use our thumb, and as apes use both thumb and big toe. It has been remarked that man has two hands but apes have four. We still have vestiges of the muscles used for working the big toe as a thumb. Together with the reduction in the functions of the toes, the mechanical arrangement of the bones of the foot is changed. Apes have a highly flexible foot, without a well-marked heel. In ours there are two fixed arches, which enable us to rise on our toes, and a well-developed heel. We are thus able to stride and to run. An ape's movement on the ground is limited much as ours is if we walk only on our heels without using the ball of the foot.

The use of the legs alone for walking, and of the arms and hands alone for other purposes, has meant a great deal in the development of man. When the walking habit evolved, our ancestors had probably already a highly-developed co-ordination of movements of the hands with sight: this, at some stage in his ancestry, had been necessary for movement in the trees. With the hands released from locomotory function, the hand-eye relationship came to have other uses. Hands could be used more and more for manipulation. All these changes took place over an immensely long period – probably several million years. There was no deliberate choice, by our ancestors, of the use to which they put their limbs. They were undergoing the slow process of evolutionary change which was discussed at the beginning of this chapter.

In most mammals the snout is the first part of the body that comes in contact with an object, and smell is usually much more important than sight. In man, as in other Primates, the hands have come to be the exploratory organs; we have no snout, our sense of smell is less acute, but our eyesight is exceptionally good. Many of our most important peculiarities, such as our eyes, our ability to breed at any season, and the muscles which enable us to make facial movements expressing emotion, are shared with the modern apes. (The dominance of the sense of sight, by contrast with smell, we share with all the Primates – the apes, monkeys, tarsiers, and lemurs.)

But apes have no *speech*. Our ability to make complex sounds, and to use them to refer both to objects or processes and to ideas, is unique in nature, and with our manual dexterity makes human society possible. The importance of communication between individuals is emphasized by the elaborate development of the facial muscles of expression; and, as M. Abercrombie has pointed out, by the development of the 'whites' of the eyes, which enable us to observe the direction in which a person is looking. Perhaps, too, the red colour of the lips, apart from any sexual significance, aids in communication since, however well we can hear a person, we are usually aided if we can also see his lip movements.

All these changes were accompanied by corresponding developments in the structure of the brain. The part concerned with smell

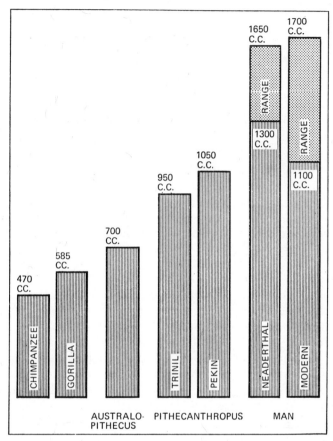

Brain Sizes of Primates. The first five rectangles represent averages: the last two give ranges

became much reduced, that with sight enlarged. Like the monkeys, but not other mammals, we have a specially sensitive area, the macula, near the middle of the retina of the eye; this area enables you to read this page, and to distinguish colours. Our vision is also stereoscopic: that is, both eyes observe the same object, instead of looking in different directions as in most mammals; this makes possible accurate judgement of distances, and of the spatial relations between objects, and consequently the accurate control of movements, especially of the hands.

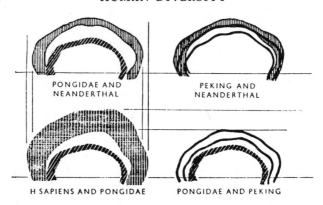

PONGIDAE AND NEANDERTHAL

PEKING AND NEANDERTHAL

H SAPIENS AND PONGIDAE

PONGIDAE AND PEKING

Ranges of Brain-Case Size. For each type, the largest and smallest brain-case is shown in outline. The Pongidae are the modern apes (gorilla, orang-utan, chimpanzee, and gibbon). Modern man has a vast range, which overlaps those of Peking and Neanderthal men

The most conspicuous difference between the brain of a man and that of an ape or any other mammal is size. Granted, the largest mammals, the whales, and even the much smaller elephants, have bigger brains than we have; but, while in man the brain constitutes about one forty-sixth of the weight of the body, an elephant's is only about one five-hundred-and-sixtieth and a large whale's about one eight-thousandth. Accordingly, in the next chapter we consider further some features of the human brain, and of the complex behaviour which it makes possible.

5

BRAIN AND BEHAVIOUR

Man has no nature; all he has is a history.
ORTEGA Y GASSETT

NOWADAYS, the brain is accepted as the most important of the organs which influence behaviour. This view has not always been held, as common expressions such as 'heartless' indicate. The present view is based partly on our knowledge of the effects of brain

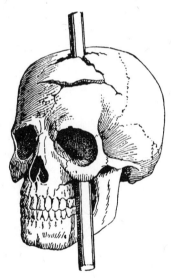

Drawing of the Skull of Phineas Gage, who survived penetration of his head by an iron bar. The tamping iron which had pierced it has been replaced

injury. Damage to particular parts of the brain may produce complete blindness, or deafness and so, of course, a marked change in behaviour. Other damage may produce partial or complete paralysis. Apart from these gross effects we find also smaller changes in

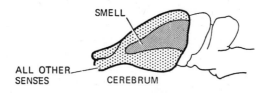

SMELL

ALL OTHER SENSES

CEREBRUM

PRIMITIVE MAMMAL

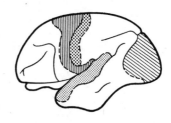

MONKEY CEREBRUM ONLY

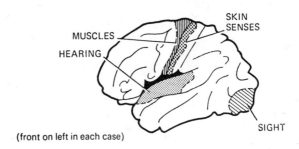

MUSCLES

HEARING

SKIN SENSES

SIGHT

(front on left in each case)

MAN CEREBRUM ONLY

Three Brains. The human brain is larger and more complex than the others: large parts (not shaded) of the cerebrum are concerned with the intellect. The drawings are not to scale

behaviour due to brain damage. Sometimes there is a measurable loss of 'intelligence'. Sometimes emotional changes occur. In one famous example, a bar of iron passed through the front part of a man's brain without killing him; and afterwards the man was described as 'not the same person', because his general behaviour towards his friends was greatly changed.

Attempts have been made to use the effects of destroying parts of the brain in the treatment of severe illness. The injury caused by the iron bar, in the case just mentioned, was to the front part of the

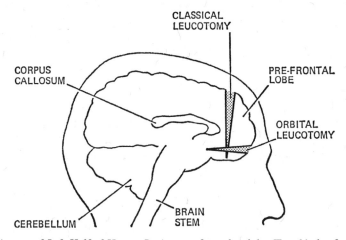

Diagram of Left Half of Human Brain, seen from the right. Two kinds of cut, used in the operation of pre-frontal leucotomy, are shown

cerebrum. Substantial damage to these pre-frontal lobes can probably lead to loss of intellectual abilities; but an adult can certainly behave apparently normally after such injury. Very severe, distressing and unmanageable degrees of madness have been treated by cutting the nerve fibres which connect the pre-frontal lobes to the rest of the brain. From a surgical point of view this is quite a minor operation: it can be done quickly and safely, at least as far as the survival of the patient is concerned. The result may be a disappearance of the most distressing features of a madman's behaviour. Less severe illness has also been treated in this way. The operation has aroused much controversy. Its effects are not predictable with any confidence. Moreover, some have criticized the ruthless interference with human personality which it entails. Its use is now infrequent, largely because the distressing features of the psychoses and psychoneuroses, for which it was used, can be controlled by drugs.

Further evidence of the role of the brain in regulating behaviour comes from the results of local stimulation during operations. In one region such stimulation evokes movements, say, of the arm: in another, the patient reports a sensation in some region of the skin. Yet other clues have come from study of the hypothalamus, a small region which lies above the roof of the mouth and is connected to the pituitary gland. Injury to one part of the hypothalamus, on

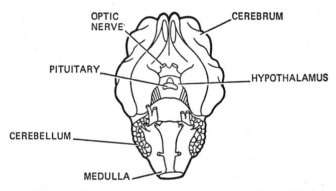

Diagram of Brain of Cat, seen from below, to show the position of the hypothalamus and pituitary

both sides, can cause total loss of appetite; or to another part, excessive eating and consequent gross obesity. These effects have been observed principally in experimental animals on which exceedingly delicate and precise operations have been performed; but similar effects of abnormal conditions of the hypothalamus are seen occasionally in human beings.

Since all parts of the human brain are much larger even than those of apes of about the same body size, a relationship between brain size and intelligence might be expected within the one human species. There is much variation of brain size among modern man: the average male cranial capacity is between 1300 and 1500 cubic centimetres, and normal individuals range from 1050 to 1800. But studies of cranial capacity and intelligence quotient (measured by 'intelligence tests') have shown almost no correlation. If there were a correlation, the Eskimo would probably be the people with the highest average intelligence, for they are said to have the largest brains.

THE NERVOUS SYSTEM AT WORK

We must now look more closely at the ways in which the nervous system operates. If a light is shone in a person's eye, the pupil contracts. This response depends on a series of events beginning in the retina of the eye. The retina includes a layer of cells sensitive to changes of illumination; these cells are connected to nerve fibres which carry impulses to the brain when they are stimulated. Within the brain, other cells are stimulated too, and some of these have fibres which are connected to a muscle which surrounds the pupil. Impulses in these fibres cause the muscle to contract, and this contraction is responsible for the visible narrowing of the pupil.

Such a simple response, or reflex, is carried out always by the same muscles or glands: it is in this respect quite unlike a complex, learnt activity such as playing the piano, in which the same note, for instance, may be played by any finger; it is also independent of the experience of the individual. Other familiar examples are the salivation, or mouth-watering, which occurs when food is placed on the tongue; and the tendon reflexes, such as the knee-jerk, which, like the pupillary reflex, are used by doctors during examination of a patient.

The mechanism of a reflex consists of a sense organ or receptor (the retina in the pupillary reflex); sensory nerve fibres in which impulses travel inwards to the central nervous system; connecting nerve cells in the central nervous system: motor nerve cells and their fibres in which impulses travel outwards; and effector organs – muscles or glands – which perform the response itself.

Our understanding of nerve function is helped by our familiarity with electrical gadgets like telephone systems, which have a superficial similarity to the nervous system. That the resemblance is only superficial can be shown by enlarging on our example of the light shone in the eye. Supposing a very brilliant light is suddenly used, the response is different: the pupil will contract as before, but in addition the eyes will be screwed up, the head perhaps turned away, and the hands may be put in front of the eyes. In this case a greater number of ingoing, sensory nerve fibres has been stimulated, and each carries more impulses than before; hence larger regions of the brain have been activated, and so the output goes to many more muscles – not only to the muscle of the pupil.

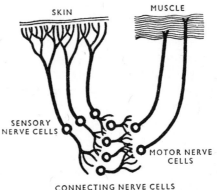

The Mechanism of the Reflex. The diagram shows a sense organ (the skin), sensory nerve cells which influence connecting nerve cells in the central nervous system, and motor nerve cells which bring about muscle contraction. All ordinary responses involve hundreds or thousands of nerve cells at each stage, linked in far more complex ways than those shown

But by far the greatest complexity arises when we *repeatedly* apply this stimulus of a very bright light. We know what would happen: either the person concerned would avoid the situation altogether; or he would come with his eyes already screwed up, in anticipation of the light; or possibly he would wear dark glasses. Certainly his behaviour would be modified as a result of experience. This implies that the connexions in the central nervous system are not all fixed: they must be highly labile, and continually changing throughout life, at least in detail. It is as if the telephone system grew new wires according to circumstances.

THE BRAIN AND COMPLEX BEHAVIOUR

The behaviour of animals with simple nervous systems consists of little more than reflexes and other immediate responses to external stimuli. Their whole activity is determined, from moment to moment, by the surrounding conditions, and they display little change of behaviour with experience. Independence of transitory sensory impulses increases with the size of the central nervous system, and reaches its maximum in ourselves. It is reflected in the 'absent-mindedness' which notoriously accompanies intense concentration on a particular problem. A man has, in his cerebral cortex alone, around 15,000m. nerve cells. Each is connected to many others, and the connexions are continually liable to change. It is not surprising that human behaviour, dependent on this intricate mechanism, is often unpredictable and baffling.

Certainly, no simple account in terms of stimulus and response fits the achievements of this vast mass of nerve cells. We may take, as an example, any skilled activity: let us say, a person reading music at the piano. At first sight the playing of a particular chord might be regarded as a complex, but straightforward, response to a specific stimulus, namely, the pattern of marks on paper. Further reflexion shows that this is incorrect, for two reasons. First, the stimulus is not specific or invariable: the chord will be played whether the music is printed, or has been roughly written by the composer; whether the type is large or small, or near or distant. There is much variation in the pattern, impinging on the retina of the eye, which induces the pianist to play the chord. Moreover, a chord may be played correctly the first time the appropriate printed music is seen. The second reason, for saying that here is no simple stimulus-response relationship, is that the details of the response itself may vary: the chord may be played by either hand, or by both, and by various combinations of fingers, yet the sound resulting may be the same in each case.

We have here, then, examples of 'stimulus equivalence' and 'response equivalence', There are many other obvious examples from everyday life. A tune is recognized as 'the same', whether played in the key of C major, or G major; we can understand words spoken in a great variety of accents, at a high or low pitch, loudly or quietly, quickly or slowly. On the side of response, a footballer can score a goal with his foot or his head, and a man who has lost both arms can write with a pencil held in his toes. Nor do these facts exhaust the complexities of our behaviour. Much of our most elaborate behaviour is 'spontaneous': that is, it arises from internal activity of the nervous system and other organs, and not from any specific, immediate external situation.

For our present purpose, the most important feature of all these diverse activities is that they are *learnt* by practice. This familiar fact is important in ways which are often overlooked. We must therefore consider the subject in more detail.

STEREOTYPED BEHAVIOUR

To what extent is human behaviour determined in advance, by a constitution fixed at conception, and to what extent does it depend, for its development, on the experience of the particular individual?

Consider an example from the hive bee. If the queen bee, the one fertile female, is removed from a colony, after an interval a curious disturbance is observed: the bees run 'agitatedly' over the combs, meeting other bees with which they lightly cross the antennae; and disorder soon spreads through the whole colony. Sometimes the bees have been described as vibrating their wings to produce 'a low, mournful lament'. Here is a notable opportunity to interpret the behaviour of very different animals in terms of our own thoughts and feelings. Bees are among the most highly organized of social insects, and the very use of the word 'queen' illustrates the long-standing habit of describing insect communities as if they were human.

But no human community has only one fertile female, the mother of all the rest. What, then, should we make of the consequences of removing the queen? If the queen is placed in a small cage within the hive, where she can still be touched and smelt by the other bees, no disturbance is observed. The situation is as if, in a human community, the most important personage had been imprisoned, in full view of the populace, but in conditions in which she can no longer take any part in communal activities.

In such circumstances, human beings would react strongly. Bees do not do so, because their behaviour depends, to a much greater extent, on particular, isolated stimuli. They respond, not to change in the situation as a whole (as men do), but to the presence or absence of a smell, a sight or a sound. Bees in the hive behave normally while a particular substance continues to emanate from the queen; in the absence of that substance, their behaviour alters.

This is characteristic of much, though not all, of the complex behaviour of animals. Many animals perform apparently skilled tasks, such as nest building, or finding concealed food, or hiding themselves: many have elaborate social activities, especially in courtship and the care of the young. In normal conditions their apparent skill is so marked, that we easily think of their behaviour as 'intelligent', or, in their social life, as displaying the emotions which we ourselves experience. Yet, as with the bees, every detailed inquiry shows how false this interpretation is. A further example is the behaviour of a bird, such as a meadow pipit, with a young cuckoo in its nest. The nestling pipits have been cast out by the cuckoo, and perhaps are squeaking just outside, in full view and hearing of the parent bird; but the latter ignores its own young, and feeds the cuckoo. It is responding to the stimulus constituted by the open beak of the cuckoo: when this stimulus is presented, in the nest, no other feature of the situation is significant for the parent bird. Like the bees, the bird fails to respond to the situation as a whole, or to adapt itself to a novel state of affairs. Such behaviour is certainly not what one would call intelligent: it is automatic or mechanical.

These responses to standard stimuli, though much more complicated than reflexes, resemble reflexes in one important respect: they are largely independent of individual experience. Standardized behaviour, typical of a whole species, has often been called 'instinctive' or 'innate'. These words have, however, led to some confusion, and so they are not used here.

THE DEVELOPMENT OF BEHAVIOUR

Some animal behaviour, which at first seems obviously 'instinctive', depends to a surprising extent on early learning. An example comes from experiments on the catching of mice by cats. Kittens were subjected to different conditions in early life. Some were brought up together with a mouse or rat; some were brought up alone after weaning; and a third group were brought up with their mothers, and allowed to see their mothers kill a mouse or rat every few days. Of those which had been brought up with a mouse or rat, only three out of eighteen killed an animal, and none killed an animal of the kind with which it had been brought up. Of twenty which were brought up alone, nine killed animals; and of twenty-one which had seen their mothers killing, eighteen were killers.

This example is especially instructive, because many people would take it for granted that mouse-catching by cats is 'an instinct'. Certainly, some cats have a strong tendency to catch mice: the three killers in the first group were, no doubt, examples. There is much genetical variation in the propensity for these various sorts of behaviour, and not only in cats. It has been utilized in the selection of breeds of dogs: some retrieve game well, some pursue sheep with exceptional efficiency after due training, yet others are watch dogs or guard dogs. But in each case, the special qualities of the animal become evident only after suitable training.

The example of the cats concerns hunting and feeding, that is, maintenance activities. The behaviour of a trained dog often seems to represent a kind of 'intelligence'. To understand how these activities come to be performed, we need to know how they develop in the individual: that is, we must study their *ontogeny*. The same applies to the development of social behaviour. H. F. Harlow and his colleagues have done important experiments on young rhesus monkeys. Given milk from a bottle, these appealing little creatures can be raised in complete isolation from other monkeys. But the result may be disastrous. As adults, they may be unable to adapt themselves to monkey society; and even their sexual behaviour may be so abnormal as to render them sexually helpless and consequently, as a rule, infertile. Here is another example, of what would often be called an 'instinctive' act, which we now find requires for its development special conditions in early life. The social and sexual behaviour of monkeys has to be gradually learnt by experience.

These examples from other species exemplify yet one more principle. There are stages in individual development during which an animal is especially capable of learning to perform certain kinds of activities. It may not be quite true that one cannot teach old dogs new tricks; but it is certainly easier to teach them to young ones. As for social behaviour, if a *sensitive period* in development is passed, without the appropriate training, it may be difficult or impossible to make up for the lost opportunity. As far as is known, Harlow's monkeys could not be socially rehabilitated as adults.

We must now consider the bearing these studies have on man.

To find fixed behaviour patterns, common to our whole species, we must turn to infancy. Every baby sucks, turns his head when his cheek is touched, clings, smiles and cries. The first two are concerned with feeding; clinging is evidently a vestige of an ancestral habit of clinging to a mother's hair. Crying ordinarily induces an adult, especially a mother, to pick up and comfort the helpless child. (It is sad that false theories, some uttered in the name of science, have occasionally persuaded mothers not to carry out this necessary act.) Smiling, which usually begins in the second month, encourages parents to cherish their infant. This statement of the seemingly obvious is supported by what happens when, rarely, a child fails to smile: the mother often becomes seriously disheartened, and finds it impossible to respond with ordinary love and care.

'Social smiling' is the response of an infant to a human face – any face, at first, or even to a hideous mask-like pattern. Here is a close resemblance to other species: a particular sight or sound leads to an equally stereotyped response. A cock robin in his territory sings at the appearance of a rival; a peacock spreads his feathers at the sight of a female; a nestling bird gapes on the arrival of a parent, and so exposes a coloured pattern inside its mouth which in turn stimulates feeding. Later the human infant becomes more discriminating: he smiles at his mother, and perhaps his father and other relatives, but embarrasses his parents by turning away from strangers. This sort of behaviour is a means by which the young of other species are kept from danger: they learn, early in life, to approach their parents but to avoid all strange animals larger than themselves.

Once infancy is passed, man no longer displays this sort of kinship with other species. In adult human behaviour there are no complex *fixed* behaviour patterns. Whether we are building a house, making love, or communicating with our fellows, we are acting in ways which – consciously or not – have been learnt by experience. Our repertoire of stereotyped performances is confined to the reflex level, as in sneezing and blinking. All our elaborate activities, including courtship, child-rearing, even our food habits, depend to a major extent on individual experience. Instead of being rather uniform throughout the species, as are the rituals of mating, nest-building and so on in, for instance, birds and fish, they vary a great deal from one community to another; they are the results of social or cultural training.

Every human being (except a few of grossly abnormal development) has a brain which enables him to develop complex behaviour such as speech; but the behaviour patterns arise during development, as a result of a process, in the child very slow and gradual, of adaptive change. Recent researches have revealed previously unsuspected ways in which the conditions of childhood influence later

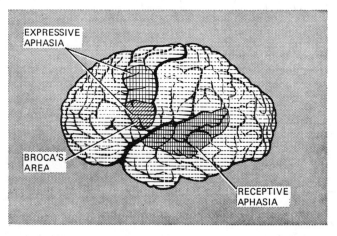

EXPRESSIVE APHASIA

BROCA'S AREA

RECEPTIVE APHASIA

The Cerebral Cortex of Man from the left. Two large regions especially concerned with speech are shown. Damage to 'Broca's' area disturbs control of the speech muscles. Injury to the area above may lead to other deficiencies, including loss of ability to express ideas in writing. The other labelled area is evidently more concerned with the understanding of speech. These large structures are distinguishing features of the human species

behaviour. One example concerns the way in which we learn to recognize the things we see. An important discussion of this problem, published in Germany in 1932, was based on studies of what happened when persons, blind from birth, had their sight conferred by operation. Later, research was done on laboratory animals.

It had been assumed in the past that human beings (and other animals) have an innate ability to distinguish at least simple shapes, for instance squares from circles. By an adult, or even quite a young child, the distinction is made 'instantaneously' and without effort. This assumption is false.

An adult blind from birth owing to cataract, and successfully treated to make vision possible, reports at first only a confusing mass of lights and colours. No object, however familiar from past experience of touching, smelling, and so on, can be identified by sight. Shapes are not identified at all: to distinguish a square or triangle from a circle, the subject has to learn laboriously to count the corners; and what is learnt on one day is forgotten by the next. If the names of colours have been learnt, and the subject is shown an orange, he may at once name the colour; but he will not identify the object as an orange until he has touched it.

We recognize the things we see (or hear) even though the exact appearance they present varies according to the distance, the angle at which we see them, and so on. This *perceptual generalization* is quite absent in those learning to see. A man who had learnt to name a square, made of white cardboard, failed to identify it when the other side, painted yellow, was shown. Objects, of which the names have been learnt in one set of conditions, are not identified when seen against a different background or in light of a different colour. Such confusions, though never made by a normal adult, have nevertheless a counterpart in adult behaviour: for instance, 'all Chinese look alike' – until we have had some experience of meeting different Chinese; or, all small brown birds look like sparrows – until we have had some experience of bird watching.

Eventually, with great persistence and after months or years, the congenitally blind person who has acquired vision may learn to make fairly full use of his eyes and even to read; but it is a painful experience.

Evidently, even the most elementary human responses are a product of learning: during the long periods of helplessness, and still longer period of dependence during childhood, all the essential behaviour patterns are being laid down, as a result of adaptive changes in the plastic central nervous system.

This applies, not only to intellectual development, but also to the growth of emotional and social attitudes. The work of Freud and his followers has made us familiar with the idea that disorders of behaviour (mental illness) can sometimes be traced, at least in part, to the conditions of early childhood. This notion has a wider application. Family relationships in childhood have an important influence on all the personal relationships of the adult: the child's attitude towards his or her father may influence later attitudes towards those in authority; a boy's feelings towards his mother may be reflected in his later behaviour to his wife; a girl's early impressions of an elder brother may induce a later competitive attitude towards men.

A notable, if controversial, study of such effects was published by the World Health Organization under the title *Maternal Care and Mental Health*. The main theme is the effects of depriving young children of mothering. 'Deprivation' means here that the child is without his mother or any substitute or foster-mother for three months or more during his first five years. Many of the studies on which this work was based were from excellently run orphanages.

Small children separated from their mothers become less active. After a few days of bitter protest they become less vocal, and sometimes appear misleadingly 'good'. Both physical and intellectual development are retarded. (These changes can be prevented if there is somebody available to become a complete substitute mother.) According to the original study, certain criminal types, notably persistent thieves, have a remarkably high proportion of histories of grossly disturbed relationships with their mothers in early years. Youths of this type lack all normal emotional responses: they are indifferent to punishment, inaccessible to true friendship and, of course, make very bad parents. Some other researches, but by no means all, have found correlations between early deprivation and later psychopathic or neurotic behaviour.

It might be thought that such youths had a 'bad heredity', and that they would have been abnormal in their behaviour regardless of upbringing. Careful studies of families have, however, failed to bring any evidence of such genetical effects. Moreover, similar behaviour can be induced experimentally in animals, in conditions which entirely exclude genetical influences. Uniovular twin kids (young goats) have been used: of each pair, one was reared normally, while one was separated for short periods from its mother. The behaviour of the deprived kids was profoundly disturbed: they did not eat normally and they displayed exceptional agitation when put in darkness. Hence, just as with Harlow's monkeys, effects observed in children can to some extent be paralleled in other species; and animal studies have in this case supplemented observations of human beings, and perhaps have helped to validate them.

The exact relationships between its family circumstances and a child's development will take a long time to unravel, but all the examples given above point in the same direction: they illustrate the diverse and complex ways in which individual behaviour is shaped by individual experience. Accordingly, we should expect to find that the social behaviour of a man or a woman is determined by the society in which they are brought up, regardless of their parentage. This has repeatedly been observed. For example, an American child was adopted in his first year by a Chinese family living in China; on returning to his native land as a young man, he found his behaviour (unlike his appearance) so wholly Chinese, that he was obliged to attend Americanization classes designed for foreign immigrants.

Other evidence comes from detailed studies of childhood in primitive societies. Among them, the Balinese are an attractive group. Many characteristic features of adult Balinese behaviour can be related to their methods of child-rearing. In Bali the incidence of muscular fatigue is less than in other societies. Correspondingly, learning in early life takes place very largely by direct manipulation of the child's body, or by encouraging imitation: there is little verbal instruction. The words that are used are mostly 'effectively toned exclamations'. Consequently, among Balinese adults, the craftsmen use only the muscles essential for the particular task: these men evidently have in high degree the valuable gift of relaxation. The Balinese also attach much importance to the position or orientation of the body, and have an exceptional dislike of drunkenness, though not on moral grounds.

In each society every child is systematically moulded in every aspect of his behaviour, his postures and movements, his ways of thinking and modes of feeling, as the result of the impressions he unconsciously receives during every waking moment from the time of his birth.

HEREDITY AND 'INSTINCT'

If environmental effects are so overwhelming, it may be asked, what becomes of the genetical influence on behaviour? The preceding section might seem to imply that genetical differences may be ignored. Yet, as we have seen in earlier chapters, this is not the case. The difficulty of sorting out genetical from environmental effects is

particularly acute for human behaviour, because the most conspicuous feature of the human nervous system is its plasticity.
Nevertheless, there is undoubtedly genetical variation, in every
human population, which influences behavioural traits. In no
imaginable environment could the writer have become a really good
mathematician. Genetical factors evidently set a limit to what each
individual can do, though we rarely, if ever, can state the limit
precisely.

This genetical variation, combined with the plasticity of the
nervous system, is essential for the development of complex
societies. Such societies require many specialists, in diverse skills.
An incomplete list of occupations, compiled by the United States
government, includes seventeen thousand titles; many of these
no doubt are unskilled, but the truly skilled trades, needing long
training, are numbered in hundreds. There is undoubtedly much
genetical variation in the ability to perform skilled work, even though
each skill is also a product of training.

The dependence on environmental influences can be illustrated
from children brought up in grossly abnormal conditions. Among
such children there are a few supposed instances of rearing by
wolves, in complete isolation from human beings from an early age.
Such children are of course without language, and effectively
imbecilic: they have no capacity at all for entering relationships with
other human beings; they have no 'instinctive' feeling of kinship
with men.

Better examples are of children, brought up by their mothers in
extreme social isolation, who have subsequently been rescued.
One was confined to a single room from the age of less than a year
until she was about six; she was fed on milk and thin oatmeal, but
no solids. When brought to a children's hospital the child seemed to
be deaf and blind; she lay limply where she was put, indifferent to
everything that went on around her. She neither smiled nor cried.
After nine months she was put into the care of one woman who had
no task but to look after her. Six months later she could walk, was
quite fat and could understand verbal instructions, though she still
could not speak.

Another six-year-old girl was found to have been brought up in
isolation by a deaf and dumb mother. This child inevitably had no
understanding of speech, and could not talk. In twenty-two months,

however, she was taught to talk intelligently and to sing, as well as the other activities characteristic of her age. None of these activities developed until they were taught.

What then becomes of the so-called human 'instincts'? We have already seen that man has no complex fixed behaviour patterns: he has no instincts in that sense. Nevertheless, writers in the past have made lists of human instincts, and many people take it for granted that they exist.

The lists of instincts describe, not particular acts of behaviour, but goals which most human beings tend to achieve. The expression 'parental instinct' is in practice a name for the fact that most people have children and look after them – but, alas, there are plenty of exceptions. The term 'instinct of self-preservation' names the tendency of most people to keep themselves alive; but again there are plenty of exceptions, as when someone sacrifices his or her life for another or for a cause.

Perhaps when some people talk of human instincts, they mean internal agents which cause people to behave in certain ways. In scientific studies today, if one seeks such internal agents, one looks in the first place in the central nervous system, and secondly in other organs, especially the endocrine or ductless glands. However, the human brain is a system of which plasticity, rather than rigidity of organization, is the most notable feature.

When human beings do behave like automata, this is still a product of early training. A cynic, reading the passages which emphasize the human capacity for adapting behaviour to new conditions, might comment on the many exceptions to be found among adults. The inflexible habits, attitudes, and beliefs, held by many even when there are good reasons for discarding them, are, however, products of early experience: they vary from one society or class to another, and from generation to generation.

There are, of course, important internal influences on behaviour, as well as the learned patterns of the nervous system. When the amount of sugar in the blood falls below a certain level we say we are hungry, and we seek food. Nevertheless, this behaviour is still partly a product of learning: the time at which we feel hungry is that at which we are accustomed to eat; if we pass this time without eating, we may cease to feel hungry, though our physiological need for food is even greater. To some extent we learn to be hungry. Our food habits – what we eat, how it is cooked and served – are still more products of cultural conditioning.

In sexual behaviour, similarly, we find important internal influences apart from training. These are clearly revealed in abnormal cases. A man with a tumour of the adrenal gland may lose interest in women, but regain it when the tumour is removed. A woman with a tumour of a particular part of the brain may be sexually over-active, but behave normally when it has been excised. Nevertheless, as we saw in chapter 1, sexual behaviour too depends on the upbringing and experience of the individual.

While nearly everyone eats, mates, preserves his own life and protects his children, partly under the influence of unlearned internal processes, the ways in which all these things are done are infinitely variable, and depend on the customs of the community in which the individual is reared.

'AGGRESSION' AND WAR

These principles can be applied to the analysis of human conflict. Some people hope that study of conflict in other species can help us to solve the problems of human behaviour. Accordingly, it is sometimes asked: Is there a human 'aggressive instinct'? To answer this we must determine the true nature of animal conflict. There are plenty of descriptions of attacks, fights and submissions in encounters between animals of the same kind. But, if the descriptions are accurate and detailed, the incidents prove to consist largely of formal postures, gestures, wrestling, perhaps harmless biting, kicking or butting, according to the equipment of the animals described; serious wounding is exceedingly rare, and death due directly to such clashes (that is, 'murder') is almost unknown among wild animals in their usual surroundings.

The wolf is a good example of an energetic predator with a peaceful home life. Wolves live in groups in which certain individuals are dominant: that is, they have prior access to food, females and other amenities. This sort of arrangement may be called a peck order (after the actions of birds in which it was first described in detail), or a status system. Dominance is determined and maintained principally by attitude. A superior male stands erect, growls and snaps his teeth; an inferior droops and remains silent.

Status systems are usual among our nearest relatives, the monkeys and apes. Baboons move about in troops within which the relationships are remarkably stable. There are occasional clashes between subordinate individuals, but they are often stopped by the mere approach of a dominant male; and, if a dominant male himself becomes violent, he may be brought to order by a group of underlings.

Status within groups disposes of anything comparable to riot or homicide, but there is still the possibility of war between different packs, herds, flocks, prides or other assemblies. And indeed, one band usually is intolerant of others; individual members of strange groups are driven away, and a mass encounter can engender quite a marked disturbance. But it is disturbance, not lethal war. A clash between groups, for instance of monkeys, seems never to be deadly in the natural habitat of the species. Howls, screams and whistles may occur; the branches of trees may be violently shaken; particular postures may be adopted. The result is not a resort to violence, but the *withdrawal* of one or both groups.

Commonly, among the larger land animals, a mated pair or larger group occupies a defended region, or territory. Territorial behaviour has been studied among a great variety of mammals, from mice to deer, but is best known among birds. Their territories are usually held by pairs. Bird territories often have particularly well-defined boundaries, beyond which the occupants do not venture, while mammals may range widely outside the region which they defend. Despite all the great variety, we find one obvious common effect of territorial behaviour: it spaces out the population of the species which display it. The usual assumption is that this prevents over-use of the food or other resources of the environment. One rarely finds starving or emaciated individuals in a natural, undisturbed population. Moreover, in a breeding season, as a rule, either healthy young are produced, or none.

In the past, many writers would have used the facts given above as a basis for moral exhortation. But systems of morals are a prerogative of man. The absence of 'murder' or 'war' in other species is a consequence, not of obeying moral codes regularly taught to the young and debated by elders, but of fixed systems of signals and responses, characteristic of each species. Most people refrain from stealing or damaging the property of others: but the training in social behaviour sometimes fails and, occasionally, we find families in which the children have been taught to be thieves or even killers. In other species apparent respect for 'property' or territory is due to a propensity to withdraw, when faced by a territory holder that makes the appropriate signals; this withdrawal is not, as a rule, gradually learnt by practice.

The list below illustrates the difference between ourselves and other species, and the first three items reflect the exceptional plasticity of human behaviour.

Other animals	Man
Stereotyped social signals and responses	Languages
'Threat' and withdrawal	Laws; but war, murder, rape
Territory	Property
Lower fertility with increasing population density	Lower fertility with increasing prosperity

One consequence of the lack of uniformity of adult human signals is the breakdown of understanding when the members of different communities meet. This is not only a matter of language. Facial expressions and gestures, too, are enigmatic in the members of an unfamiliar culture. This sometimes holds even when the *language* is the same. Its consequences are felt in such situations as those of soldiers trying to interpret the attitudes of young women in a foreign country, and psychiatrists attempting psychotherapy in a strange society.

Similarly, the laws concerning respect for other persons and for property are learnt, usually in childhood, and vary greatly between communities. There are no standard signals or responses, common to our whole species, which regulate our encounters with other people, and our attitudes towards their belongings. This allows, not only great diversity of laws and customs, but also the breakdown of social order, as in rape, murder and war. This dark side to our behaviour does not, however, justify talk of a fixed 'aggressive instinct'. Granted, any person can be provoked to violence; nevertheless, a habit of violence has to be developed by practice: this is what most military training has attempted, at least in the past. It is often gratifyingly difficult to instil martial 'virtues' in an ordinary person.

The contrast between man and other species is equally clear if we compare the territorial behaviour of animals with property-holding by people. Territories are maintained by formal signals, common to a whole species. Every adult or group of each species holds a territory. Man displays no such uniformity: even within a single community, vast areas may be owned by one person, while others have none. There is, even today, ownership in people. But in some countries private ownership is confined to personal property. In a few tribal groups even minor possessions are held in common. Man has, in fact, no more a 'property-owning instinct' than he has an 'instinct to steal'. Granted, it is easy to rear children to be acquisitive; yet the form of the acquisitiveness, and the extent to which it is sanctioned by society, varies greatly from one country to the next, and from one historical period to another.

Debate on the human propensity for aggression or greed needs to be balanced by acknowledgement of our much more marked gift for peaceful social behaviour. Should we say, then, that man has an innate tendency, or instinct, for cooperation – or love? Though both true – in a sense – and agreeable, this adds hardly more to our understanding than statements on the 'aggressive instinct'. The important questions are how social behaviour develops in each individual, and how this development sometimes fails.

On this, exceptionally, there is a clue from work on another species, namely, the experiments already mentioned, of H. F. Harlow and his colleagues on rhesus macaque monkeys. These animals, in their normal environment, form stable colonies each with a typical status system. Yet their social behaviour in general, and their sexual behaviour in particular, both depend, for normal development, on experience in early life. Neither is 'instinctive', in the sense of highly stable and fixed in development. Young macaques, reared during their first months without other monkeys, on release into a colony behave abnormally: instead of soon conforming to the status system, they attack and injure others. The result is disruption of the colony. A very few females reared in isolation have been mated. These mothers brutally maltreat their young: they attack them, and rebuff them when they pathetically try to cling. These maltreated young, in turn, when they grow up, are sexually over-active and abnormally aggressive.

These observations seem to parallel those, mentioned above, on children who have been deprived of ordinary parental care during their early years. The notion that parental love is important for the emotional development of a child is hardly new. Moralists, among others, have been urging it for millennia. Unfortunately, other moralists have, for a similar period, urged the importance of strictness and punishment in the upbringing of children. This is yet one more example of the absence of standard patterns of social behaviour in our species. What is new is that we are now beginning to analyse just what parental care consists of, and what features of it are crucial for emotional development. This is of great practical importance for the conduct, say, of orphanages, and for the way in which young children are treated when they have to make a stay in hospital. Perhaps this sort of understanding will help to prevent the development of anti-social, aggressive behaviour in children without ordinary family life.

The preceding paragraphs equate aggression with violence. It may be argued that much 'aggression' is expressed in other ways. When a business firm advertises for 'aggressive salesmen', the advertiser is not, presumably, seeking men eager for unarmed combat. There is, in fact, a shift in meaning here. One needs to distinguish between animosity, on the one hand, and dominance (in the everyday sense), on the other. Failure to make this distinction led a speaker at a scientific conference to ask whether it is desirable to control aggression in man. He was not inciting his colleagues to murder or assault; his remark merely reflected the use of the word 'aggression' for qualities which, sometimes at least, are thought socially desirable.

The absence of standard means of regulating our behaviour is reflected in the growth of human populations. Other species, at least of mammals and birds, probably regulate their densities through their social behaviour – especially territorial behaviour. If we did this, there would be no crowded cities and no population problem; we have a singular capacity to huddle together in vast numbers, and the ability to rear our children so that they continue to live in crowds with remarkably little conflict. This adaptability has its disadvantages: since crowding does not impair fertility, we are obliged to adapt ourselves still further, by devising methods of birth control.

But perhaps we possess some trace of ancestral territorial behaviour? Is it possible that crowding does increase animosity? In fact, there is no evidence for this. Presumably, if it did so, there would be a high incidence of assault at holiday camps and other seaside resorts. More seriously, the animosity might be aroused, but suppressed as a result of training, with indirect ill-effects.

We know all too little about the effects of life in cities on mental health, but it must be doubted whether studies in terms of population density alone would be profitable. In the kinetic theory of gases, each molecule of a given substance, such as carbon dioxide, may be thought of as identical with every other; and each encounter between two molecules is of the same sort. By contrast, a kinetic interpretation of human encounters obviously will not do. The effect of a meeting between two people can be influenced by the precise circumstances at the time, the general social training each has undergone and their own particular personalities. Each of these in turn is influenced by many factors. Moreover, an encounter between two strangers in a sparsely populated region might be decidedly alarming, whereas in a city it is a commonplace and unremarkable.

Psychologists and others will certainly continue to observe monkeys and rats, even when their proper study is man. They may reasonably hope, in this way, to throw light at least on human physiology. Our hormones we share with the rest of the mammals (and others); and all the major features of our brains are represented in other species. Any improvement in our understanding of the nervous systems depends almost entirely on experiments on laboratory animals. Moreover studies of species closely related to ourselves can suggest hypotheses on the development of behaviour: they may help, for example, to validate, or to modify, psychoanalytic notions on the influence of early relationships in the family.

If we are to apply the results of such experiments to man, we need an accurate chart of the gulf between ourselves and other animals. A purely scientific survey (which omits much) reveals two prominent features. First is the vast scope of our ability to adapt our behaviour to circumstances. This faculty dominates, not only matters of intellect, but also the development of social behaviour. A human being, even the most free and independent, cannot avoid being moulded by the community in which he is reared. Second, we are correspondingly deficient in predetermined abilities which regulate our behaviour. We have inescapable needs, but the means by which to satisfy them have to be learnt.

Hence, we have, in the end, to control our own behaviour by making decisions based, not on knowledge of other species, but on awareness of ourselves.

SOCIAL AWARENESS

There is also awareness of others. Other animals respond to stimuli, or 'signals', given by members of their own species. This by itself does not constitute what we call here 'awareness'. A bird may display before its mate, or a rival, but this does not imply any appreciation that the other individual is also perceiving, and responding to, the display.

How do we distinguish awareness? In ourselves, we are subjectively conscious of it, but there are also objective tests. The important test is: does each individual modify the signals he gives – sounds, movements, and so on – to ensure that they are audible, visible, or, in general, intelligible, to other individuals? It is doubtful whether any animals other than man, and perhaps his nearest relatives, correct their signals in this way. In man, such correction is usual; but it is far from universal, as the study of the behaviour of lecturers quickly shows.

Subjectively, we experience thoughts and feelings which make up our consciousness; and we assume that others have similar thoughts and feelings. This sort of awareness is an essential basis of human social behaviour. Man is not merely a highly social animal, like the hive bee; he is also a communicating animal, at a level of complexity without parallel in the rest of the animal kingdom. There is nothing, in the social signals given by other species, to be compared with human languages, even the simplest ones. By means of language, we communicate both facts and feelings, and we do so on the basis of our knowledge, not only of our own feelings, but of those of our fellow human beings.

This may seem an arid way of saying that men love, and depend on the love of, their fellows. It would, however, be absurd to attempt an account of human behaviour, and then to omit this, its most distinctive feature. A difficulty is that the language in which we are accustomed to speak of these facts is not that of science.

In this book for the most part the language of science is used since, for matters of fact, it is the most effective. This chapter might have been called 'the human mind'; it was not so called, and the word 'mind' has not been used, because in practice scientists do not find it convenient to discuss their observations in terms of mind. Granted, many scientists do speak of 'mind' as opposed to 'body'; 'psychological' medicine is often sharply distinguished from 'physical' medicine, and 'mental' disorders from others. Nevertheless, scientific observations of human behaviour today are usually described in terms of actual behaviour (including speech, where that is involved), and of the changes in the nervous system, endocrine glands and other organs. We are only at the beginning of this scientific psychology. In everyday language it is still implied that each person has a 'mind' which in some way influences his behaviour.

In primitive communities this 'natural' way of speaking is usual, not only for other human beings, but for animals, plants, and even inanimate objects like rivers or mountains. Each of these is said to have a resident spirit working from within, just as we say a person has a mind. This mode of expression arises from our awareness of ourselves and of others. We are aware of thoughts and feelings in ourselves; we call them our mind, our consciousness, our spirit or perhaps our soul; and we attribute them also to others. It follows that these others too have minds, spirits, or whatever they may be called.

It is a short step from this way of speaking of people, to saying that these internal agents exist independently of the body, and may even become separated from the body.

In science none of these assumptions is necessary, and indeed the facts contradict them. Intelligence, moral behaviour, every aspect of personality, and life itself, depend on the functioning of the bodily organs – the organs studied by physiologists. We have our feelings and our thoughts but, as we saw at the beginning of this chapter, they are not independent of our brains: they are an aspect of our bodily function. This, at least, is the point of view from which the present chapter is written. It does not alter the fact that men live, work, and play together, and depend for their lives on doing so: it is one way of describing the behaviour involved.

CONCLUSIONS

Although man is a product of the slow process of organic evolution described in the previous chapter, the most important changes which man undergoes now are those of social evolution – a far more rapid process than the biological sort. Human social behaviour, so overwhelmingly a product of learning, is determined by tradition, handed down by example or verbally from generation to generation. Tradition is commonly thought of, rightly, as a source of social stability; but it is also an essential basis for social change.

Changes in social organization involve drastic changes in human behaviour; and they in turn depend on the fact that human behaviour is plastic and not fixed. We see the absurdity of the notion that 'human nature cannot change'. This commonly made assertion always implies that human *behaviour* is essentially fixed: it is therefore the exact opposite of the truth.

This account of man is very different from that of even a century ago. It can be traced, in part, to the Darwinian theory of evolution by natural selection, according to which the order we observe in the living world is a product, not of a divine plan, but of a process which can be studied rationally and even investigated experimentally. This attitude to the organic world led biologists to look at animal behaviour as a product of natural selection: the complex and elegant adaptations, shown by each species, to a particular way of life, came to be seen as existing by virtue of their 'survival value'.

This matter-of-fact approach was reinforced from another source. During the same period the science of physiology developed rapidly, largely by applying the concepts of physical science to the body. Thus, in the age of machinery, the body was studied in part as a machine working in accordance with the laws of mechanics, in part as a chemical system. Some people find this way of speaking of human behaviour distasteful. Sometimes it is called 'inhuman'. It would certainly be ridiculous to say that the present scientific account of human behaviour is anything more than tentative and provisional: it omits much that is of importance to any ordinary loving and hating human being, and any scientific worker in this field knows how vast is the unknown compared with the known.

Our present knowledge does, however, give us some insight into our nature as social beings. A schoolteacher or employer – even a parent – still often labels persistent unsatisfactory behaviour in the young as naughtiness, wickedness, or laziness or some such thing, instead of enquiring into the actual causes of the behaviour. These causes may include illness, malnutrition, emotional disturbances, and many other factors outside the child's control. It is quite unpractical to dismiss this rational approach as 'theoretical', or as 'softness': it is as unpractical as if a motor mechanic, faced with an automobile which refused to go, gave the bonnet a kick and said the machine was lazy. Indeed, it is worse: an automobile has no feelings.

Hence the attitude presented here is not only scientific: it is also humane. Science is the knowledge which can help to guide men of goodwill in improving the lot of mankind. The emphasis on the importance of the environment, for the development of human behaviour, does not imply that human beings are mere puppets, pulled this way and that by outside influences. We are not only influenced by our environment: we can also change it.

⑥

HUMAN TYPES

The world in all doth but two nations bear,
The good, the bad, and these mixed everywhere.
ANDREW MARVELL

IN THIS chapter we turn from fundamentals, to trivialities to which an unjustified importance has been attached. These are minor differences of structure or chemistry found in the human species today, and particularly those, such as skin colour, which have a well-marked geographical distribution. Technically, man is said to be *polytypic*: that is, different physical types comprise the populations of different regions.

THE 'RACES' OF MAN

The human species is sometimes classified in three main groups distinguished primarily by the structure of their hair.

The *Negriforms* have spiral hair and broad noses (plate 1); they include Bantu-speaking Africans, the South African Bushmen and Hottentots, the Negroes of West Africa, the pygmy Negrito and Negrillo of Malaysia and Africa, the Andamanese and the Melanesians. The Negriforms vary greatly in other respects: they may be black, brown, or yellow; their jaws may be prognathous (projecting) or not; and their skulls may be broad or narrow, although most of them have narrow skulls.

The second group, the *Europiforms*, have wavy hair and narrow noses (plates 2–4). They inhabit Europe, the Mediterranean countries, Asia Minor, and India; they are also, as a result of recent emigration, the main inhabitants of North America. The Ainu of Japan are Europiform, but in respects other than hair and nose shape resemble their Asian neighbours. The Europiforms may have white or brown skins, and broad or narrow skulls.

The third group, the *Mongoliforms*, have lank, straight hair; their noses are intermediate in width (plates 5–9). They include most of the inhabitants of Asia, apart from India, and the indigenous peoples of the Americas from the narrow-nosed Eskimo of the north to the Fuegians in the south. Apart from the Eskimo and certain Asian and American groups, their skulls are for the most part broad.

There is a fourth, much smaller group, which does not fit into the three main ones. The *Australiforms* (that is to say, the original inhabitants of Australia) have wavy, Europiform hair, but broad noses like those of Negriforms (plate 13). Their skin is often as dark as that of Negroes, but this may well be the product of a separate evolutionary development. The aboriginal Australians have perhaps been almost or quite isolated from other human groups for most of the time during which modern man has existed. Their average male cranial capacity is 1300 cubic centimetres, which is below the average for modern man as a whole; the head bones are thicker, and the teeth rather large. Some authorities believe the Australiforms to be derived from a mixture of two or more human types which had come together as a result of emigration. Nothing conclusive can be said on their precise status.

The question is sometimes asked, which of the three main groups is the most primitive? and the answer is sometimes supposed to be that the Negriforms are primitive, because, on the whole, they have not developed such advanced societies as have the others. But if we consider anatomical features (and the three groups are defined anatomically), we find that things are not so simple. We first have to decide what we mean by 'primitive', since it is easy, but unprofitable, to use the word as an undefined term of derogation. In biology one type is said to be more primitive than another when it is regarded as the more similar to a common ancestor of both types. Since the ancestors of man were apes, primitive men must be those that are most ape-like. But we know very little of the structure of the apes from which both men and present-day apes are sprung, apart from their skeletons, and so comparison is often made between man and his nearest contemporary relatives, the chimpanzee and gorilla. These have undergone evolutionary change, just as man has, during the last few million years, and so are not a reliable guide to what is primitive. And if we make the comparison we find no clear picture. The Europiforms are ape-like in having a good deal of hair on their bodies, in having wavy hair, and in their thin lips; on the other hand, in the formation of the face they are least ape-like. The Negriforms are ape-like in their broad noses, but less ape-like than Europiforms in their thick lips and the structure and distribution of the hair. Evidently no definite statement can be made on which of the main human groups is anatomically primitive. Men and women of the four types described can and do intermarry and produce offspring of mixed characteristics without any difficulty apart from social barriers. Consequently, wherever there are mixed populations intermediates are found (plate 12).

This applies even more obviously to the sub-divisions of the three principal groups. Anthropologists have subdivided the human species into thirty or more 'races', but this classification, based on average measurements of surface features, is not of much use. As an example, three main European types have been described. The 'Mediterranean' is defined as having a mean stature of about 160 cm (5 ft. 3 in.), a narrow, oval face, and very dark eyes. The 'Alpine' is very broad-headed, with brown or black hair, broad nose and medium stature. The 'Nordic' (made notorious by Hitler and the Nazis) is tall, has reddish-white skin and light colouring, and tends to have a narrow head. Such definitions are not only vague but make use of characters, such as stature and skin colour, which depend a good deal on the environment in which the individual lives.

Almost any European can, by looking at the people he meets every day, see that intermediates exist between the three types just described. Nevertheless most people in any given region might belong to one type. It is, indeed, easy to get this impression from some writings. However, the impression is misleading. In one instance 250 Swiss soldiers, from German-speaking cantons, were studied. None was found to have the combination of height, narrow-headedness, light eyes, and blond hair of the Nordic type; 9·2 per cent had the Alpine combination of characters; 0·8 per cent had the Dinaric combination (which is similar to the Alpine); and 0·4 per cent that of the Mediterranean. Hence only 26 of them, or 10·4 per cent, belonged to one of the anthropological types, and the remaining 224 showed a mixture of characters. Even in Sweden, which has the highest proportion of Nordics, army recruits in 1897-8 were found to include only 11 per cent of the Nordic type.

Not only are there no populations in Europe today of which most of the members are of one type; there never were such populations. The existence of a good deal of variation within the various species of fossil man was mentioned in chapter 4. When a group of human fossils is found in one place, and belonging to the same period, whether of our own or another species, the degree of variation in the skeletons is similar to that found in the mixed populations of today. In comparing populations, one has to speak in terms of the distribution of characters, as described in chapter 3 (page 87): populations do not, as a rule, differ sharply, but only in degree, or quantitatively.

The existence of a great deal of variation in human populations is due partly to differences in genetical constitution: each individual has a unique combination of genes. If we consider characteristics that are largely independent of environment we find that every possible combination of them exists: blue eyes can appear with both dark and fair hair, Negriform hair with a fair skin, and so on. Different combinations are, indeed, found in members of the same family: when both parents are European one child may approximate to the Nordic type and another to the Alpine. It is because of this occurrence of many combinations of characters that man was classified above primarily on the basis of hair structure, since this is a single character of which the development is not significantly influenced by change of environment. In defining the Negriform, Europiform, and Mongoliform types it was also possible to use the shape of the nose, since the distribution of the nasal types coincides with that of the hair types. The main exceptions are found where there has been intermarriage between groups, among the Australiforms, with their combination of Europiform hair and Negriform nostrils, and in some smaller groups (plates 10, 11).

SKIN AND HAIR

The anatomical features commonly used to differentiate human groups are nearly all superficial in the most literal sense: that is, they are external features. If the bodies of, say, a Negro and a European were both flayed, so that skin and hair were removed and the face obliterated, it would be impossible to tell for certain which was which. 'Racial' differences, it has been said, are only skin deep.

The most obvious of these differences is in skin colour. The colour of a man's skin is mainly determined by three things: first, the amount and distribution of a black pigment (melanin); second, the outer layer of dead cells, which varies in thickness; and third, the blood in the vessels below the surface. Melaninsare the only substances responsible for the major differences of colour between the people of different parts of the world: there are no different black, brown, and yellow pigments, and the many shades are due to the combined effects of the three factors just mentioned. People of northern countries would have very nearly white skins, instead of pink, but for the effect of the blood; this whiteness can be seen in an anaemic person, or in one who has lost much blood. It is not due to a white substance in the skin, any more than is the whiteness of a cloud or a mist, but to the scattering of light by the surface cells. Some black pigment is present in the skins even of the palest people. The only exceptions are albinos, who typically have no pigment in the skin, hair or iris of the eye. (They consequently have pink eyes, since the blood shows through.) Albinism is a rare condition which may occur in any human group, including those with the darkest skins; it is usually a recessive character like bright red hair.

In general, the greater the amount of strong sunlight in a country the darker are the indigenous inhabitants. The main exceptions are the American Indians, who are all rather similar in colour from Alaska in the north to Tierra del Fuego in the south; but these men are in America as a result of a relatively recent immigration, of less than ten thousand years ago, and so presumably retain the hue of their nomadic ancestors.

The dark skin of a Negro is not due to the *direct* effects of the sun: Negroes have the capacity to form melanin in their skin without exposure to the sun. This capacity varies in a fairly regular way in different groups of men between the poles and equator, and the differences between individuals in this respect are clearly genetical in origin. (The capacity to respond to sunlight by melanin formation, as when we go brown in summer, also varies, but that is a separate point.)

The dark skin of tropical peoples may be a product of natural selection, since it gives protection against sunburn. It is believed to be important in protecting the sweat glands from damage. In view of this probable biological usefulness (or *survival value*) of very dark pigmentation it may well have evolved separately in human groups inhabiting different tropical areas. Another possible function of dark skin is protection against the cancer-causing action of sunlight. In very sunny countries light-skinned people are more likely to develop such cancers than dark people.

Colour variation is, of course, familiar in other species, and particularly in domestic animals. Race-horses vary a great deal in colour, and there is no connexion between their colour and desirable qualities such as the ability to win races. As we shall see in the next chapter, there is a parallel here with man.

The next obvious external feature is *hair*. Human hair varies in structure, colour, and distribution on the body. The essential difference between Negriform, Europiform, and Mongoliform hair is the shape of each individual hair. Within the first two types there is a good deal of variation. The Papuans and Melanesians have long hair, Negroes have short, spiral hair, and Bushmen very short, tightly-coiled hair. Similarly, Europiform hair may be almost straight or quite curly. Whatever the structure of hair its usual colour is black, and only among some European peoples are there many exceptions to this rule. The pigment responsible is the same melanin as that found in the skin. Red hair, however, has a special pigment; it turns up here and there throughout Europe and western Asia, but is especially common among the Irish and Welsh, the Scottish highlanders, and among Jews and Finns. As for the distribution of hair on the body, Europiforms tend to have most body hair, and Negriforms least. Apart from the temporary effects of permanent waving (or straightening in Negro women), environmental influences have little or no effect.

An instructive curiosity concerning hair was described in 1931. Although they have no Negro ancestry, many members of a Norwegian family have 'woolly' hair of the Negriform type. The condition is inherited as a dominant trait, like that illustrated on pages 171 and 173: that is, it is present, regardless of sex, in successive generations; and a couple neither of whom has woolly hair never have woolly-haired children. This is an example of a so-called 'racial' character appearing in a people utterly remote from those who usually display it.

FACE AND HEAD

Other facial characteristics can be dealt with shortly. *Eye colour*, that is, the colour of the iris, is generally brown or black, but where the skin and hair are lightly pigmented blue, grey, and green eyes are quite common. It is, however, possible for dark people to have grey or blue eyes, and for blonds to have dark eyes. The function of the iris pigment is probably to protect the interior of the eye from the harmful effects of sunlight; consequently light-eyed people are at a disadvantage in sunny countries, and often wear dark glasses.

Eye form varies owing to differences in the arrangement of the

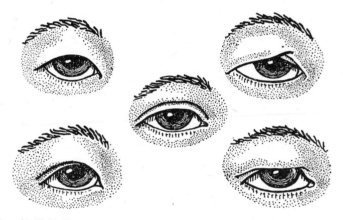

Epicanthic Fold. Centre, no fold, as of a European; other drawings show different kinds of fold, seen principally in certain Mongoliform types

skin around the eyes. Mongoliforms tend to have 'slit eyes', and some, particularly in Asia, have the 'epicanthic fold', a fold of skin that covers a part or the whole of the edge of the upper eyelid. This fold can occur in Negriforms and Europiforms, but among them it is rare.

As for *nasal form*, the flat, broad type of nose (platyrrhine) is probably primitive. Probably the leptorrhine, or narrow-nosed condition, is a result of natural selection: in general, the hotter and moister the air, the broader the noses of the native inhabitants; in colder climates it may be an advantage to have a high, narrow nose in which the air is warmed before it reaches the lungs.

We come now to a feature to which anthropologists have in the past attached much importance: this is *head form*. There are many ways in which the human head varies, including the flatness of the face and the degree of projection of the jaws (prognathism); but the character most studied has been the ratio between the maximum breadth and the maximum length. This can be measured in a living person, and is then called the cephalic index; in a skull it is called the cranial index. If the maximum breadth is x and the maximum length y, the index is

$$\frac{x \cdot 100}{y}$$

On this basis heads are classified in three groups:

Index of or over 82; brachycephalic (head relatively short or broad);

Index from 77 to 82: mesocephalic (intermediate);

Index under 77: dolichocephalic (head relatively long or narrow).

On the skull these limits are conventionally two units lower. The

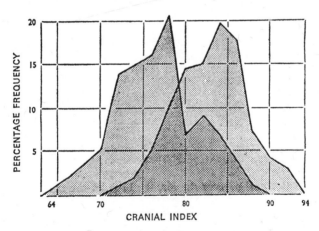

Cranial Indices. In the fifth to eighth centuries skulls in Switzerland were narrower (more dolichocephalic) than those of the nineteenth century. The polygons show the two distributions, nineteenth century to the right. It is impossible to tell to what extent genetical change or environmental differences have influenced this variation with time

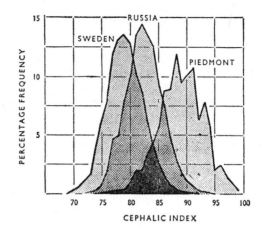

Cephalic Indices. The distribution of cephalic indices in three European groups. This sort of variation, with different averages but greatly over-lapping distributions, is typical of differences between human groups, or 'races'. Cranial or cephalic index is of no social or biological importance, as far as is known, nor is it correlated with characters of social significance

classification is quite arbitrary, and the selection of figures a matter of convenience.

The broadest heads are found among Mongoliforms, the narrowest among Negriforms. Some Asian groups average 86·8, and one West African people 71·8. European averages vary a great deal. Central Europeans, including Germans, are decidedly brachycephalic (a non-Nordic characteristic); in the north, in Britain and in Spain averages are mostly between 76 and 79. However, in every European population, and indeed in most populations throughout the world, there is great variation, and some people are decidedly narrow, others broadheaded.

BODY FORM

The tallest men are the Negroes of the Sudan and the Lake Chad region in Central Africa, the shortest the pygmies, also of Central Africa, with an average height of only 150 cm. (4 feet 6 inches). The Negro neighbours of the pygmies, who eat similar food, are 10–15 cm. taller. Why there is this great difference is quite unknown.

There is great variation among the members of nearly every group. This variation is partly due to differences of environment, as well as genetical differences within each nation. For instance, the Japanese are commonly regarded as a 'short race'. Certainly the average height of Japanese adults in Japan is less than that of Europeans or Americans; but to speak of them as a short *race* suggests that their stature is determined genetically and is consequently unalterable, except possibly by selection during many millennia. This is not the case. The children of Japanese emigrants to the United States or Hawaii are a good deal taller, on the average,

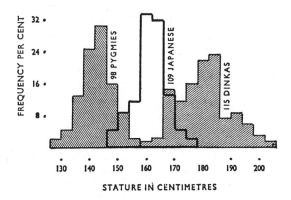

Stature in Human Groups. Histograms showing the distribution of stature in three groups (two of them extremes), illustrating overlap

than children in Japan itself: in one large-scale inquiry it was found that for boys of fifteen years the difference is about 10 cm. Chinese show similar differences. Probably they are due to improved diet and perhaps to less infectious disease.

The importance of food is illustrated by celebrated experiments, performed in the 1920s, in which the diets of various groups were fed to rats. The rats, which were all genetically similar, reflected in a remarkable way certain of the characteristics of the group whose diet they received. The Pathans are physically impressive, and the rats fed on their national diet were large, developed very little disease, had large litters, and had a low infant and maternal mortality. Madrassis, at the other extreme, are physically much inferior; rats fed with their diet (largely rice) were small, had poor coats, much disease, small litters, and high death rates. Hence some apparently 'racial' differences between Indian nationalities are probably due to diet.

If we turn from stature to *body-build* (or somatotype) we find less information on what determines it, but what there is reinforces the impression gained from the study of cephalic index and stature. Every kind of body-build is found in almost every human community, though in varying proportions. Probably environment can influence body-build. Both in the United States and Japan there are more tall, slender individuals among the rich. It has also been stated that peasants and farm labourers tend to the opposite type. These facts – if they are facts – have been attributed to environmental influences, including differences in nutrition and in occupation.

There is little satisfactory evidence that particular temperaments are regularly associated with particular physiques. 'Let me have men about me that are fat', said Caesar,

> Yond Cassius has a lean and hungry look:
> He thinks too much; such men are dangerous.

But it is doubtful if he was justified. The attempt has been made to relate physical differences between human groups to glandular function. A change in the functioning of the system of endocrine or ductless glands can produce drastic physical and behavioural changes: for instance, thyroid deficiency causes cretinism, abnormality of the pituitary gland may cause giantism and several endocrine glands influence sexual development and behaviour. There is, however, no evidence that, for example, pygmies are of small stature owing to thyroid deficiency, or that the tall, slender Negroes of the Nile region owe their physique to a subnormal production of the sex hormones.

CLIMATE AND MAN

Physique may, however, be related to climate. The effect of climate must be indirect, because (it is assumed) it is a result of the natural selection process. It is not like the darkening effect of sunlight on a pale skin (which is a case of individual adaptation), but is evidently due to the fact that, in a given region, some types survived longer and so produced more offspring.

This probably applies to dark skin colour in hot countries, and perhaps to narrow nose form in cold ones. Certain writers further believe that some groups, long isolated in particular areas, have evolved special characters, through natural selection, which adapt them in still more detail to their particular climates. Desert peoples, for instance the Tuareg of North Africa, the Somali of East Africa, and the Aborigines of north and central Australia, tend to be lean and skinny, with long limbs and shallow bodies; these have the greatest possible surface area relative to body weight, and so promote heat loss. One general principle supports the theory that body-build has been influenced by climate: over a long period only a very slight advantage of one genetical type over another can lead to the complete elimination of the inferior type.

This argument could also be applied to the peoples of the lands which surround the Arctic Sea. They are thickset, and so perhaps lose body heat at a relatively low rate; hence they may be supposed to be better able to cope with a very cold climate. The typical appearance of the Mongoliforms of eastern Siberia is also supposed to reflect the climate of the area. They have flat faces, which reduce the chances of frost-bite; their slitty, fat-lidded eyes may be protected against sun glare as well as frost; and their scanty beards possibly reduce the condensation of moisture from the breath around the mouth (plate 5). The theory is that this type is the product of a selective action during the rigours of the ice ages. Since then, they have multiplied and spread into some of the warmer parts of Asia, and into the Americas.

The idea of selection for certain bodily characters, especially in the extremes of hot deserts and the northern steppes, sounds plausible, but must inevitably be speculative. Recent studies of the Eskimo, who flourish in one of the most adverse environments occupied by man, show why some anthropologists remain sceptical about 'climatic engineering'.

There are about 60,000 of these people, spread along the north coast of North America and among the many arctic islands. They are often nomadic; they live in small groups; survival depends on their skill as hunters of seals and other large game, from which they get clothes and fuel as well as food. They live in snow igloos or skin tents. The Eskimo are often described as fat but, though they are usually stockily built, they, and their neighbours the Aleuts and

Siberian Mongoliforms, are lean. There are two small groups of rather tall Eskimo. Their clothing is excellently designed for activity in arctic conditions; their kayaks, or canoes, are skilfully constructed and managed; they wear slit goggles to protect their eyes from snow glare; and they have an elaborate system of customs and techniques which enable them to cope with low temperatures, ice, snow, wary game and sparse plant food. Evidently these cultural features are crucial in the 'adaptation' of the Eskimo to their environment. There is no conclusive evidence that body-build is of primary importance.

There are also difficulties in applying the concept of natural selection to the occurrence of pale skin in northern Europe. The blond, with his lack of skin pigment, and light coloured irises and hair, may appear occasionally in any group; in the fog-wreathed lands of Britain and Scandinavia he is evidently, at least, at no disadvantage, as he might be, in primitive conditions, in hotter lands; and the absence of skin pigmentation may promote the formation of vitamin D in the skin, under the influence of sunlight.

Whatever the truth about natural selection and climate, all healthy men and women, of whatever type, are highly adaptable. After a few weeks, Europeans can work as well as indigenous peoples in the tropics, further; both Asians and Europeans undergo the same changes of adaptation when transferred from one climate to another. Moreover, men of a particular physical type may live in widely different climates. This does not apply only to the populations of European origin, now worldwide. There are the American Indians who live all the way from Tierra del Fuego in the Antarctic to the tropical Amazon; there are the Negroes of the West African tropics who resemble the highland Basuto; and the Australiforms who live in both deserts and high mountains.

The hazards encountered in the past by Europeans living in hot countries were not strictly climatic. In part they were psychological; in part they were diseases such as malaria which can now be overcome. Today, in any case, we are coming increasingly to create our own climate in our houses; not only can large buildings continuously maintain a sub-tropical climate even during a northern European winter; they can also, in tropical lands, maintain a temperate climate: the refrigeration, as well as the heating, of houses is being increasingly used.

WHAT IS RACE?

The facts of geographical variation are sometimes confusing, especially since it is usual to speak of human groups as if they were sharply distinct from each other. They are not in fact clearly marked off, and different physical features can occur in any combination. An example, already quoted, is the occurrence of spiral hair, of Negriform type, among Norwegians. Another is provided by the Polynesians, who have a combination of Europiform, Negriform and Mongoliform characters. At the same time, there are marked differences between large groups; many are genetically determined, and some at least seem to be products of natural selection. On the other hand, some important features, such as stature, are much influenced by environment, and such features may change conspicuously in one or two generations.

The question may be asked: what then is race? This question presupposes that, because there is a word *race*, there must be something corresponding to it – something of which it is the name. This is very far from being the case. Any dictionary gives many meanings for the term race, and if you look in the writings, not only of laymen but also of specialists, you may find it difficult or impossible to make out which meaning the term is supposed to have.

However, most people have something fairly definite in mind when they speak of races. They may think of human groups well marked off from each other, such as Negroes and Europeans (ignoring for convenience, the existence of intermediates due to intermarriage). Or they may think of differences such as those between Scots and Greeks, although in this case there is a great deal of overlap and the distinction is one of averages: for instance, the average degree of skin pigmentation, or the proportion of blue-eyed individuals. And sometimes they may even think of national, or cultural characters. Always, however, or nearly always, the characters are thought of as fixed, and unalterable by environmental changes. We have already seen to what extent both structural and behavioural differences depend on environment, and the next chapter gives more examples still.

The division of mankind into 'races' by genetically determined characters, or, better, by actual genes, is usually based on the assumption that, if an individual possesses genes determining, say, black skin, then that individual must be more closely related, by descent, to all others with these genes, than to those without them. But this does not follow. We have already had the example of the appearance of spiral hair among Norwegians. Apart from oddities of this sort natural selection may have independently produced similar effects on large populations in different regions: perhaps the Australiforms and the African Negroes have separately developed heavy skin pigmentation as a result of natural selection in hot climates. We shall see, in chapter 8, that there is clear evidence that this sort of thing has occurred. For this reason, no attempt is made here to outline the attempts at classification of mankind by means of blood groups. The genetics of blood grouping are well established, but the biological significance of variation in blood character is less clear. In particular, we cannot be certain that similarity of one population to another, in the proportion of blood groups, necessarily indicates close relationship.

Meanwhile it is possible to give a reasonable definition of the word race, so that if the term must be used at all it can be used precisely. A race may be defined as a group which shares in common a certain set of genes, and which became distinct from other groups as a result of geographical isolation. The possession of genes in common is not sufficient: no biologist would speak of the race of albinos, for example, or the race of red-haired people. Races in this sense arise as a result of isolation from other groups.

But a definition of this sort, though fairly precise, is not much help in the study of human differences. It helps mainly in avoiding the errors that come from the use of a term that is undefined, or has a number of different and incompatible meanings. These errors are the more likely to arise when the term is often used to arouse emotion rather than to give information. In fact, the question 'What is race?' is not a very profitable one to ask. The important question is: what are the *facts* about human diversity?

7

RACE THEORY

Of all the vulgar modes of escaping from the consideration of the effect of social and moral influences upon the human mind, the most vulgar is that of attributing the diversities of conduct and character to inherent natural differences.

JOHN STUART MILL

FEW of the qualities discussed in the last chapter have any direct social importance. A man's physique may qualify him for some types of work, and disqualify him for others, but the shape of the head or the amount of melanin in the skin are not likely to be considered by a foreman recruiting stevedores, or by the examiners for a medical degree. Most people, if they had to make a list of the socially desirable qualities, would no doubt suggest some of the following: emotional stability; health and energy; intelligence and initiative; moral behaviour. They would not include any particular eye-colour or nose shape. Some, however, if the point were raised, might assert that there is a connexion between, say, skin pigment and moral behaviour: for example, the now completely discredited Lombroso describes the Negro as follows:

> The principal thing is always ... the stifling of the primitive. Even if he is dressed in the European way and has accepted the customs of modern culture, all too often there remains in him the lack of respect for the life of his fellow men, the disregard for life which all wild people have in common. To them, a murder appears as an ordinary occurrence...

This rubbish has its cruder counterpart in what some South African whites say if asked to discuss the status of Negroes. Later we return to attitudes of this kind. In the next sections we examine dispassionately the evidence bearing on behavioural (psychological) differences between human groups.

INTELLECTUAL ABILITY

Unfortunately, it is much less easy to measure intellectual and moral qualities than stature or muscular strength. The behavioural quality that has been most measured is often called *intelligence*. The measuring is by systems of tests. The tests do not measure mechanical or mathematical ability, or emotional stability, or initiative, or imagination, or moral outlook; but a high score can confidently be taken to imply a high degree of verbal ability, even when the test itself is not verbal. In general, university teachers make high scores in intelligence tests, and so do members of the other learned professions. This must be expected, since the tests were designed by professors. It does not signify that they are useless. The research of which they are a result represents an attempt to get an objective, quantitative expression for an important human quality. Intelligence tests have been of undoubted value on a vast scale in, for example, the British and United States armies, in both of which they have been successfully used (together with other tests) in the selection of men and women for different tasks.

Intelligence tests were originally designed to assess the educability of children. A system was needed to enable teachers and psychologists to compare children of different ages. This is what the *intelligence quotient* (IQ) does. The method is this. For a given community, such as London, a representative sample of school children of all ages from five to fourteen are given tests, and the average achievement for each age is worked out. Afterwards, any child can be tested and compared with the norm. If a child of ten scores the average mark for ten-year-olds his mental age is ten; if he scores the average for eleven-year-olds his mental age is eleven. To calculate IQ:

$$IQ = \frac{\text{mental age} \times 100}{\text{age in years}}$$

Hence the IQ of the ten-year child with a mental age of eleven is 110. Up to fourteen years mental age increases at a regular rate, but after that the rate of increase slows down. In England it is considered that an IQ of 120 or more is required if a child is to profit from a higher education; and children with IQ of less than 70 are classed as dull and backward, and may be given special schooling.

Since IQ is calculated by comparing mental age with age in time, it cannot be applied to adults. A man of forty scores no higher, as a rule, than he did at twenty: although his age in time is doubled, his mental age remains unchanged, or nearly so. In this and the next two chapters, therefore, in discussing the results of these tests on different human groups, the letter I is used to refer to scores obtained in intelligence tests by adults, irrespective of the particular set of tests used. 'Intelligence', like 'race', is popularly used in a variety of ways, and this is not the place for a discussion of its various meanings; the word is therefore best avoided.

To compare average I's, say, of American Negroes and whites, we can interpret the figures correctly only if we know how I is influenced by heredity and environment. It is still sometimes believed that the results of intelligence tests are unaffected by environmental changes: that differences in health and education, for instance, are not reflected in the intelligence quotient. Chapter 2 gives the general, biological grounds which justify us in doubting assertions of this sort, and there is now much direct evidence that I is considerably influenced, not only by genetical variation between individuals, but also by environmental differences.

Illness, accident, and malnutrition may affect IQ, but their influence is demonstrable only in extreme cases. Changes that have permanent effects on IQ are those which last for some years, and this applies particularly to changes that occur before the child is seven years old. Attendance at nursery school, for instance, raises IQ and, in general, schooling has more effect than the economic or cultural circumstances of the home. This effect of schooling is reflected in a rise in IQ that takes place in Negro children in the United States when they are brought by their parents from country districts to cities. The earlier they come to town, the more nearly, on the average, do they approximate in IQ to the white children in the same schools.

It is in the United States, with its very mixed population, that the greatest volume of work has been done on racial and national differences of I. For example, literate Negroes have, on the average, lower I's than literate whites. This was clear from the results of testing army recruits in 1917. Recruits from the different states gave widely different averages, although within each state the Negro average was always lower than the white. The differences were so great that Negroes from some northern states scored *higher* than whites from the south. Since the southern states were, and still are, backward in educational matters, there was evidently an environmental effect arising from variation in schooling. The lower average of Negroes in each state might, it follows, be due to the fact that nearly everywhere in the United States Negroes are economically and socially inferior to whites, and have correspondingly inferior facilities for their children. Negroes *can* reach white average levels, or even surpass them. In 1923, 500 Negro children tested in Los Angeles had a mean IQ of 104·7, which was a little above that of the whites.

It has been suggested that results of this sort can be accounted for by selective emigration of the more able Negroes to places such as Los Angeles. The migration theory is, however, pure surmise. The IQs of children of parents who have emigrated do not differ from those of the non-migrant children shortly after migration has taken place.

The results of testing American whites and Negroes can be summarized in Klineberg's words: 'The most probable interpretation', he says,

is that when American Negroes live under relatively favorable environmental conditions their test scores are correspondingly high, and when whites live under relatively poor conditions their test scores are correspondingly low. It is apparently not 'race' but environment which is the crucial variable. As for the factors in the environment which are mainly responsible . . ., it is likely that the nature of the available schooling plays a major role. A glance at the figures for per capita expenditure for Negro and white children in the segregated school system of the South brings into sharp focus the handicaps of the Negro children; the figures also reveal that Southern white children suffer similar, though not such extreme, handicaps.

The results of comparing Negroes with whites have been given at length, partly because there is a widespread belief in the inferiority of dark-skinned persons, and partly because of the abundance of evidence. These results are, moreover, quite characteristic of those obtained from any study of the correlation between features such as skin colour, nose shape and so forth, and I. Investigation has, for instance, shown no correlation at all between head shape and I, or between hair colour and I. Comparison of individuals of Nordic, Alpine, and Mediterranean types in Germany, France, and Italy has revealed no significant differences between them, although, in each country, city dwellers (as in the United States) scored higher, on the average, than country folk. Once again, it seems, we have an example of the importance of environmental differences. Perhaps, however, the tests themselves were weighted in favour of town dwellers.

There is evidence, in some recent work, of a slight positive correlation between stature and the intelligence quotient of children, but this has at present no practical significance. Even if further investigation shows correlations between such characters and I, we can be certain that every large human group overlaps every other in the distribution of I among its members; every group includes people of both high and low I. The results of intelligence tests are not likely to justify social discrimination against any group. We can look forward to the appearance of many men and women of intellectual ability from 'races' and nations which at present produce none, or very few; what is needed is the improvement of educational and other facilities.

CRIME

We cannot yet measure many other aspects of human behaviour as we measure I. Some types of behaviour of social importance are, however, reflected in the figures of conviction for various crimes. Since it has often been held that some 'races' are prone to certain types of crime, it is useful to examine the evidence.

Statistics of crime are very difficult to interpret. This is clearly shown by the difficulties met with in the United States, with its mixed population. Suppose, for example, that the Irish and the Italians in America are to be compared, we can hardly hope to learn about the criminal propensities of the Irish and the Italians in general: the immigrants from the two countries may constitute two quite unrepresentative samples: the best types of Italian might be reaching America, and the worst Irish, or vice versa. If, on the other hand, the figures for the Irish in Ireland are compared with those for the Italians in Italy, the comparison is vitiated by differences in laws and in enforcement in the two countries. Even in a single country

6

different groups may be treated differently: it is a commonplace, accepted by American sociologists, that Negroes in the United States (and especially in the south) are more likely to be arrested for criminal offences and, once arrested, more likely to be convicted, than whites.

Another type of difficulty is met if the attempt is made to compare the criminality of Jews and non-Jews. W. A. Bonger, a Dutch criminologist, has published figures for the criminality of Jews in Germany and other countries for various years from 1883 to 1916. Jews were less likely than others to commit crimes of violence, sexual crimes, theft, or embezzlement. Murder and theft, in particular, were about three times as common among non-Jews. But Jews had a worse record for fraud and forgery. This might be held to support the view that Jews are 'naturally' dishonest. In fact, it gives us no evidence on this question at all. A very high proportion of Jews in most countries are shopkeepers or are employed in business, and a correspondingly low proportion in manual work. Manual workers, whether in town or country, have little opportunity for fraud or forgery, and even those with criminal tendencies are therefore unlikely to commit these crimes. To get significant figures we should therefore have to compare, not Jews in general with non-Jews in general, but, say, Jewish shopkeepers with non-Jewish, and so on. If such a comparison showed marked differences it would then be necessary to see whether the differences could be ascribed to features in the family life and upbringing of the two groups, or whether there was evidence for 'natural', or genetical, differences.

There is, in fact, no evidence whatever for 'racial' or genetical differences in criminal tendency between large groups. On the other hand upbringing has obviously a very marked effect on behaviour. What in most communities would be called murder is in some regarded as a virtuous and even necessary act: in such diverse areas as Sicily and parts of India vendetta and family feuds are, or have been, a normal element in the life of the people.

> The wildest dreams of Kew are the facts of Katmandu,
> And the crimes of Clapham chaste in Martaban.

What is more, the effect of upbringing in such matters can be shown not to be transmitted from generation to generation; this is done by studying families which have migrated to a new environment. Here, for instance, are the figures for persons committed for homicide or assault in Massachusetts in 1915:

Group	Commitments per 100,000
Born in Italy	192
American born, one or both parents born in Italy	24
American born of American parents	24
American born, one or both parents foreign but not Italian	22

The amount of crime is strongly influenced by the environment, in particular the 'culture', in which people are brought up. Another example illustrates a further point. Here are the figures of convictions of first and second generation Irish immigrants in Massachusetts in 1908-9:

Offence	Irish Immigrants	Second Generation	Native Whites
Homicide	2·3	1·0	0·5
Rape	0·0	0·3	0·7
Gaming	1·2	2·7	3·6

Hence a change of environment may influence not only the amount of crime, but also the nature of the crimes committed.

It does not follow that we are all alike in our inherited capacities for crime or for virtuous behaviour. There is, no doubt, genetical variation in the ability, in any particular environment, to become law-abiding or the opposite. But the differences between large human groups, in the amount of anti-social behaviour that they display, reflect primarily differences in custom; and these differences can be rapidly altered. As far as we know at present any group can, given the appropriate conditions, produce large numbers of crooks; equally, given other conditions, we may suppose that any group can reach a state in which the behaviour of its members is almost uniformly lawful.

THE ORIGINS OF RACE THEORIES

Since no valid case can be made for theories of the inherited and unalterable superiority of one human group over another, it is reasonable to ask how 'racism' has become so widespread. The defeat of the German fascists, the most notorious of the propagandists of race theory, put views on the superiority of a German or 'Aryan' race in the background. But there are still plenty of Englishmen who think that men with dark skins are their natural inferiors, and Americans who think the same of Negroes and Asians. And there remain in 1971, two countries, South Africa and Rhodesia, whose administration is based on racism.

This is a point where it is not possible to separate human biology from sociology and politics. Colour bars, for instance, are found where men of one physical type are ruled by aliens of another type. This is or was recently the case in the colonial empires of Britain, France, and Holland. This political structure is often supported by biological assertions. A slightly different situation is found in the United States, where the blacks are in a minority, and are the descendants of slaves brought from Africa.

Certainly the ruling group have sometimes an obviously more advanced type of society than the ruled. The important question is whether this relationship should be regarded as permanent. In the most advanced modern societies it is taken for granted that every individual should enjoy certain rights, including a free education up to a specified age and the vote in elections for central and local government. But these rights are denied to a great part of the world's population. History suggests that we are not justified in thinking this situation permanent or inevitable. Countries such as China, India, and Egypt, which until recently were colonial or semi-colonial, have in past times had civilizations far in advance of those of Western Europe. Chinese emperors have been in a position to treat white ambassadors with contempt, and dark-skinned North Africans have written of the immature barbarians of northern Europe. The facts given earlier in this chapter confirm the plasticity of human behaviour from generation to generation (also discussed in chapter 5). Theories of racial superiority may be regarded as reflecting the political situation in a particular historical period, but as having no biological foundation.

This is not the whole story: it does not account for race *hatred*. It is sometimes thought that dislike of one human type for another is inevitable. This is certainly untrue, since children of different types brought up together show no special antagonism. Race hatred exists only where it has been taught. The ease with which it can be taught is perhaps one of the most remarkable things about it. A full explanation – if one existed – would require a complex, psychological discussion, but one important factor is the common desire for a scapegoat. When the Germans were going through a bad time the anti-semitic doctrines of the Nazis encouraged them to put the blame for their difficulties on the Jews. Most people have aggressive tendencies more or less kept in check; some give them an outlet by playing strenuous games or by watching films about gangsters. However, it is convenient to have some class of people, marked off fairly sharply from one's own group, towards whom one can direct this aggressiveness without offending the neighbours. This fact was exploited by the fascists in Britain: in the East End of London they tried to generate anti-semitism; in Cardiff they attacked the Negro community; in Liverpool the immigrant Irish were the target.

These tendencies are encouraged by all who profit from racial and national divisions. In some parts of the world even today dark-skinned people form an important source of cheap labour for farmers and industrialists. If their wages and conditions of work were improved profits might fall, or disappear. In one gold-mining district of South Africa in 1937 the 36,000 European workers had an average annual income of £390, while the 280,000 non-Europeans received £47. If all types of workers combined in trade unions, as has happened in some parts of the United States, the inferior position of the non-Europeans would no doubt rapidly improve, to the disadvantage of their employers. Hence in South Africa, as in some other countries, it is to the advantage of the ruling and employing group to maintain 'racial' divisions, and to support them with lies about human biology.

THE JEWS

The so-called 'Jewish problem' resembles the problems touched on in the last section in having political, economic, psychological and religious aspects; some of them have already been mentioned. Anti-semitism is so profoundly irrational that it can hardly be made the subject of a straightforward, biological discussion; or at least if it were, the argument would have no effect on anti-semites, and would be superfluous for anyone else. However, the biological facts about Jews are not well known, and are worth summarizing. The Jews do not form a nation (except those in Israel), nor are they at all uniform in structural features.

During the Roman Empire there was a great increase in the numbers of Jews, as a result of the conversion of people of many types in many countries to Judaism. In appearance the Jews today vary greatly, and in each country they tend to resemble the non-Jewish natives. This is due to mixed marriages with non-Jews, and is most apparent in Jewish communities which have been established for many centuries. Chinese Jews are Chinese in appearance, Abyssinian Jews resemble other Abyssinians. The so-called Jewish nose resembles that often found in persons of the Armenoid type, and is not by any means universal among Jews nor confined to them. In parts of Poland, and in Alsace, a high proportion of Jews are blonds, although typically Jews (like most people) are dark. There is no uniformity in head shape or in stature. Many people say they can identify Jews by their appearance, but when their claims are tested on large numbers of people they make many mistakes: they often fail to identify Jews as such, and they may identify as Jews people, for instance Armenians, who are not Jewish at all.

Statements about the Jewish character have been sufficiently dealt with already. Not only are the Jews not a race in any sense of the word, but their behaviour, social or anti-social, is just as much a product of the conditions in which they live as is that of any other group. This has been ruthlessly demonstrated by the conduct of the Israelis in their new nation-state.

MIXED BREEDING

Another question which arouses much emotion is that of the desirability of marriage between persons of widely different physical type. Where racism and colour bars exist, such intermarriage is certain to be regarded as a grave impropriety, and in some countries it is illegal. In British colonies white women have received terms of imprisonment for cohabiting with Africans. Even where the law does not intervene, convention often makes intermarriage difficult and dangerous.

The question is whether there are biological objections to intermarriage. This is sometimes believed because the children of such marriages are sometimes unsatisfactory. This, however, is a *non sequitur*. Where there is a colour bar it is often the poorest people of the two colours who intermarry, and poverty alone (as we shall see in the next and later chapters) is a severe handicap. Moreover half-breeds may be despised by both elements, and so suffer other disadvantages.

Intermarriage does not necessarily produce either biological or social difficulties. In New Zealand there has been successful inter-marriage between Maoris and whites: there is little colour feeling, and a Maori has been acting Prime Minister. In such diverse regions as Hawaii and South America 'race crossing' has been and is practised without ill effects. A traveller in South America describes 'a blond Negro talking Spanish to a red-headed Chinese'.

Attempts have been made to show that marriage between certain types, such as Negroes and English in Liverpool, produces children in whom the different parts of the skeleton do not conform: in whom, for instance, the teeth of the upper and lower jaws fail to fit together in a normal manner. The observations used to support this view have, however, not taken account of the effects of malnutrition, and are therefore unconvincing.

If the whole of history is examined, 'race mixture' is found to be frequent, and it is impossible to show that it has had undesirable results. In general, 'race crossing' is a social, not a biological problem. Biologically, the marriage of diverse types presumably produces new genetical combinations. From this point of view it is desirable, since it increases the possibility of genotypes of especial value to society.

THE INEQUALITY OF MAN

*We hold these truths to be self-evident: that all men are created equal;
that they are endowed by their Creator with certain unalienable rights;
that among these are life, liberty, and the pursuit of happiness.*

AMERICAN DECLARATION OF INDEPENDENCE

SINCE man, like most animal and plant species, reproduces sexually,
his genes are combined in new groups at the beginning of every
person's life; and, apart from uniovular twins, each individual is
genetically unique. There is consequently much genetical variation
within each human group.

The subject of innate inequality has become peculiarly confused
with the political question of equality of opportunity. Despite the
magnificent prose and admirable intentions of the American
Declaration of Independence, it is not true that all men are created
equal. The Declaration was primarily concerned to assert the right
of every person to life, liberty, and the pursuit of happiness; but this
holds irrespective of genetical differences between individuals. The
main source of the confusion has been the attempt by some to claim
especial virtues for particular classes: just as some 'races' have been
said to be superior to the rest, so genetical superiority has been
claimed for the middle or upper classes within a single nation.

EUGENICS

This sort of claim has been especially associated with eugenic
propaganda. The founder of the eugenic movement was an English-
man, Francis Galton. Galton was a brilliant mathematician; he was a
pioneer of the use of statistical methods in biology; he invented the
finger-print method of identification; and he interested himself in a
wide variety of research problems, including some unconventional
ones, such as the statistical investigation of the efficacy of prayer.
He was the first President of the Eugenics Education Society (now

the Eugenics Society), which was founded in London in 1908.

Some of the early pronouncements of leading members of this society, including scientists, were of a kind to bring the ideas of eugenics into disrepute. A distinguished mathematician remarked that the upper classes contained all the finest examples of ability, beauty and taste. It was asserted that the poor were genetically less fit than the wealthy, and on these grounds old age pensions (five shillings a week at the age of seventy), and free meals in schools, were opposed, since such measures were held to encourage the improvident poor to breed more and so to produce an excess of inferior types. Attention was drawn to the fact that, at that time, the richer families produced fewer children than poorer ones. The eugenics movement has been called a passionate protest against the fact that the meek do inherit the earth.

These views have been, and still are, supported by transparently false arguments. The legends of the 'Jukes' and the 'Kallikaks' are still repeated in supposedly serious publications. These concern two families, of which the second has been given an invented name. In both stories it is implied that an initial pairing of two persons has given rise, solely because of bad heredity, to numerous degenerate, defective, or criminal descendants. In the second story, that of the Kallikaks, it is alleged not only that the union of a soldier with a defective girl produced many inferior descendants; but that the marriage of the same soldier to a respectable young woman founded a family of upright, hard-working, worthy citizens. These tales originated when knowledge both of genetics, and of the social effects of bad conditions, was slight, and the most responsible eugenists no longer make use of them. The importance of environmental agencies, such as nutrition and housing, has (as we shall see in chapters 12 and 13) become so clear that poor physical development is no longer attributed to 'bad inheritance'; and mass unemployment has made it difficult to regard poverty as an inherited character. Similarly, in the past, infectious diseases such as leprosy and tuberculosis, and diseases of malnourishment, have been attributed to heredity; but now such conditions can be prevented by improving environments. It is therefore easier to consider the question of eugenics in a matter-of-fact way, and to inquire to what extent our knowledge of human genetics could be used for eugenic purposes.

There is, in principle, nothing absurd in the idea of the planned breeding of human beings. The selective breeding of domestic animals is so well established that men have inevitably thought of applying similar methods to themselves. Such speculation did not await the development of human genetics: the subject was discussed in the ancient world. In the fifth book of Plato's *Republic* we find this:

And those of the youth who have distinguished themselves, whether in war or anywhere else, ought to have awards and prizes given them, and the most ample liberty of embracing women, so that under this pretext likewise the greatest number of children may be generated of such persons.

However, neither the Greeks nor any other large human groups have yet tried to put the principle of selective mating into practice. (The Germans under the Nazis were perhaps an exception.) There are primitive peoples among whom children thought to be defective or superfluous are killed; but, although this practice may have a favourable effect on the populations concerned, it is not advocated by modern eugenists.

Most eugenic programmes aim at preventing the breeding of the 'unfit'. This is *negative eugenics*, by contrast with positive eugenics aimed at promoting the breeding of the especially gifted. The means of preventing reproduction include propaganda and contraceptives; the segregation of persons in institutions; and sterilization, either optional or compulsory. Among other countries Denmark, Norway, and Sweden have sterilization laws, and some States of the U.S.A. In Nazi Germany a sterilization law giving very wide powers was passed in 1934. Legislation has been proposed for the United Kingdom, but has not been before Parliament.

What can sterilization do? This depends on the precise way in which defects are influenced by the genes. Some conditions can be said without qualification to be inherited, because environment plays no significant part in their advent. Of these, several are dominant. Brachydactyly, or short fingers, due to a failure of normal growth in the middle bone, is passed on by an affected person to half his or her children, on the average. The condition is transmitted only by affected persons, and never skips a generation. Brachydactyly is itself a not very severe defect, and does not prevent a useful and normal life.

On the other hand, lobster claw, or split hand, which is sometimes transmitted as a dominant condition, is a severe handicap. Even worse is yet a further disorder of growth, achondroplasia, a kind of dwarfism in which bodily proportions are distorted. It too is dominant. At least sixteen defects are known to be transmitted in the same way, but some of them are relatively slight. Moreover, they may vary

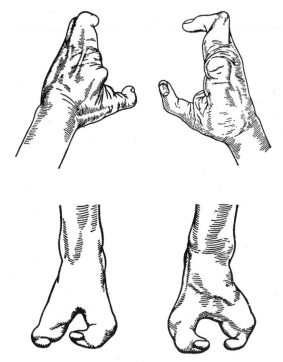

The Hands and Feet in Dominant Ectrodactyly, or 'Lobster Claw'

in severity: for instance, lamellar cataract may consist of a large opaque body involving most of the eye lens and causing nearly complate blindness, or only a small defect compatible with excellent sight.

Sterilization of all persons with lobster claw would bring about a rapid reduction in the number of people with that defect. Since the gene responsible takes effect in every individual who carries it, all such individuals can be identified. But not all dominant conditions could be eliminated by controlled breeding. Achondroplasics usually fail to reproduce. (Our knowledge of the genetics of this condition comes from the rare exceptions who marry and have children.) Since most are naturally barren, their continuing appearance in all large human populations must be due to mutation. The result of sterilizing all achondroplasics can be calculated: the incidence of the condition would be lowered by only twenty per cent. Other examples of defects usually due to recent mutation are retinoblastoma and epiloia (mentioned in chapter 3).

Another dominant condition presents a different kind of problem. Huntington's chorea is a severe disease of the nervous system in which there are involuntary movements of progressive violence. The difficulty arises because the disease often becomes evident only in middle or old age. The affected person may already have had several children. In this case, even the most ruthless advocate of sterilization is frustrated by often not knowing whom to sterilize until it is too late.

Some diseases are recessive. Among them, too, the problem of mutation arises. An example is haemophilia. As we saw in chapter 3, haemophilia is a recessive condition due to a sex-linked gene; it is almost confined to males, who derive the gene from their mothers and who rarely survive to have children. The repeated appearance of haemophilics in a population is due to mutation; the gene responsible mutates at the rate of about one in fifty thousand. This is probably an unusually high rate.

What of defects which are recessive but not sex-linked? It is unusual for individuals with these conditions to have affected parents. Just as a red-haired person may have parents both of whom have non-red hair, so a child with, for example, 'congenital' deaf-mutism may have normal parents; each parent has passed on one gene responsible for the complaint. Sterilization of all persons with congenital deaf-mutism would do little to reduce its incidence: according to one calculation, there would be no noticeable effect in fewer than thirty generations. Normal persons carrying the gene would continue to produce deaf mutes as before.

So far we have considered only diseases and defects determined in a relatively simple way. But advocates of negative eugenics have commonly been more concerned with conditions, such as mental deficiency, which are far from simple genetically. Intellectual attainment, like stature and some other qualities discussed in

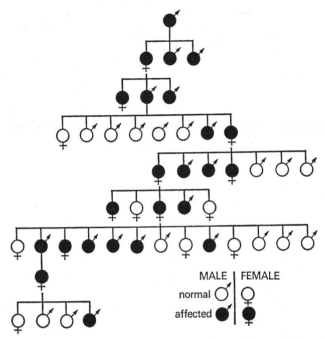

Transmission of a Dominant Character. Part of a pedigree of 'congenital' stationary night-blindness, a dominant defect. It appears regularly in each generation; it is transmitted only by affected persons (of either sex), but not to all their offspring

chapter 3, is influenced by many genes. The level of intelligence of whole populations is sometimes said to be threatened by the excessive breeding of mental defectives. If 'mental deficiency' were a simply defined condition, like albinism, and transmitted in a straightforward way from parent to offspring, it might be possible to make a rational plan to reduce its incidence. But it is not. The children who attend special schools for mental deficiency include a great variety of types, each owing the deficiency to a different set of causes, not all of them genetical. Some are curable, for instance by psychotherapy. At least five, and perhaps as many as twenty per cent can, by the application of existing knowledge, be so improved as to become useful and normal citizens. As for the genetics of mental deficiency, out of every hundred children with one or both parents defective, about seven or eight are themselves mentally deficient. A larger proportion are backward, but most are normal. Just as mentally defective parents can have normal children, so can normal parents have mentally defective children. Indeed, most defective children have normal parents.

Evidently, eugenic measures can do little to prevent the appearance of mental defectives; and if all defectives were sterilized or otherwise prevented from breeding, this would prevent the production of many more normal children than of defectives.

GENES AND ENVIRONMENT

It does not, however, follow that we must always resign ourselves to the appearance, in every population, of people handicapped by the effects of disadvantageous genes. Sometimes straightforward treatment, that is, environmental action, can reduce the ill effects of such genes. Severe short sight, for instance, is a grave handicap which makes a person almost blind for distances of more than one metre; but spectacles or, if necessary, contact lenses, can provide a complete correction. A very different example is diabetes, in which, too, there is a genetical element: many diabetics, some of great distinction and giving valuable service to the community, have been kept alive and vigorous for many years, by means of insulin. Preventive measures are also possible.

But there is a more fundamental point to make here. Improving the environment probably can, and does, reduce the number of disadvantageous genes in a population. This is so surprising, and so important, that it deserves a rather full treatment.

One of the most notable biological features of human populations is their *polymorphism*. We have already seen that man is highly polytypic: that is, geographical groups show marked differences which are in large part genetically determined. But within each group, or population, there is also great variation between individuals; and this variation, too, depends partly on genetical differences. Obvious superficial examples are in facial structure, general physique, and hair colour. (This statement does not contradict the assertion that such characteristics may also be influenced by environment.) This variation within each group leads us to say that man is highly polymorphic. How is this polymorphism maintained?

This question most clearly arises when we consider the continued appearance of disadvantageous genes. This is sometimes, as with haemophilia and retinoblastoma, a consequence of repeated mutation of normal genes. Mutation counteracts the effects of selection against the abnormal genes, and ensures that a few people with these abnormalities appear in every generation. But for some conditions

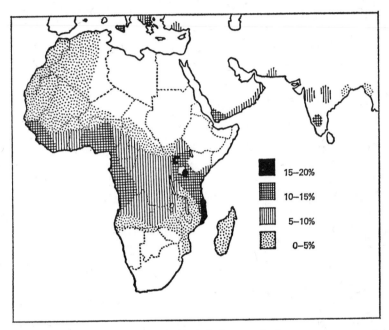

The Distribution of the Gene for Sickle-Cell Anaemia. Its frequency corresponds to the distribution of sub-tertian malaria

the numbers in the population are too large for this explanation to be valid: there must be some other effect which maintains the unwanted genes despite the disadvantages which they confer. It is, of course, just these genes which eugenists wish to eliminate by restricting breeding.

An explanation of the presence of these genes has been put forward on theoretical grounds, and has recently been confirmed. Sickle-cell anaemia, a disease of the blood, is found in people who inherit a particular gene from both parents; such people are said to be homozygous for the gene, and to have the genetical constitution SS (see chapter 3). The disease is often fatal early in life, and only a small proportion of such homozygotes survive to have children. Persons with only one of this type of abnormal gene (heterozygotes, of the constitution Ss) are normal, except that their red blood corpuscles, in certain conditions, become sickle-shaped; there is no evidence that heterozygotes are at any disadvantage compared with people with two normal genes (ss). Most people in the world have this last constitution, but among certain groups, notably some African Negroes, there is a high frequency of the abnormal gene which we denote by S, and therefore a considerable incidence of sickle-cell anaemia.

How is it, then, that the abnormal gene is not eliminated as a result of selection against the homozygotes? If there were no opposing effect, a gene which conferred such a disadvantage in the homozygous state would soon disappear. The answer cannot be mutation, because mutation rates are far too low to account for this case. The suggestion is that the heterozygote (Ss) has an advantage over both homozygotes (SS and ss); and that the advantage is more than enough to balance the selection against SS.

This is what actually happens in certain regions. Heterozygotes for the sickle-cell gene are almost completely immune to a dangerous form of malaria (sub-tertian). This disease is prevalent in parts of Africa, exactly where the incidence of the gene is high. Sub-tertian malaria occurs also in the south of India, and here too the population includes many with the sickle-cell gene (see map, page 175).

As we saw in chapter 6, the possession by Africans and Indians of this gene in common is *not* by itself evidence for 'racial' affinity: it reflects the fact that the two groups have been subjected to a similar environmental influence, and so to a similar selection pressure. When the environment is changed selection pressures change too. Africans in North America, where there is no sub-tertian malaria, have a greatly reduced incidence of the gene. The gene is being eliminated, as a result of the disadvantage it confers on the homozygote, since – in the absence of this type of malaria – the heterozygote is evidently at no advantage.

Sickle-cell anaemia is not the only example of this sort. Cooley's disease is another form of anaemia fatal in early life. It is a recessive condition: if the gene is Th, sufferers have the genetical constitution

ThTh. Heterozygotes, with only one Th gene, have a mild abnormality of the blood and, like sickle-cell heterozygotes, are malaria-resistant. This gene is common in lands around the Mediterranean, where one of the malarial parasites, *Plasmodium falciparum*, occurs. Other examples are provided by the blood groups of the ABO series. Whether your red blood cells carry A or B antigens, or both, or neither (group O), is determined in a simple way by the genetical constitution of your parents. If your group is O, your resistance to plague is probably below average. This accords with the proportion of O in different populations: it is high among the American Indians, Australiforms and Polynesians, who have no history of plague infection. Where plague is endemic, as in India, group O is rare.

Probably, disease has been an important agent of natural selection in human populations. The examples just given are of populations with a genetically determined resistance to disease. The other side of the coin appears when explorers or invaders reach a long isolated group. The inhabitants of Tierra del Fuego, and the Polynesians, were nearly wiped out by infectious diseases carried by the Europeans who first reached them.

Evidently, many genes may be maintained in populations by selection of the kind which operates for the sickle-cell gene. If this is so, there is a clear eugenic implication: to eliminate such genes, the most effective action is to alter the environment to remove the selection pressure which enables the genes to persist. Probably, this has already happened on a large scale in communities in which (as will be discussed in chapter 13) many formerly common diseases have been prevented. Had the genes been eliminated, by some eugenic measure, before the diseases had been disposed of, the result would have been to weaken the resistance of the population to infection.

The most general lesson to be learnt here is the complexity of the problems which face a eugenist. If we wish to improve the genetical constitution of a human population, we cannot safely proceed on any simple assumption: we cannot say merely that 'like produces like' (for it often does not), and therefore encourage the breeding of the people we approve of, and discourage breeding by those whom we deplore. If this were done, the results might be very different from those we desire or expect. When it becomes possible to construct a detailed eugenic programme, based on knowledge, it will be much more complex and subtle than anything so far proposed.

MEASURING 'INTELLIGENCE'

Even if negative eugenics, in the usual sense of the term, can be of little use, there might still be important genetical differences between classes. We have seen that no socially important differences can be demonstrated between 'races' or nations; but they might be found between, say, the professional and managerial group on the one hand, and the unskilled labourers on the other. This is a difficult question to investigate, because in most countries the conditions in which the children of these two classes grow up are exceedingly different. Environmental diversity has important effects on height, weight, strength, and length of life, but on genetical differences we have no precise knowledge.

To consider psychological differences we have, as before, to fall back on measurements of intelligence quotients. But first something further must be said on their limitations.

Ordinary examinations, as applied to large numbers of children in, for instance, the General Certificate of Education, are most unreliable tests. In experiments, not only have different examiners given widely different marks to the same paper, but the same examiner has given equally different marks when faced with the same paper on different occasions. Sometimes, in subjects such as English, the difference may be that between failure and distinction. Ideally, intelligence tests should overcome these difficulties, by providing an objective and reliable means of assessing general educability.

A major question, then, is whether the tests have 'predictive value'. To be useful in the prediction of future performance, the result of one test on a given child must be very similar to the result of testing the same child after an interval of years. If a group of people is tested, and the average is taken, then that average is usually much the same years later. This is the justification for the discussion of group averages in the previous chapter. A steady group average could, however, conceal much variation among individuals, if some improved and some declined in the ability to answer the tests.

To find out whether intelligence tests are reliable, it is first necessary to establish test-retest correlations. At best, the retest, made shortly after the first, would give exactly the same score as the first: the correlation would then be 1·0. In fact, such correlations are usually about 0·9. In a typical test, this means that, of ten children scoring 100 on the first, one will score above 112 or below 88 on the second. This is hardly satisfactory, when it is realized that some decisions regarding a child's future are determined by a much smaller margin of marks. But, worse than this, the correlations are far lower if retests are made after an interval of years.

Intelligence tests given to children of, say, five or six years, have virtually no predictive value: the correlation with the results of tests given later is so low as to make the tests useless. The rate of intellectual development evidently varies; one child may do well early in life, and slow down later; another may do the opposite. In fact, the IQ of a normal child may vary by as much as 50 points over a period of years. These facts are of great practical importance. Many English primary schools divide the children, at eight years, into three streams, on the basis of tests, and the A stream, consisting of the highest scorers, are prepared for entry to grammar schools, while the remainder, taught at a lower intensity, are expected to go to a modern school. In Scotland, too, there is a similar segregation, for some children, at five years.

This system must cause much injustice and waste of ability. The remedy is being applied by some local authorities: it is the development of 'comprehensive' secondary schools, that is, schools which take all the children of over eleven or twelve years in a given locality, regardless of their supposed attainments. Every child then has access to every type of secondary education. Only such schools can allow for the known facts regarding the development of ability in children. At later ages intelligence tests have some predictive value, but they are never more than, at best, a very rough guide to the ability of any particular individual.

Today, more than half a century after the tests were invented, their limitations are becoming widely known. Better still, psychologists are beginning to develop new tests – not to replace those devised by Binet but to measure other qualities just as important. One quality has provocatively been called 'creativity' (it might have been 'imagination'), but this is as bad as calling the IQ, 'intelligence'.

The new tests are amusing but not, perhaps, always as easy to mark as the old ones. Among them there is this: 'Write down as many meanings for the following words as you can: *bit, bolt, pink, port...*' Another requires as many uses as can be proposed for an object such as a barrel. These questions are 'open-ended': the second,

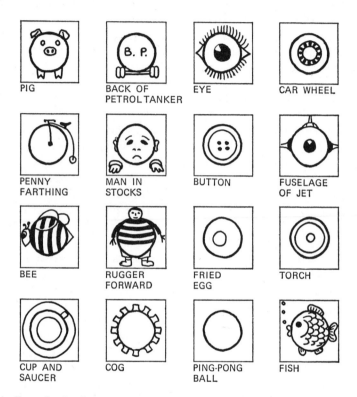

An Example of a Response to an Open-Ended Test. The subject is required to make drawings all based on the same circle

especially, offers virtually unlimited opportunities. Conventional questions, by contrast, have only one correct answer.

Some of the new tests go even further. 'Make a drawing with the title "Zebra Crossing".' One response was a picture of a Zebra crossing itself. (Another suggestion, previously unpublished, is a Zebra in coitus with a horse.) This test is, however, not typical.

Among English 'public' schoolboys, at least, those beginning to specialize in literary subjects score high on open-ended tests, while the physicists and chemists do better in the old ones. Biologists evidently have the best of both worlds, for they do not fall clearly into either class. A question which urgently demands study is how the two types of ability develop. Do we want educated people capable of the meticulousness of a good physicist and also free to accept and even propose novel ideas? If so, how do we produce them?

WASTED ABILITIES

Despite the serious defects of intelligence tests, it is sometimes possible to draw at least tentative conclusions from studies of the IQs of large groups, such as the different classes making up a nation. There are two questions which may be usefully asked. First, is there any connexion between IQ differences and genetical differences? In other words, do we have IQs similar to those of our parents, *irrespective of environmental influences*? The second question is: What is the distribution of IQ in the different social classes?

As for the genetical effect on IQ, there is ample evidence for a high correlation between children and parents, and between sibs. This could be attributed to similarity of environments. A check has been made by a study of children in orphanages, who are found to show a slight positive correlation in their IQ with that of their parents. In particular, orphanage children of professional class parents show a slightly higher average IQ than the rest. Since members of the professional classes have higher IQs than other sections of a population the orphanage results presumably reflect a genetical difference. A clearer illustration of the genetical effect is given by tests on twins. Uniovular twins on the average show much closer resemblance in intelligence tests than fraternal twins. On the other hand, as we have seen, tests of uniovular twins show also that the environment *can* have a marked influence on IQ. This is what we should expect from the importance of learning in the development of human behaviour, discussed in chapter 5. An example of the same thing is given by the children of English bargees. Up to the age of six these children do not differ significantly in IQ from other children, but after that age their IQs fall below normal. This is evidently a result of lack of schooling during their life on the canals.

The second question, that of the distribution of IQ in the social classes, is partly answered in the figure below. In England the highest income group has the highest average IQ, and the highest proportion of very gifted individuals. On the other hand, there is a big overlap: even the lowest group has a considerable proportion of individuals with high IQs. In fact, since the lower income groups

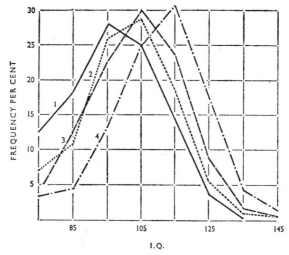

'Intelligence' Quotient. Distributions of ability to answer 'intelligence' tests among children of different economic classes in England. Group 1 parents unskilled; 2 semi-skilled; 3 skilled handworkers; 4 'brain-workers'. The wealthier children score better, on the average, than the poor, but there is a big overlap. The lower average of the poor is probably due largely to environmental effects

form the great majority of the population, they include more individuals of exceptionally high IQ than the higher groups.

We cannot say to what extent the difference between the classes is genetically determined. Some, at least, is due to the inferior amenities of the poor. The immediate conclusion to be drawn, for practical purposes, is that there is no sharp distinction in IQ scores between the different classes: all classes have individuals with both high and low scores, and intelligence tests provide no grounds for educational discrimination between them.

The crucial question of opportunity is brought out by the test scores of pupils in different types of school. Consider first children of nine to twelve and a half in England and Wales in the 1930s. Out of every hundred with IQs of 120 or more, about eighty-four were in the free schools (attended by the poor) and sixteen in the expensive schools. This would not have mattered if the opportunity for higher education, entry into the professions, and other advancement were the same for all classes. But this was, and is, far from being the case. All the children of the rich who reach the necessary standard can get into universities, but most of the able children of the poor are unable even to take the examinations which give entry.

During the period 1928 to 1960, in England and Wales, the proportion of the young who went on to full-time university doubled, from 2·9 to 5·8 per cent. In 1928 the chances of a child of a non-manual worker going to university were 6·5 times those of children from a manual worker's family. *The corresponding figure for 1960 was exactly the same.* A contributory factor to this discrimination between classes has only recently been recorded. The progress of large numbers of British children has been followed from birth to adulthood; and with age the IQ of middle-class children has tended to rise, that of working-class children to fall. Here is a demonstration of an effect of an intellectually impoverished environment, and a challenge which has not yet been faced by the liberal democracies. The retention of educational privilege for a minority is not only grossly unjust; it also squanders one of the most valuable resources of a nation, its supply of ability.

Even in the United States, with its far higher proportion of university entrants (and of drop-outs), the poor remain under a substantial handicap. A Harvard committee has written:

If ... the social environment of these young people should improve materially, more of them would almost certainly show higher promise. There is experimental evidence that ability can be improved as a child's early surroundings are improved – evidence which, as was said, the growth and spread of talent which have accompanied the decline of privilege in the modern era tends to confirm.

The waste of ability is, of course, far greater in the under-developed countries. In 1959 nearly all the people in Europe, the U.S.S.R. and North America were literate: that is, about ninety-six per cent could write a letter and read a newspaper. In Central and South America the corresponding figure was below sixty per cent, in Asia below forty and in Africa below twenty. But here there is rapid progress. The world figures for 1959 are already out of date in the 1970s. China, one of the most backward countries in 1947, amidst all its upheavals, is rapidly becoming an educated nation. In the transformation of vast peasant communities to a modern, technological way of life, the U.S.S.R. has acted as a pacemaker. In 1918 its people were mostly unlettered, and many in the West assumed they would remain so. Today the U.S.S.R. produces as many engineers, for every million of population, as the U.S.A., and so indicates the rate at which change is possible.

DECLINING INTELLIGENCE?

The evidence of plentiful ability among the poor and unprivileged conflicts with a widely propagated belief that the 'national intelligence' of Britain, America and other countries is declining. The argument is this: the rich (that is, the professional and managerial class) have children whose average IQ is higher than that of the children of the poor; but the poor on the average have larger families than the rich; the difference in IQ between rich and poor is, at least in part, genetically determined; therefore, the proportion of those with high intellectual ability is being steadily reduced.

This view has been criticized on various grounds. For instance, as we shall see further in chapter 14, the differential fertility between rich and poor may be only temporary. More important, it has been suggested that the difference in IQ between rich and poor children may be a product of the inferior conditions, both physical and intellectual, of the poor. The theory has now, however, been directly tested. In 1932 87,000 Scottish children aged eleven years did intelligence tests; in 1947 nearly 71,000 eleven-year-olds did similar tests. Out of a maximum score of 76 points the average in 1932 was 34·5; in 1947 it was 36·7. Evidently the IQ of Scottish children had risen during the period of fifteen years covered by the investigation. We do not know what caused the rise: it may be improved environment, especially nutrition; it may be 'test sophistication', which is a name for the fact that children and their teachers can undoubtedly get wise to the tests, and prepare for them. Whatever the explanation, two further large-scale studies, in England, have also brought evidence of a general, though slight, rise in intelligence quotient.

The 'declining intelligence' hypothesis has also been criticized on theoretical grounds. Persons of exceptionally high 'intelligence', as measured by tests, do tend to have fewer children than the average. The same is true of imbeciles and idiots. But both classes of persons continue to appear in the population, often as the offspring of near-average parents. Ordinary people are on the whole more fertile than individuals at either extreme. This principle applies generally. It could be predicted, for instance, that the 'national stature' of many countries must be declining, on grounds exactly comparable to those on which the declining intelligence hypothesis is based. But stature is, if anything, increasing in these countries.

The question of fertility has therefore, very recently, been examined more closely. The statement that low IQ accompanies high fertility is based on studies of people who have children. But a substantial number have none. Are these barren individuals, on the average, high or low scorers in intelligence tests? In fact, there are more childless people among the *lower* scorers. Suppose now one takes at random, say, one thousand people of below average 'intelligence', and one thousand above, and that the childless are included. Which group produces the larger number of children? In the studies so far made, differences between the two groups have been very small; but, where they have been significant, the *higher* IQ group has produced more children.

We know little of the selective influences which act on human populations, or of the genetical changes taking place in them. But there is no longer a rational basis for alarm about declining intelligence. Our anxieties should rather be directed towards our failure to give scope to all the talent that exists.

SUMMING UP

Any large group, whether defined geographically, or by physical features, or by economic status, can produce persons of high ability, and also some of low. Some groups may differ genetically from others but, if they do exist, the differences certainly do not justify reserving educational privilege, or entry into certain professions, for members of a particular class.

We have so far ignored the need of human society for many widely different types. Most individuals, given education and opportunity, could find something useful and pleasant to do among the available occupations. Even the mentally deficient can work at simple tasks. Hence, to assess the worth of an individual we must say exactly what sort of life he is to live.

To sum up, every 'race', and each economic class within a nation, can produce its quota of the good and bad, intelligent and stupid, strong and weak. This is just as well. Every human being is entitled to certain essentials of civilized life, including food, clothes, and shelter, with some leisure in which to enjoy them in his own way. If this principle had to be applied to large populations unable to make a contribution to world prosperity, the outlook would be depressing: the more advanced peoples would have to accept for many decades a lower standard of life, while a large fraction of what they produced went to the less fortunate and less capable. The actual outlook is quite different. Once depressed nations and classes are set on the road of social development, they can make a contribution to the material and intellectual wealth of mankind commensurate with their numbers.

⑨

SEX DIFFERENCES

Social progress can be measured with precision by the social position of the female sex.

KARL MARX

THE most obvious aspect of human variety, the division into two sexes, remains to be discussed. Unfortunately, precise knowledge on sex differences, apart from the obvious ones, is surprisingly small, while misunderstanding and prejudice are correspondingly great. A Scottish religious leader, John Knox (?1513–1572), wrote:

To promote a woman to bear superiority . . . is repugnant to nature, contrary to God, and . . . the subversion of good order and all equity and justice.

There are still plenty of men, Scots and others, who cling to this sort of belief – and some women, too.

In most societies the different social positions of men and women are based directly on their roles in reproduction: women bear children and suckle them, and so are tied to the home and to household duties; men undertake the outside tasks: hunting in primitive conditions, tilling the fields in a peasant community, and carrying on the various trades and professions in a modern society. It is natural to take this situation for granted, and to believe that women are not fitted for the tasks normally carried out by men. A century ago there were no women doctors, and many assumed that women had no capacity for the practice of medicine. Such assumptions are often based on nothing more than local custom: in the third century A.D. a Greek, Athenaeus, exclaimed, 'Who ever heard of a woman cook!'

PHYSICAL DIFFERENCES

From before birth there are sex differences in growth rates and in the development of various organs. Boys, on the average, are slightly

187

heavier than girls at birth; but the development of the skeleton of girls is more advanced. There is no possibility of these differences being determined environmentally. As for the adult skeleton, it is usually possible for an anatomist to determine the sex even of a quite small part, such as a fragment of the skull. About one skeleton in forty may be difficult to place. These differences may be influenced by the different conditions in which the sexes are brought up, but it is reasonably certain that they are mainly genetical.

Boys are not only slightly heavier, on the average, at birth, but also (among Europeans) about 8 mm taller. This superiority of height does not persist: by eleven years the average heights of the sexes are about equal, and at thirteen girls are about 18 mm taller. But girls slow down and stop growing earlier than boys. In addition, the vital capacity of the lungs, and the number of red cells of the blood, increase in adolescent boys but not girls.

All this certainly reflects genetical differences in growth capacity, even though environmental agencies may play some part. In some societies the growth of most women is checked prematurely by early child-bearing, and the difference of stature between the sexes is thereby increased. Perhaps there are less obvious environmental effects operating even among children in the Western World today. Some may act in the opposite direction. In Italy, for instance, boys are more prized than girls, and better looked after, and as infants they are kept more carefully in the shade; but the action of sunlight on the skin produces vitamin D, and in times of food shortage, as in the period after the Second World War, this may be important. Doctors doing relief work found a higher incidence of rickets (which is caused partly by vitamin D deficiency) among boys. Whatever moral one draws from this, it is an example of an environmental effect influencing the two sexes differently.

Males are not only bigger than females; they also have a higher metabolic rate on the average: that is, chemical changes in their bodies go on more rapidly, and so males on the whole require more food for a given body weight. This is evidently because women have more adipose tissue than men – again, on the average. If metabolic rates are calculated for body weight minus fat, they are the same for the two sexes.

Muscular strength parallels growth changes. In one study of eighty-seven girls and eighty-nine boys, in California, grip, pulling, and thrusting strength were measured regularly throughout school and college life. Sex differences were small up to the age of thirteen; after this the rate of change became much less in girls, but greater in boys. As a result, after sixteen almost no girls reached even the average performance of boys, and nearly all the boys were above the girls' average. It is hardly possible to attribute this difference to environment, especially since all the children studied had plenty of opportunity for developing muscular strength through games, and nutritionally they were all in much the same state.

Muscular *skills*, on the other hand, seem to be distributed in a more complicated way. As a rule boys throw better than girls. This might often be because they are encouraged to play more ball games. But probably a more fundamental difference is involved. The form of the limbs is different in the two sexes: in particular, a girl's forearm, but not a boy's, makes an angle with the upper arm. So girls, for anatomical reasons, may be obliged to throw in a less effective way than boys. And the anatomical differences are presumably determined genetically.

Throwing is, perhaps, not of much importance. In some other skilled activities girls do better than boys from an early age. Anything requiring the performance of delicate movements is done better by girls: for instance, they learn to dress earlier. Differences in the capacity to carry out fine movements have been reported as early as nine months. This may be a correlate of the general greater maturity of girls; the same applies to their earlier achievement of bladder control.

So far, then, there is some objective basis for referring to women as 'the weaker sex': they are measurably less strong than men, on the average, (though not less skilled) and the difference is probably mainly genetical. But in another respect men are the weaker sex. They die more easily. This is largely due to a lower resistance to infection which holds throughout life. This does not, however, apply everywhere: in India and similar countries, where women suffer conditions especially bad for health, the death-rate of women is higher than that of men at most ages.

INTELLECTUAL DIFFERENCES

It might be expected that, on coming to intellectual differences, the first step would be to compare the average IQs of the two sexes. Unfortunately, modern intelligence tests are so *designed* that boys and girls of equal age give the same average performance. However, it is a different story if we examine special abilities. Boys have superior mechanical ability and are more likely to excel in mathematics; but girls from a very early age are more articulate: they talk more, and more intelligibly. They are also superior in 'aesthetic sense': for instance, they discriminate colours better than boys. Their memory too is said to be better, at least in early childhood. Later, they are better at languages. A general difference is that boys vary more than girls: there are more extreme types among males, for instance more with a very high IQ and more imbeciles.

An important question is whether intellectual development parallels the changes in growth and physiology during adolescence. Girls stop growing earlier, and their 'intelligence' has been said to reach its maximum before that of boys. (To show this, one must, of course, use tests which do distinguish between the sexes.) Earlier maturity or not, there is a great overlap of intellectual ability between men and women. There are no grounds for denying women a higher education in any subject.

Although the differences just described are quite likely to be mainly genetical, we are entirely justified in remaining sceptical on that point. It is extraordinarily difficult to discern the more subtle environmental influences, and to distinguish their effects from genetical ones. We saw something of the complexities of early learning in chapter 5. In most societies girls and boys are treated differently almost from birth: they are dressed differently, talked to differently, and *expected* to show different interests. We cannot say to what extent this attitude has prevented the appearance of women eminent in the arts and professions. The difficulty in allowing for the effects of social convention is probably greatest if we try to deal with differences of 'character' or 'temperament'. Child psychologists and others commonly assert that, for instance, boys are more aggressive than girls, and girls shyer. We need not doubt that this is true, but unfortunately it is not easy to measure aggression or shyness, and so it is difficult to make statements of this kind quantitative and precise. It would be very rash to say that a difference of this sort is quite independent of the child's environment. In any case all these statements concern the averages shown by groups: they tell us nothing about particular persons. When Samuel Johnson was asked, 'Which have the most brains, men or women?', he replied, 'Which man, which woman?' His reply could not have been more to the point.

WOMEN IN THE COMMUNITY

To assess environmental effects further, we may examine different types of society. National groups show great plasticity of behaviour in response to different environments. Do the two sexes show a similar plasticity?

In some respects they obviously do. The behaviour of a well-to-do business man in Western Europe or the United States during the late nineteenth century might be contrasted with that of the dandy of less than a century before. Similarly we may make the obvious comparison of the Victorian lady dressed, perhaps, in ankle-length skirt and bustle, and the mid-twentieth century young woman in slacks or mini-skirt.

This type of comparison, however, though interesting, is superficial. In 1869 John Stuart Mill went much further when he wrote:

What is now called the nature of women is an eminently artificial thing, the result of forced repression in some directions, unnatural stimulation in others. It may be asserted, without scruple, that no other class of dependents have had their character so entirely distorted from its natural proportions.

The character of men, too, in 1869, as today, was no doubt 'distorted from its natural proportions'. Mill's emphasis on women was a protest against their position as dependents. The buying and selling of wives had not long been given up in England when Mill wrote.

The protest against the subjection of women, and the demand for their emancipation from all the social and economic disadvantages imposed on them, has been supported by pointing to societies in which the roles of the sexes have seemed to be the inverse of those familiar to us. In our society women are expected (on the whole) to play a passive part in love-making; to be dependent rather than self-reliant; to be modest, chaste, home-loving, and motherly; and to be particularly interested in self-adornment. It is said, however, that in some civilizations, notably those of Sparta and ancient Egypt, these characteristics have belonged on the whole to men, and not to women; and that this inversion was related to the economic subjection of men which was characteristic of these societies.

The extent to which this account of these ancient societies is accurate has been questioned. But in some primitive societies today, such inversion has been reported from direct observation. The best-known work of this kind was done by Margaret Mead in New Guinea. Of three tribal groups in that country, she states that one, the Tchambuli, has a relationship between the sexes the exact opposite of what we accept as usual. In both the others, however, there is 'no idea that men and women are different in temperament'. Of these two, among the Arapesh the behaviour of both men and women is uniformly gentle and unaggressive, and what we should describe as maternal and passive; this group practises agriculture. On the other hand, the Mundugumor, who are head-hunters, are, men and women alike, aggressive and 'masculine'.

The observations made by anthropologists remind us forcefully not to take for granted the patterns of behaviour to which we happen to be accustomed. This is especially important now. The control of conception, combined with modern housing, is beginning to release women from permanent domestic serfdom, even in communities in which women are expected to cope with all the child-rearing and all the management of the home. Hence both men and women have to adapt themselves to a new situation: men will have to treat their wives as equals, and not possessions, and women will face wider responsibilities. The benefits from these changes may well accumulate over several generations.

15 THE DESERT – The Algerian Sahara.

16 THE SOWN – Terraced, irrigated rice fields in Java.

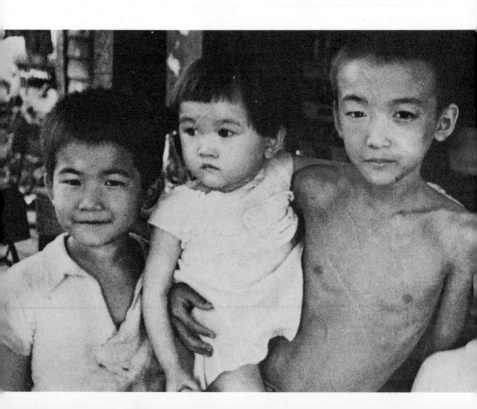

17 STARVATION – This baby girl of Thailand has the pot belly, spindly limbs and apparently enormous head of severe undernutrition.

18 RECOVERY – The same baby at 3.5 years, after a period of proper feeding.

19 PLAGUE – In a Calcutta slum a sanitary squad sprays dead rats to kill the fleas.

20 MALARIA – This Indian woman, lying in the open with an attack of fever, was brought to a WHO malaria team in the Terai Region, for treatment. Malaria is estimated to infect 300 million persons in India every year, and to kill 3 million.

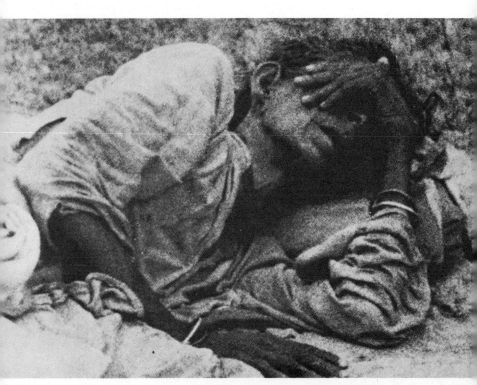

21 MALARIA: CONTROL – Spraying with DDT in a temple in Thailand, to kill malaria-carrying mosquitoes.

MALARIA: CONTROL – Spraying with dieldrin, a more toxic substance than DDT, to kill malaria-carrying mosquitoes in the Philippines.

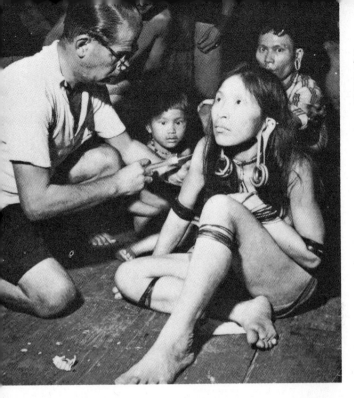

23 MALARIA:
TREATMENT – A
doctor treating a
Punan woman in
Sarawak.

24 TYPHUS –
Members of an
Afghan
government team in
Kabul, dusting
children to kill lice
which carry the
germs of typhus.

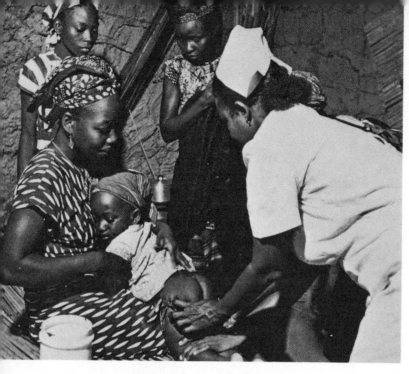

25 PUBLIC HEALTH – In Liberia a nurse treats a baby for yaws. This infection, common in large parts of Africa, is rapidly cured with penicillin.

26 PUBLIC HEALTH – Vaccination against smallpox in a Liberian village.

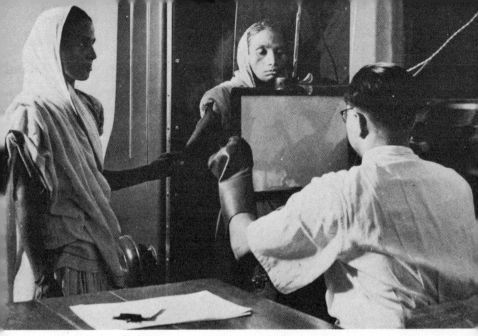

27 TUBERCULOSIS: DIAGNOSIS – At Patna, in Bihar, the Indian government have a demonstration and training centre, with help from WHO and UNICEF. Modern techniques of examination are used for early diagnosis of tuberculosis, which greatly increases the chances of recovery.

28 TUBERCULOSIS: TREATMENT – In India, as in countries further west, tubercle is one of the most serious health problems, and sanatoria are few. Here a doctor from Ceylon examines a patient in his home, while a WHO nurse advises the family about the patient's needs.

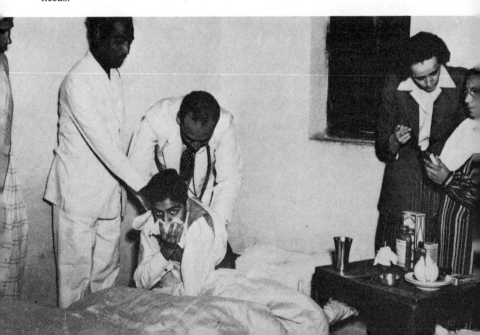

29 BILHARZIASIS – In Egypt the snails which carry this dangerous infection are trapped on palm leaves for investigation.

30 BILHARZIASIS – In the Philippines a farmer clears the banks of an irrigation canal.

PART THREE

LIFE AND DEATH

The first human societies were small family groups, and only when agriculture was invented, perhaps eight thousand years ago, did populous human communities come into being. Gradual improvement in the techniques of cultivation made it possible to produce a food surplus, which could support those who grew no food but worked in industry or trade, or administered the state; this was the foundation of civilization. But food supplies have never been entirely reliable for any large human population. Today we can see the world's food problem as a whole, and also discern the biological and economic changes required to solve it.

The other major biological problem of the twentieth century is the conquest of infectious disease. Much of the world still suffers from the same epidemic and endemic scourges as our ancestors of centuries ago, although it is known how to prevent them. In the advanced countries, where they have been prevented, there remain formidable problems such as high infant mortality, tuberculosis, and 'mental' illness, but these too can be solved.

If full use is to be made of biological knowledge for human benefit, human populations, most of which are increasing, must attain an equilibrium with their environmental resources. This can be achieved if schemes of development, especially of undeveloped areas, are given adequate priority, and effective methods of birth control are made generally available. The crucial problem for twentieth-century man is to apply knowledge, not to destruction or private profit, but for the general good.

10

MAN AND SOCIETY

Thou shalt eat the herb of the field; in the sweat of thy face shalt thou
eat bread ...

GENESIS

THIS chapter is a connecting link between the fourth and fifth on
human evolution and behaviour, and the four which follow on food,
disease, and population. It deals with the evolution of human
society. In chapter 4 man was described biologically, and his
relationship with other mammals, especially the apes, was
emphasized. But, as we saw in chapter 5, man is distinguished by
a unique form of social organization. It is unique because other
highly social animals, such as ants and bees, have the patterns of
their behaviour fixed independently of experience, whereas one
of the most notable things about man, compared with other animals,
is his capacity for learning, especially in his early years, and the consequent plasticity of his behaviour. The single species, *Homo sapiens*,
has therefore produced many types of society; and in some areas
(such as Western Europe, or Central Asia) society has changed from
one type to another very rapidly.

There is a notion that some kinds of human existence are more
natural than others, though what *natural* means in this context is
rarely explained. The 'state of nature' in which primitive man exists
is sometimes contrasted with the 'artificiality' of modern times. The
implication is that primitive men live like most other animals, without social organization, tools, or speech. But this is not true. Even
before *Homo sapiens* appeared there were all these things, together
with fire: wherever and whenever he has lived man has assembled
in groups and has altered his surroundings so as to satisfy his needs.
This is what is meant when it is said that man 'creates his own
environment'.

Social organization probably developed from family groups.
Among apes today the group consists typically of a single dominant

male with a number of subordinate males and females and their young. There is no division of labour between the sexes and all have to forage for food. Among primitive men monogamy is typical. The women contribute to food-getting by gathering food plants, and the men hunt. The division of labour between the sexes also makes possible greater protection for the young by the mother; as we know, this is essential, since human social behaviour depends on the young gradually learning appropriate habits and customs.

SAVAGERY

This early type of society is technically called savagery, though not in any pejorative sense. It refers to the state of all pre-*sapiens* man; and *Homo sapiens* himself has lived for ninety per cent or more of his time in the same state.

Savage man is usually nomadic. The present tense can be used here, not merely as a literary device but because there are several groups which have never progressed from savagery (at least, until very recently indeed): for example, the Australian aborigines, the Eskimo, and some of the inhabitants of Malaya and of Central and South Africa. He lives by collecting food, plant or animal, over a wide region, and a great area of land is needed to support each individual, compared with that required in an agricultural community. The sparse population is divided into family units which may include twenty persons. Occasionally there may be larger gatherings, since at a season of plenty, when much food can be gathered in a small space, members of different groups may meet. Only on such occasions is there opportunity for the exchange of knowledge and views. However, both knowledge and ideas are likely to be very restricted. In small groups there is less opportunity for division of labour apart from that between the sexes, especially when nearly all waking time is needed for food collecting; and without it, technical advance cannot go far.

The tools of savages, to judge by the behaviour of apes today, may first have been sticks; but by the time of Peking man stone choppers had long been manufactured. As containers there are gourds, shells, skulls and perhaps baskets, but no pottery. For coverings skins, grasses, and bark may be used, but there are no textiles. There are no domestic animals, either for food or for draught. There is private property in weapons, digging sticks, collecting bags, and trinkets, but not in food.

Neanderthal man – our immediate predecessor in Europe – probably had all these resources. Stone tools were more skilfully made, by flaking, than were those of earlier man; in particular there were well designed scrapers and points. There were a few bone tools. Traps were made. Burial of the dead suggests some kind of religion or magic, and cannibalism, which was also practised, may have had a similar foundation since, as in the Christian ritual, the eating of a person's body is sometimes supposed to confer the strength or virtue of the eaten on the eater.

This takes us to the end of the whole of the lower palaeolithic period, including the Mousterian culture for which Neanderthal man was responsible. ('Palaeolithic' means 'old stone age'.) More information is given in the chart on page 201. In the upper palaeolithic we come to the stage, called the higher savagery, at which our own type, *Homo sapiens*, first appears. A few men remain today in this phase of social development, but in the Mediterranean area certainly, and no doubt in other parts of the world, men of modern type lived in this way during a period beginning at least 70,000 years ago and ending less than 10,000 years ago. The variety of cultures that existed during this long period is only imperfectly known: large parts of the world are almost unexplored for possible remains, and most of our present knowledge comes from France and the North of Spain; North Africa and parts of Asia have, however, yielded valuable material. Even in these rather small areas it is possible to distinguish a series of distinct phases, in each of which the designs of tools and clay vessels, artistic styles and mode of life all have characteristic features.

The different cultures do not correspond to the different physical types shown by skeletal remains. One culture, called the Gravettian, has left widespread traces in Western Europe; Gravettian equipment was used both by 'Cro-Magnon' man – a type regarded as typically 'European' – and by the Grimaldi type which in skull character has been held to resemble a typical Negro. Both are found together in the Guttes de Grimaldi at Mentone. This fact gives further support to the conclusions on race differences reached in chapters 6 and 7.

H. sapiens, from the first we know of him, had much more

elaborate flint tools than his predecessors. After a large fragment had been struck from the main mass, much skilled secondary flaking was done to get the desired shape. Bones, antlers, and teeth also were used as instruments. Stone lamps, pestles and mortars were made. There was still no pottery, but clay modelling was done. Remarkable works of art, including figurines, are found in the caves used as dwellings, but we do not know the significance of these works to their makers. Skins were probably used for clothing, and

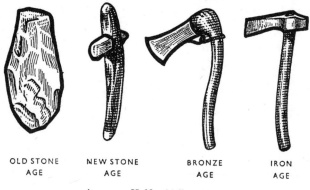

OLD STONE AGE   NEW STONE AGE   BRONZE AGE   IRON AGE

Axes over Half a Million Years

sinews for bows and harpoon lines. Spears and arrows had flint or bone points.

Thus from the first *H. sapiens* has displayed much manual skill, together, perhaps, with an aesthetic sensibility. Nevertheless, for tens of thousands of years man remained in the pre-agricultural phase, and lived by hunting, shooting and fishing, and by the collection of wild plant food and honey. As a rule, there was probably a seasonal nomadism, in which the movement of the small family groups was determined by the travels of game in search of food and water. In winter, caves, or simple structures with the floor below ground level, were occupied. A typical group would perhaps occupy four or five huts, each housing several people.

The use of well-constructed huts was developed in Europe in the latest pre-agricultural period. This new phase, the mesolithic, or middle stone age, lasted a rather short time before it blossomed out into the agricultural revolution. The characteristics which distinguish it from the old stone age are the domestication of the dog for hunting; the use of nets, hooks, and lines for fishing (but perhaps these have been preserved only from this more recent phase); and the construction of canoes, paddles, skis, and sledges for transport. There was a greater variety of technical skills, but no fundamental difference from the paleolithic. In general, savagery, whether 'higher savagery' or not, whether carried on with mesolithic equipment or that of the old stone age, is a precarious existence. The human population of the world before agriculture was practised was probably fewer than 10m. – about the number now living within twenty miles of the City of London. England is believed to have had a population of about 250 at that time and 2000 when agriculture began.

Another way of describing that rare animal, man before agriculture, is in terms of population density. The aborigines of Tasmania, when first studied by Europeans, averaged about one person for every hundred square miles. This is a low figure, even for men in a state of savagery. In the most favourable savage conditions there was probably one person for every square mile. Of course, the spread was not even; it is better to say that a typical family group occupied, say, twenty square miles.

PRIMITIVE BARBARISM

The great change came about 8000 years ago. At that time cultivation of domestic plants began in the sub-tropical zone which includes North Africa, Syria, Iran and Turkestan; the whole area today is dry and largely desert, but during the Pleistocene it had had a good rainfall. At first, cultivation was no doubt confined to the most favourable regions, such as the Nile valley, where there was plenty of water. The type of cultivation was that called 'extensive': that is, there was frequent breaking of new ground as the old lost its productivity. This is a less permanent type of settlement than is found among people practising intensive cultivation – the continued use of the same plots of land for an indefinite period. (Extensive cultivation was still being used in Western Europe after the collapse of Rome.)

No doubt men had already used the seeds of wild grasses as food. Flint sickles found at Mount Carmel suggest that cereals were eaten by the mesolithic cave-dwellers, probably before 6000 B.C. The first step in agriculture was to induce suitable grasses to grow annually on selected plots within a settlement. In the Mediterranean area wheats, wild Einkorn and wild Emmer, were domesticated, together with wild barley. Rye and oats came much later, at first as weeds of wheat and barley fields; their advantage was their capacity to give good yields in more northern climates than wheat would stand. The earliest known civilizations, those of Syria, Mesopotamia, and the valley of the Indus, occupy an area roughly coinciding with the distribution of the wild ancestors of wheat and barley, and' the civilizations of Europe and Western Asia are founded on the productivity of these two plant species.

The domestication of animals for food began at about the same time as cereal cultivation. The dog had preceded agriculture, as an adjunct to hunting. Cattle, sheep, goats and pigs were brought in early. The use of the horse, ass, ox and camel for transport and traction came later. The early stages of settled agriculture, with both cultivated cereals and domestic herds, have been most studied at the ancient settlements of the Faiyum and Merimde in Egypt, and Sumer in Mesopotamia. It is at the latter that the use of sheep's wool for clothing is first recorded, probably 4000 years before the present era. Dairy farming also seems to have begun in Mesopotamia, perhaps 1000 years later.

The type of culture associated with the most primitive agriculture is called neolithic – the culture of the new stone age. The Maoris of New Zealand were still at this stage in 1800. Our knowledge of the neolithic phase throughout the world is exceedingly fragmentary, but agriculture probably arose independently in several regions. Certainly the maize and potato agriculture of Central and South America owes nothing to the ancient Egyptians, and in China that based on millet and the pig may have been a separate development.

Wherever it was adopted agriculture had the most profound effects on human life. Its primary function was to ensure a greater and more reliable supply of food, but in doing so it made possible a vast number of new techniques and activities which, in their combined effects, transformed man from a rare creature into the dominant species that he is today. The earliest agricultural communities were probably ten to twenty times as large as the nomadic groups of savagery. Among several hundred persons, specialization of labour became possible, and this in turn gave rise to more complex and more skilled operations. Among the earliest trades so established were those of the weaver, the potter, and the flint

DATE	ECONOMIC SYSTEMS (Mode of Production)	TECHNICAL PERIOD (Tools and Materials)	INVENTIONS AND INNOVATIONS
2000–	**CAPITALISM, wage labour** [Europe and N. America] WESTERN EUROPEAN CIVILIZATION **FEUDALISM, serfdom** [Europe]	MODERN	INVENTIONS OF MODERN ERA Steam engine [1781] Printing [1381]
1000–		IRON	Crop rotation
0–	GRECIAN & ROMAN CIVILIZATION		
			Watermill
1000–	**ANCIENT CIVILIZATION** Slavery [S. Europe, N. Africa, Middle East especially; also India, China, Central and South America]	BRONZE	Iron used
2000–	INDUS CIVILIZATION		
		NEOLITHIC	
3000–	FIRST EGYPTIAN AND MESOPOTAMIAN CIVILIZATIONS		Wheeled vehicles Plough
4000–			Sail
			Copper smelting
5000–	**PRIMITIVE BARBARISM** that is, agriculture and stockbreeding without cities		STOCK-BREEDING AGRICULTURE
6000–		MESO-LITHIC	
7000–	**SAVAGERY**		

The Development of Human Society in the West

The approximate relations in time of the stages in the development of civilization, and of some major technical advances. The sequence shown applies mainly to the Mediterranean area and Europe

polisher. There was at this stage, however, no major technical advance from savagery, apart from the development of agriculture and stock-breeding themselves. The possibility of great technical developments depended, in the first place, on the acquisition of sufficient skill to produce a *surplus of food* from the soil. This made possible the existence of people, such as skilled flint workers and other specialists, who produced no food for themselves.

An important contribution to farming technique was made by the traction plough – the plough drawn by oxen (or, later, by the horse): this greatly increased the arable area that one man could cultivate. The use of domestic animals as a source of power was in fact of fundamental importance. Another technique of the greatest value was that of irrigation, which was developed on a large scale in Egypt and Mesopotamia. The immediate consequence of these advances is illustrated in the Faiyum: in this prosperous community of between 6000 and 5000 B.C. there were two groups of silos, numbering sixty-seven and ninety-eight respectively; each held, on the average, about 400 kg of grain, which was probably the yield of two or three acres. This figure, then a great achievement, is low by modern standards. In the 1950s in England and Wales an average of about 1350 kg of wheat was produced per acre, and in Ontario about 1000 kg (but this was high for North America).

CIVILIZATION

Civilization has been called the culture of cities. Cities are themselves primarily large gatherings of men not engaged on food production. They are, of course, much more than that also. They appear first in the valleys of the Nile in Egypt, the Tigris and Euphrates in Mesopotamia, the Indus in northern India, and perhaps simultaneously the Yangtse-kiang in China. A further, separate civilization arose in Central and South America. We have seen that an important function of a food surplus is to support workers in crafts and industries other than agriculture and stock-breeding. The surplus, however, does more than that. From very early it was also a basis for trade. Certain important commodities are found only in a few places: raw materials such as flint, and later copper, tin and iron were mined and transported long distances, either in the crude state or in the form of finished products such as axes, vessels, shields or ornaments; and other consumer goods such as pottery and trinkets entered largely into the trade of early civilization. As human communities became more complex, they came to need a central administration, a legal system, and machinery for keeping order and enforcing the law. Cities were the centres, therefore, not only of craftsmanship and trade, but also of administration; and the food surplus had to support a ruling class of priests and kings who took taxes or tribute in the form of food. This was the origin of the *state*, the apparatus of government and control by a small ruling class.

A series of new discoveries and inventions followed. In the fourth millennium B.C., that is, between five and six thousand years ago, the wheel was invented, and used both for transport and in the making of pottery. Oversea trade led to the development of the sailing ship, and this in turn to the establishment of navigational methods. Navigation requires a knowledge of the stars, and so is one of the sources of the science of astronomy. The other early source is the needs of agriculture itself, since to plan the sowing of crops according to the seasons a calendar is required. The great pyramid of Egypt is so designed that the dog-star, Sirius, is visible in a central chamber only at the equinoxes. The Egyptians had a year of 365 days and no leap year, and this calendar was probably used first in 4242 B.C. Knowledge of astronomy and of the working of the calendar was no doubt a prerogative of the priest-kings, and since this knowledge was a source of their power, we can guess that they guarded it jealously: they provide an early example of the restriction of learning to a particular class. The association between religion and the calendar is exemplified in England by the famous neolithic temple at Stonehenge, which is so arranged that on midsummer day the sun rises in line with two marked points.

In Egypt the needs of agriculture stimulated the growth also of geometry, owing to the necessity for re-surveying the fields each year after the Nile floods had obliterated all landmarks. The history of ancient civilizations illustrates very clearly the way in which the development of science is related to human needs.

The use of written numbers and alphabetic scripts dates from about 3000 B.C., and is contemporary with the Asiatic discovery of bronze. At this time the civilization of the Indus valley had reached a very high level of development. Among the technical problems that arise in all cities are the supply of clean water and the disposal of liquid waste. At the city of Mohenjo-daro, on the River Indus, there was a well-organized system of aqueducts and drains, and there is evidence of town-planning by the city government.

Civilization not only creates material wealth and an elaborate technology, but by making leisure possible it leads also to development of the arts. At the same time the media for artistic expression are augmented. The artists of the higher savagery took advantage of the leisure made possible by a plentiful game supply to paint and draw on cave walls and on bone. The artists of civilization could express themselves also as architects, with inorganic materials for building; and in Egypt a heptatonic musical scale was invented. In this way, on the basis of a successful agriculture, the main features of all civilizations up to 200 years ago were developed nearly 5000 years before the industrial revolution in Europe. Even a money economy was established in Mesopotamia.

Between the ancient civilizations and the present there was a long period of continuing, slow technical and economic change. Stone implements gradually gave place to metal: at first copper was used, and later tin and copper together, to make bronze; later still iron, which is more difficult to extract from its ores but far more plentiful, came into general use, and only now, in the twentieth century, are other materials, such as aluminium, replacing it for some purposes. There were improvements in power production. First, water power, which began to be used in the late Roman Empire, for processes such as grinding wheat and separating ores, became very important in some areas; second, the invention of the horse collar in medieval times, in place of a strangling yoke, greatly increased the effective muscular power of horses. This, with the invention of iron horseshoes, enabled the farmers of the middle ages to cultivate lands hitherto inaccessible to the plough. Another simple invention, the stirrup, gave the mounted knight, for a time, military supremacy – until yet a further technical innovation, gunpowder, unhorsed him.

With the development of wood pumps men were able to mine more deeply and more widely, and the mineral and technical wealth of human communities increased correspondingly. New techniques and new ideas came from many lands. The Chinese provided sailors with the magnetic compass; and with the introduction of the rudder, and the invention of methods for sailing into the wind, sail conquered the high seas. China also provided gunpowder – a decisive instrument of war until the other side acquired it; and, again from China, came paper and printing – both essential for the foundation of a large educated community.

Economically, the great iron age civilizations of the Mediterranean – of Italy, Greece, Palestine and North Africa – were based largely on slavery, at least for industrial production. Productive and other manual work was done by classes sharply marked off as of inferior status, and a small ruling group had the prerogative of administration and access to a good education. The consequent separation of those with clerical knowledge from the people with practical skills had an ill effect on technical and scientific development which is still reflected in administration and education today. In Europe, after the fall of Rome, this system gave place to feudalism, under which the cultivator was typically a serf, limited to working on one particular patch of soil. This led to an increase in the productivity of the soil in the temperate forest area, where regular rotation of crops became customary. It was accompanied by the development of guilds of craftsmen and merchants which led to an improved status for their members.

The conventional account of the middle ages is that given by historians interested primarily in political and perhaps economic history, and in the arts. Here we are concerned rather with techniques, and especially those which played an important part in agricultural and industrial production. Some historians indeed consider that this aspect is a key to the understanding of the period. In the words of an American, Lynn White:

The cumulative effect of the newly available animal, water and wind power upon the culture of Europe has not been carefully studied. But from the twelfth and even from the eleventh century there was rapid replacement of human by non-human energy wherever great quantities of power were needed or where the required motion was so simple and monotonous that a man could be replaced by a mechanism. The chief glory of the later Middle Ages was not its cathedrals or its epics or its scholasticism: it was the building for the first time in history of a complex civilization which rested not on the backs of sweating slaves or coolies but primarily on non-human power.

THE SCIENTIFIC AGE

Today civilization has begun a change greater than any of those of the past. It is taking place with remarkable rapidity on the historical time-scale, though with painful slowness for those who live through it. In 1850, in Western Europe, the efforts of three-quarters of the population were needed to provide a food surplus adequate for the remaining quarter not engaged in food production. Today, in advanced areas, the figures are reversed: one quarter produce enough surplus for three-quarters of the population. In such countries as France, the United States and New Zealand (all of which normally export food) fifty per cent of the population live in towns. In Great Britain, which imports food in exchange for manufactured goods, the figure is eighty per cent. On the other hand, in the whole of Asia, where, except in the U.S.S.R., modern agricultural techniques have, until recently, hardly been practised, only about fifteen per cent of the population are reckoned to be town dwellers. The change in agricultural productivity per man is partly a reflexion of the technical advance of industry. The invention of machines which enable us to make use of the energy in coal and oil has made it possible, in the advanced countries, to replace the muscle power, not only of man but now also of domestic animals, by more effective installations. Large numbers of workers have been released from food production, with a great potential increase in material wealth and leisure. This state of affairs is at once based on and has led to the development of our knowledge of the physical sciences. The other basis of modern agriculture is applied biology, of which some features are discussed in the next chapter.

The economic counterpart of these technical developments is capitalism, which had replaced feudalism in most of Europe by the end of the nineteenth century. Under capitalism not only land, but also capital goods such as mines, factories and transport services, are privately owned; or if they are not, they are operated by a state which is itself controlled by the owners of large capital installations. It was indeed the single control of big productive units that made the large scale application of modern techniques possible: previously the individual craftsman had often owned his own tools and equipment, but a blast furnace, the machinery for a mine, or a steam loom, could not be worked by single individuals, or even by a family;

in practice they were worked by a number of wage-earners and owned by the employer. Today capitalism in its turn has in some countries already been replaced by yet a further economic system, socialism, under which private ownership is restricted to personal property, and the means of production are communally owned and controlled.

None of these phases of human society is the prerogative of any particular biological type. We have seen that this applies to palaeolithic cultures. The great invention of agriculture itself seems to have been made separately by widely different groups. Again, the early civilization of the Indus has been described as the product of 'peoples of mixed origin and diverse racial types'. The various prehistoric cultures of Europe are often attributed to groups of contrasted physical types, such as 'tall long-heads' and 'lightly built round-heads'. Certainly the various migrant or conquering groups differed on the average in such physical characters as stature or cephalic index, but there was continual intermingling of peoples and exchange of ideas and techniques. In the same way, today, the modern culture originating in western Europe has been absorbed, in many of its features, by such diverse groups as the New Zealand Maoris, the Japanese, and recently primitive peoples in northern Siberia.

In the first nine chapters of this book the topic has been human diversity in time and space: what determines human differences, and the social consequences of the differences. But when we study civilizations and cultures we can look at mankind as an entity – not indeed, because there is any uniformity of cultures, but because wherever he is, and of whatever type, man has certain fundamental problems to solve. The different kinds of society, with their various types of economy and techniques, represent his attempts to solve those problems in the varied circumstances in which he lives. Among them are the three great biological ones: the supply of food, which has already been partly discussed in this chapter; the prevention of infectious disease; and the maintenance of the population by the bearing of children. These are the subjects of the next four chapters.

11

FOOD AND SOIL

One of the most ruinous limiting factors is the capitalistic system – and this is one of the gravest criticisms that can be leveled against it. The methods of free competition and the application of the profit motive have been disastrous to the land. . . .

Throughout virtually the entire world, land is not used to produce the crop best adapted to it on a permanent basis but to produce as much cash as possible, as cheaply as possible, and as quickly as possible – the same system exalted by the manufacturer.

WILLIAM VOGT
Chief of Conservation Section, Pan-American Union, in 1948

IN 1954 a hydrogen bomb was tested at Bikini. The explosion produced the expected radio-active fall-out on a number of Pacific islands, and also scattered debris over thousands of square miles. As a result, dangerous radio-active materials appeared in the small plants which live in the surface of the sea; these were eaten by small animals which in turn were eaten by larger animals, notably the tuna fish which are an important article of diet in Japan. Hence a number of Japanese ingested quantities of radio-active food.

This disgraceful occurrence reminds us that we are not set apart from nature, but are inextricably involved in the nexus of living organisms. On a cosmic scale, our planet is a cinder of matter, revolving around an average star. On the faintly irregular surface of this cinder is a patchy film of carbon compounds which contains all the million or more species of tellurian biology. Despite the appearances of conflict between species – or even within them – the most prominent feature of their relationships is interdependence. The whole of tellurian life may be regarded as a 'macrobe'. For one species to survive and prosper within this macrobe, it must be in equilibrium with the rest.

To descend to a more familiar scale, some parts of the world have supported prosperous peasant communities for many centuries – even millennia. Famines may have occurred; but on the whole the peoples of the most fertile regions have grown rice, wheat or maize and have lived in equilibrium with their environment. The soil has been conserved; pests have not multiplied calamitously; floods and drought have been prevented; natural forests have been left standing in spaces between cultivated regions. The important innovations – new strains of plants and animals, new techniques and new systems of management – have originated in these stable areas.

Nevertheless, none of the advances in food production has yet prevented food shortages. Increased food supplies lead also to great increases in the density of human populations, and when their food supply fails the disaster is correspondingly great. This sort of thing is familiar enough to biologists: animal populations are prevented from indefinite increase by *limiting factors*, and food supply is sometimes the factor which determines the maximum size of a population. Other possible factors are the amount of space for breeding, and the number and efficiency of predators or parasites: for instance, the cats of a village may influence the maximum population of mice. Man himself is a limiting factor, or creates such factors, for many animal and plant populations: in the attempt to grow or to capture food for himself he is obliged to reduce the food available for other species, to destroy their living-space and sometimes to kill them directly, either because they themselves provide food or because they interfere with his activities.

There is thus a complex interaction between human populations and the populations of other species, both plant and animal, in all the regions of the land and sea where man lives or works. The study of this interaction, which is a part of the science of ecology, is important for many reasons, including the fact that it is a necessity for a scientific agriculture. The need for science in farming has become especially obvious during the twentieth century. One reason for this is the increasing consciousness of what scientific method can do, when it is applied to such problems as the improvement of soil or the breeding of better strains of crop plants or domestic animals. A second reason has been the enormous scale of human food production during this century, accompanying the increase of human populations in every continent; these changes have led to disruption of balanced communities of animals and plants in many parts of the world, and consequent loss of soil fertility and other natural resources. Yet a third reason is that, for the first time, feeding the world is being considered as a single problem: as we shall see in the next chapter, it is now possible to say with some precision what constitutes an optimum diet, and to show that many people do not get one.

A PLUNDERED PLANET?

The wealthy civilizations, with their dense populations and advanced techniques, are a measure of the success of agriculture in providing a surplus of food beyond the needs of the producers; this success is reflected also in the recent rapid growth of human populations, of which the figures are given in chapter 14. These expanding human communities have displaced previously existing communities of other species. In North America, for instance, when European colonization began, the number of indigenous human beings was of the order of 1m., but there were probably 50m. bison, and vast herds of other large mammals such as elk, deer, caribou, antelope, and moose. All these species now exist in only small numbers, or are on the verge of extinction. It is believed that in Canada alone there were 50m. beavers, and this number was reduced to 1m. before protection was introduced. There has been a similar destruction of large mammals in East and South Africa.

More obviously, increasing human numbers, and the expanding need for more agricultural land, have led to the destruction of forests over vast areas. Britain and Western Europe, for instance, were formerly for the most part forest lands except in the higher mountains, but only small wooded patches now remain.

Changes of this sort are, up to a point, inevitable if large human communities are to exist at all. They can, however, lead to further changes which in the long run make a prosperous agriculture impossible. The most serious of these changes are in the soil. If forests are removed from sloping ground in areas of fairly high rainfall, the soil, deprived of its protective covering, is liable to be washed away down to bare, unproductive rock. This is *water erosion*, and it is going on now in great areas of fertile ground in the Americas, Africa, and Asia. (Soil erosion must be distinguished from the much slower process of rock erosion referred to in the chapter on evolution.) Another form of water erosion takes place in the plains below the despoiled hills: a result of the destruction of forests is to alter the character of the rivers and streams; instead of flowing at an even rate they dry up in the dry season and during the rains become raging torrents which cut deep grooves, or gullies, in the soil of the plains.

In the dry season, on the other hand, there is drought: the soil dries and becomes powdery, and may be blown away, as is seen in plate 15. The same result often comes from loss of plant cover due to overgrazing. This is *wind erosion*, and the spectacular effects it sometimes produces have made it famous. Fairfield Osborn describes 'the shock that came to the people of America in 1934':

In that year a vast transcontinental dust-laden windstorm, darkening the sun, broadcast the fact that large once-fertile portions of five western states ... had become a desolate dust bowl. This catastrophe was the result of overgrazing by too large herds of cattle and sheep and of ploughing for crops grasslands that should never have been converted to this use.

H. H. Bennett, another American authority, has said:

In the short life of this country we have essentially destroyed 282m. acres of land, crop, and rangeland. Erosion is destructively active on 775m. additional acres. About 100m. acres of cropland, much of it representing the best cropland we have, is finished in this country. We cannot restore it.

It takes nature from 300 years to 1000 years or more to bring back a single inch of topsoil and we sometimes lose that topsoil as the result of a single rain, if it is an especially heavy torrential type of rain.

The first examples of soil destruction have been taken from North America because that area has been very fully studied, and because there the destruction has been exceptionally rapid. But every other continent has suffered erosion, and it is believed that a total of nearly 200m. acres is affected. Some extinct civilizations seem to have been helped on their way by the disappearance of their agricultural resources. The Maya civilization of Guatemala created deserts by the destruction of forests, just as today the soil of Mexico is being washed into the sea as a result of ill-planned attempts to cultivate land on the steep slopes of the mountains. North Africa was once an area of a dominant civilization, but is now principally desert; this could probably have been prevented with a different system of cultivation. The area between the Tigris and Euphrates was once, in Osborn's words, 'a land suggestive of the Garden of Eden, a rich land whose people lived well, built flourishing cities, established governments and developed the arts'. Its degeneration into desert seems to have been helped by the cutting down of forests, perhaps by over-grazing of grassland, and finally by the wrecking of the irrigation works which coincided with political collapse.

It is not suggested here that the collapse of these ancient civilizations is to be simply explained by defects in their methods of land management. It might indeed be argued that the errors of the farmers should be attributed to imperfections of economic or political organization, and that these were the significant causes of collapse. The facts that are fully established are the creation of deserts in once fertile lands by a series of civilized communities, from three thousand years ago up to the present day.

It has been suggested that these calamities have been brought about, not by man's activities, but by climatic influences. Climate has obviously played a part, but it is extremely doubtful whether this can anywhere have been a decisive one. Serious soil erosion occurs only where agriculture is practised; it follows that climate can be blamed for it only if there have been climatic changes for the worse since agriculture began. There is little evidence for such changes; olive groves can still be made to flourish in North Africa, in the very places where they were cultivated by the Roman colonists; indeed, a few have survived the past two thousand years. Palestine, extensively eroded, can nevertheless support the same crops as were grown in biblical times, given proper care. In India and China there has been much erosion, but alongside the areas of bare rock are terraced and irrigated lands which have been continuously cultivated for three thousand years. Soil erosion cannot be considered as anything but man-made.

The material destruction of soil is the final result of bad land management, and much damage can be done before erosion itself occurs. In Africa the Sahara is said to be advancing in some areas at the rate of half a mile a year, but this is only one consequence of the mismanagement of the grass-covered savannahs. The great plains of North Africa, potentially fertile and capable of carrying a prosperous agriculture, have a dry season which is sometimes as long as eight months; only a carefully preserved plant cover, either of grasses or larger plants, can prevent severe drying and loss of fertility. Excessive grazing by domestic animals, of which the goat is particularly destructive, is in vast areas eating away the plant cover, and ruining the land. From America Vogt gives another example:

Virgin soils in Ohio, with unimproved seed and no insect control, yielded a hundred bushels of corn per acre, and sixty bushels of wheat. Crops now average forty-two bushels of corn and twenty of wheat. And even this yield per acre in one of the most advanced states in the Union, where there is greatly increased knowledge of disease and pest control, fertilizers and plant breeding, is being maintained with difficulty and at great expense.

THE 'BALANCE OF NATURE'

Soil erosion and loss of fertility can be regarded as results of the upsetting of a natural balance or equilibrium. Forests or grassy plains can remain stable for very long periods; rivers change their character only through millions of years. If there are grazing animals their numbers may be restricted by predators (such as lions), by the water supply, or by other limiting factors. Soil losses are made good, probably more than made good, by material derived from dead plants and animals.

Agriculture cannot avoid upsetting this balance. The vital necessity is that it should be replaced by another equilibrium, one chosen by man to suit his own ends. This is not only a matter of preserving the soil: it involves also allowing for the activities of many plant and animal species which are indirectly, and often quite unexpectedly, affected by agriculture. The most obvious of these species are the pests, and especially those which attack crops in the fields. By greatly increasing the growth of some plants, particularly cereals, man has created conditions favourable for the rapid multiplication of various fungi, insects, and rodents, many of which had probably been hitherto comparatively rare species.

The most spectacular of the onslaughts on our crops are those due to locusts; there are seven important species, and between them they cover the Americas, Africa, the Near East, central Asia, India, China, Indonesia, and Australia. Unwise cultivation may increase the number of swarming grounds. In the Americas plagues of the related grasshoppers cause similar damage as well. Other spectacular disasters to field crops are due to field mice: the grain-producing areas of Europe, Asia, and North America are subject to periodic plagues of small rodents which do damage on a scale similar to that of locusts. The third main group of pests are the parasitic fungi: the potato blight swept Europe in the nineteenth century and caused the total loss of the potato crop in Ireland in 1846; in 1870 another fungus, a leaf rust, wiped out the coffee plantations of Ceylon, and the country was saved from ruin only by the establishment of the tea industry. In Central America and the West Indies the Panama disease has come near to causing the complete destruction of banana cultivation.

These dramatic effects of pests and disease organisms are well enough known, and they are of first-rate importance. But a great proportion of the food losses due to pests goes on continuously and unobtrusively: the pests are there all the time, and they take their regular toll which may account for ten or fifty per cent of the total. This is especially the case with the losses of stored food. Food may be stored by peasants in a rolled mat, a bamboo cylinder, or a pit in the ground; by farmers in corn rick or barn; by merchants in warehouse or silo: in all these places the concentration of foodstuffs encourages the multiplication of rats and mice, weevils and other insects, mites, and moulds. So universal are these pests that throughout the world farmers and warehouse-keepers often regard their presence as inevitable. World transport has further ensured that, however narrow the original range of a particular species, it has good opportunities of spreading to every country in which suitable conditions exist: the brown spider beetle, as one example, which probably came from Tasmania, has so spread during the past 70 years that it is now found in every grain warehouse in Europe and North America.

These are examples of fairly direct and simple connexions between human activities and changes in animal and plant populations. There are many more complex interactions. In North America agriculture chronically suffers severe losses from small rodents. These pests are preyed on by carnivorous mammals, such as foxes, by birds of prey, and by snakes. All these predators have been systematically persecuted by farmers, and by those who preserve game, who have thus, in all probability, greatly increased the rodent damage.

Sometimes whole systems of species come under the axe. Some

farming communities favour the careful preservation of hedgerows and small woodlots, others destroy them. There is in fact a strong case for keeping such semi-natural communities of plants and animals: they add beauty to the countryside; and they also help the farmer. Research in Germany has made it possible to estimate that hedgerows increase grain yields by twenty per cent in some conditions of farming: one of their effects is to reduce the evaporation of water from the fields by cutting down the force of drying winds; this can be equivalent to increasing the rainfall by one-third – an extremely important factor in rather dry areas with fertile soils. They are also nesting places for small birds and spiders which eat injurious insects, and for humble bees which pollinate clover and other desirable flowering plants. Incidentally, hedgerows are an important source of timber. And the trees give shade, not only to people but also to domestic animals. It is doubtful whether the increased area for ploughing, acquired by destroying the hedges and replacing them by wire, can be justified.

The importance of balanced communities of plants and animals is very general. It has been illustrated, especially in recent decades, in two ways. First, increasingly vast areas have been planted with single crops such as wheat or coniferous trees. This provides parasites and pests of crop plants with the ideal opportunity to multiply with explosive speed and to cause the maximum amount of damage in conditions in which the difficulties of prevention or control are greatest. Second, more and more species of plants, animals and fungi have been taken across the world, deliberately or by accident, from their usual ranges to somewhere quite new. Once in a new environment, uncontrolled by their natural enemies, they may spread widely and disrupt the stable systems of organisms which have evolved together for tens of millions of years.

A famous example is the insect called the cottony cushion scale (a 'bug', or Hemipteran, related to green-fly) from Australia, which got into the orange groves of California and threatened to destroy them. Fumigation with hydrogen cyanide gas had some success, until the insect evolved a cyanide-resistant strain. Eventually, after much loss and great expenditure, it was brought under control by bringing in another insect from Australia; this was a ladybird beetle which is a predator living largely on the scale bugs. This is an outstanding, and rather unusual, example of biological control. Another example is the Asian fungus, called chestnut blight, which was introduced into the U.S.A. about 1900 and in fifty years had killed all the native sweet chestnuts except some in the extreme south. This fungus is harmless in its native areas. In this case the only remedy, after vast losses had occurred, was to introduce the Chinese chestnut which is not harmed by the fungus.

The example of the scale bugs illustrates two attitudes. One response to pests, parasites, weeds, inconvenient trees and other obstructions is to try to alter the ecological pattern, and to achieve a new equilibrium. The other is to attack them directly. The second method gets rid of unwanted organisms without regard to the total effect of doing so, and it has certainly had some success; but it can also have unintended consequences. The famous insecticide, DDT, has had immensely beneficial effects in killing disease carriers such as mosquitoes, and insect pests of farm crops. At first sight this triumph of modern chemical industry seems an unqualified blessing. But, on examination, it has proved also to be a menace.

DDT is poisonous, not only to the insects we wish killed, but also to birds and mammals, including ourselves. It is a very stable substance, and it has been used on a vast scale. Hence it is increasingly circulating among living things: it has been absorbed into the natural cycles of matter, on which all organisms depend. DDT is now in the air we breathe, and hence in the bodies of animals all over the world – even the Antarctic penguins – and the fatty tissue of human beings. When an animal dies, the DDT it contains returns to the soil or the sea, where it is picked up again by plants. DDT is sometimes sprayed from aircraft over large areas, in order to kill insect pests. About half of it is then carried as crystals into the upper air, where it is dispersed like radio-active fall-out.

The concentration of DDT varies greatly among different species, since it depends largely on the position the species occupies in food chains. First a plant is eaten by a plant-eating animal; in the sea or fresh water this may be anything from a microscopic crustacean to a large fish, and on land, from a mite to an elephant. Many plant-eating animals are themselves eaten by predators such as salmon, owls, weasels and men. Some of these are in turn eaten by larger predators. As DDT ascends a food chain, its concentration increases. Plants may contain by weight less than a tenth of one part per million; at the other end a large predator may contain twenty-five to seventy-five parts per million. These concentrations are rising. At about ten times their present levels they can kill; at lower levels they can prevent breeding. The ecological consequences of such interference with animal populations cannot be fully predicted. If many predators are killed, one result can be the proliferation of pests which would otherwise be eaten by them. Eventually, after disastrous upheavals, many species might, by a kind of natural selection, become resistant. But at present the only species known to include resistant forms are among the flies and other insects which DDT was designed to eliminate.

At least one government, that of New Zealand, has already, in the 1960s, banned the use of large numbers of substances which could be a danger to livestock; some, such as aldrin, dieldrin and DDT itself, are household words for farmers all over the world. Eventually, no doubt, there will be international agreements to regulate the use of all dangerous or dubious poisons.

Many more examples could be given of the workings of the living nexus in relation to man. Some could be of successes; others of dangers or disasters. But the main lesson is obvious. Whether we are concerned with the production of food or timber, with protection from pests, with conservation or with building new cities, we need to know what we are doing, what is happening to other species and what is likely to happen to them in the future. This holds for the sea as well as for the land. Only deliberate planning, on the largest scale, based on detailed knowledge (which entails much more research), can any longer keep our own species in a satisfactory relationship with other organisms whether these are useful, harmful, beautiful or apparently neutral.

FEEDING THE WORLD

So far in this chapter the emphasis has been on difficulties and problems. But the history of food production is not one only of blunders and mismanagement. There are examples even of very primitive groups in which admirable principles of land management have been applied. In New Guinea some of the mountain dwellers, with a neolithic economy, use a system of crop rotation combined with terracing which ensures the preservation of the soil and its fertility; they also use the vegetation for green manure, as they clear ground for planting. In the lowlands the neighbouring peoples use a system of ditching which both drains swamps and also provides new, unexhausted soil to spread over the surface. In many parts of Africa the Africans have used crop rotations in which leguminous plants are sown at regular intervals to replenish the nitrogen of the soil. The most important principles of land management, such as irrigation and drainage, terracing, manuring and plant selection seem to have been developed independently in the Old World and the Americas, some of them before civilization began in either group of continents.

All the great civilizations have depended on a successful and stable agriculture. We have seen that some, such as those of North Africa and the Near East, collapsed and their agriculture with them. But others have continued. Large areas of China have sustained a stable agriculture for thousands of years, by the use of irrigation, terracing to prevent erosion, and extensive manuring (commonly with human excrement) to preserve fertility. There is, however, considerable erosion both in China and India. In Western Europe, on the other hand, the plentiful and evenly distributed rainfall, and the relative flatness of much of the ground, have made possible an even more stable system of cultivation; moreover, since Western Europe was the original home of modern science, scientific methods have been extensively applied there, and so the productivity of both arable land and animal stocks is quite high.

The problem which now faces the whole of humanity is to develop these existing systems so that every human being is adequately fed. How far short of this they fall today can be only roughly estimated; some of the estimates are given in the next chapter. But hundreds of millions chronically suffer actual hunger, and even more are malnourished. Moreover the population of the world is increasing at the rate of 20m. a year. The next chapter deals with this problem from the point of view of the needs of human beings as consumers of food. Here we are concerned with production.

The total land surface of the world is 36,000m. acres, but the greater part of this is totally unfit for any form of agriculture at present imagined. The limiting factor is water: the annual rainfall must be at least fifteen inches for cultivation to be possible, and there are difficulties if it is less than eighteen inches; in equatorial lands, with high evaporation, the necessary minimum rises to forty inches. It is estimated that on this basis about one-third of all land could be cultivated. To what extent is this 12,000m. acres actually used by the two-thirds of humanity who still live on the land?

The answers to this question vary with the method of estimation. Probably about ten per cent of all land, or less than one-third of the land that could be used, is in fact cultivated, but only four per cent of all land is used for crops which provide human food:

> of total land surface:
> land that could be cultivated = 34 per cent
> land that is cultivated = 10 per cent
> land used for human food = 4 per cent

These estimates imply that there remain enormous areas still to be opened up, but they are misleading if they are taken to show that it would be easy, within a few years, greatly to increase the world's cultivated area. Two hundred years ago there were vast fertile plains in the New World, Australia, and elsewhere, waiting to be ploughed and sown with wheat. Today all the easy ground has been occupied (and some of it, as we have seen, plundered). A great deal of what remains is tropical forest.

Despite the difficulties, attempts are already being made to cultivate the tropics. Modern machinery, such as bulldozers, and the new insecticides, have helped to make such projects feasible. On the general prospect of the use of forest lands a recent report of the Food and Agriculture Organization is optimistic:

Here is virtually a new continent, the unused forest, equal in area to the whole of Asia (excluding the U.S.S.R.), which remains to be explored and used for human benefit. These forests could contribute not only fuel and lumber but also, by chemical transformation, pulp, plastics, sugar, ethyl alcohol, yeast, and fodder cellulose. It may be that in time they will provide a large proportion of the world's clothing materials and animal feeding stuffs, thus releasing important areas of cropland for food crops.

When the attempt is made to develop a backward area, or even, perhaps, an advanced one, special problems may arise with the human population. At first sight it might appear that a big productive scheme would be certain to benefit the native inhabitants of the area, but in fact it can do so only if their customs and needs are properly considered. Primitive customs are quite unadapted to modern, large-scale agriculture. It follows that, unless a policy of ruthless exploitation and contempt for native needs and abilities is adopted, all such schemes must include provision for education and a general raising of living standards.

The need for the planning of an area as a whole, and for ensuring that those taking part do so willingly and with knowledge of its value to themselves, has been recognized in a number of big schemes of land development in advanced countries. Of these the Tennessee Valley Authority is an example of what modern engineering can do to make soil fertile by irrigation, provided that all possible means are used for the development of the area, including education and financial help. Similar schemes have been proposed for the Missouri Valley, for the Jordan River in Palestine, for various Indian rivers, for the Niger River in French West Africa, and for a number of others. The Amazon Basin is the subject of a United Nations plan.

One of the biggest schemes began during the 1930s in a vast area of the U.S.S.R. A very large part of the Soviet Union is too cold for ordinary agriculture (which is one reason why so much work has been done there on cold-resistant wheats and other crops); and of the remaining land much is liable to severe drought. The remedy in the dry areas is irrigation, and this is planned on an unprecedented scale. An area the size of Europe, west of the Caspian, until recently desert, is being transformed, not only by irrigation but also by afforestation and the application of every aspect of scientific agriculture, from pest control to the study of the mechanics of soil particles.

THE IMPROVEMENT OF AGRICULTURE

Although vast schemes of conservation and development are essential, they are not the only means of increasing food production. Throughout the world agricultural methods remain for the most part primitive and, without increasing the cultivated area or any drastic change of method, production could be greatly raised. The output of food per man in advanced countries is estimated by the Food and Agriculture Organization to be about ten times what it is in the backward lands. The population of the backward areas is nearly three-quarters of the world's total. In Britain the productivity per acre and the output per man are three or four times higher than even the more backward areas of Europe; and on the average about four times as much milk is produced by each cow. Yet even British farming could be improved, since some farms, in which every advantage is taken of technical improvements, have a productivity twice that of the average. Indeed improved farming in

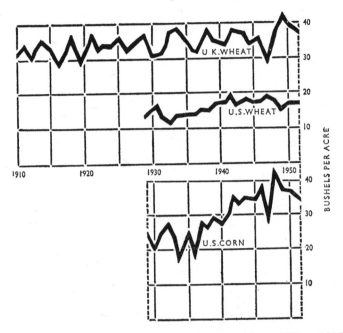

Rising Food Production. Slow but steady rise in wheat yields in U.K. and U.S.A. during recent decades, due to gradual improvement in the standard of husbandry. The increase in maize yields in the U.S. after 1936 was due to the introduction of hybrid maize – a product of applied genetics

temperate lands would probably yield a greater increase of food than could be got from tropical development.

The general, all-round raising of the standards of cultivation depends on the systematic improvement of every aspect of farming practice. Improvement is needed, and is practicable, in the plants and animals themselves; in the fertility of the soil; in the control of weeds and of animal and fungal pests; and in the number and design of the machines used.

The milk yields of many herds, even in Western Europe and the U.S.A., can be doubled in two generations by proper breeding; such breeding can be greatly accelerated by the use of artificial insemination, which enables the best bulls to serve at least ten times as many cows as would otherwise be possible. The scope for improvement in the wretched cattle of the backward areas of the East is far greater. Stock can also be bred for cold climates. Recently the cattalo, a hybrid between buffalo and domestic cattle, with some admixture of yak, has been produced to deal with the conditions of parts of Canada in which ordinary cattle fail. The cattalo has a heavy coat; it will eat shrubs or paw through snow to get herbage; and it stores much fat in its body against the winter. It is an excellent source of beef.

Besides the improvement of stock by breeding, much can be done by better feeding, for instance by the development of pasture of higher quality. Indeed, breeding and the improvement of stock management must go together, since breeding can be done effectively only if a suitable environment can be provided for the herd. The development of the grasslands themselves also depends partly on genetical methods: in the past it has been usual to regard 'grass' as a natural phenomenon not much amenable to human interference, but today, on the best pastures, it is treated like any other crop: special seed mixtures are used, selected for the particular conditions of soil and climate, with corresponding improvement of the sward and of the livestock that feed on it.

The use of special seed from selected plants is one of the most important means of raising crop production generally. A famous example is hybrid maize. The usual method of preserving a good strain of plant or animal species is to inbreed among individuals of the strain (as was described in chapter 2) so as to preserve the favourable genetical qualities; but if this is done with maize a loss of yield results. Inbred lines are therefore grown only by seedsmen in breeding stations: to produce the seed for the farmer the inbred lines are crossed, and hybrid seed is distributed for use on the farms, where it gives a high yield. Hybrid maize has made possible yields twenty-five per cent higher than before, and more than ninety per cent of the maize now sown in the Corn Belt of the United States is hybrid.

Breeding is capable of producing not only improved varieties, but quite new types with unexpected combinations of characters. Much has been done on these lines in the U.S.S.R. (There is a story of some botanists trying to develop a radish–cabbage hybrid: they succeeded, only to find that the new plant had the leaves of a radish and the root system of a cabbage. Fortunately, further effort gave the desired result.) Among the new hybrids is perennial wheat, a result of crossing wheat with wild couch grass. One variety is drought-resistant, fungus-resistant, and has an exceptionally high gluten content. It is not cold resistant, but can be grown in the southern areas of the U.S.S.R., where wind erosion is serious and the protection of a perennial covering for the soil is most needed. It is reported to give at least two crops a year, and of course does not require annual sowing.

A better known example of the possibilities of plant breeding is the production of highly productive wheats which are also resistant to the fungus disease called stem rust, which is exceedingly destructive in North America.

Much more of this sort of work remains to be done: research on rice, which is the staple food of at least one-third of mankind, is far behind that on the wheats and on maize, though what has been done has given valuable results in India, where some new varieties have very recently produced a record harvest. Research on millet, another important staple of the East, has hardly begun.

If we turn to the improvement of the soil we find a similar picture. The importance of fertilizers and manures is well known: nearly every gardener uses both inorganic fertilizers and manure derived from a compost heap (which may have been chemically treated) or possibly from the leavings of horses in the street outside. Primitive systems of cultivation, as we have seen, rely on human and animal manure, and on plant residues, to replenish essential elements taken from the soil by their crops. We must still do the same, and on a larger scale; the sewage from the great cities is a valuable source of manure, and far too little is returned to the fields; it has been referred to as a river of valuable elements awaiting recovery. But we can also supplement the organic manures with synthetic nitrogenous substances: it has been estimated that in Britain the addition of 50 kg of ammonium sulphate to each acre of average arable land can increase the yield of wheat by 125 kg. To get the best result potassium and phosphate must be added as well. In advanced countries such practices are commonplace, but over the greater part of the world they remain almost unused. The quality as well as the quantity of plants can be improved by synthetic nitrogenous fertilizers. For instance, the protein content of grass can be doubled, with corresponding benefit to the livestock that feed on it.

Recently, there have been important refinements in our knowledge of soil chemistry. In large areas of Australia a serious condition of livestock, called pining disease, was found to be due to a mineral deficiency of the soil which affected the plants of the pasture and through them the grazing animals. The element that was deficient was not any of those well known to be important, such as nitrogen, phosphorus, or potassium, but a comparatively rare one, cobalt. Since then similar phenomena, involving several elements besides cobalt, have been found in many parts of the world.

We are, however, only at the beginning of a systematic knowledge of the effects of soil chemistry and physics on plant growth. We still do not know as well as we should what justification there is for ploughing, harrowing or even allowing ground to lie fallow; in the U.S.S.R. one procedure is now to plough very deep only once in every four years. We still have to discover why some plants ('lime lovers') can grow only on alkaline soil, while others must have acid soil. Even the significance of humus for plant growth is controversial. Interesting research is now in progress on the use of soil improvers – substances which increase the water-holding powers of the soil and so enable the soil to support more plant growth. If these materials prove effective, they may both increase yields in fertile lands, and contribute to the reclamation of deserts.

Care of the soil requires more than attention to its chemistry. Irrigation may be needed to prevent excessive dryness and consequent loss of fertility and eventual wind erosion. Irrigation is indeed one of the oldest means of preserving soil fertility. The Nile Valley is probably the longest irrigated area in the world, but in the last half-century it has nevertheless been extensively developed, and the system changed from basin irrigation, or one-crop agriculture based on the annual flooding, to perennial irrigation which allows the growing of several crops a year. For some months in each year no Nile water enters the sea direct: the sea receives only water that has been pumped from the main drains after passage through the irrigated soil. India, with 70m. acres, has the largest irrigated area of any country, three times the area in the United States. There is nevertheless need for much more irrigation in India, and still more elsewhere, and the great river valley plans are largely based on schemes of irrigation.

Erosion is controlled also by preventing loss of plant cover due to overgrazing, by the planting of woods and forests to act as windbreaks, and by special techniques such as ploughing along the contours of hills to prevent a too rapid drainage of water down the slopes. Even beavers have been pressed into service in North America: in areas where water erosion was serious small numbers of beavers have been introduced and allowed to build dams. In one area, where water erosion and flooding were causing loss of orchard trees, twelve beavers were released; two years later sixty new dams had been built and the flooding greatly reduced. Beavers have been used also to conserve water for irrigation.

The various methods of soil conservation are capable of bringing dramatic improvement in regions where bad management has not gone too far. Even in the notorious dust bowl of North America agricultural production is higher than ever before.

The very fertility of cultivated soils, however, gives rise to special problems: having made soil fertile we inevitably encourage the growth of unwanted species as well as crop plants. But weed control has recently made great strides: substances, sometimes called plant growth hormones, which in some conditions can be used to stimulate the growth of parts of plants, can also be used as selective weed-killers; by destroying the unwanted species, but leaving the crop plant unharmed, they can double the yield per acre on some agricultural land.

We have already seen that, just as fertile ground attracts weeds, so does the accumulation of food on cultivated land and in stores attract animal and fungal pests. Here again we are not obliged to resign ourselves to extensive losses. The detailed study of the way of life of particular pests has made possible their large scale destruction. Locusts have for thousands of years made their inexplicable and unpredicted descents on cultivated land, leaving starvation behind them. Only since the First World War has it been found that, when they are not swarming, locusts live as harmless grasshoppers of different appearance from that of the swarming phase. Swarms develop only in limited outbreak areas and are induced partly by climatic influences, some of which are known. It is now possible to predict outbreaks of the red and the migratory locusts, in Africa, before they occur, and by the use of new insecticides, such as gammexane, the swarms can be intercepted and destroyed before they do any harm. In the early 1930s swarms from a single outbreak area near the Middle Niger swept over nearly the whole of Africa, and did enormous damage. During the 1940s similar outbreaks threatened; but by that time a control organization existed, and for the first time in history Africa survived a period of locust attack without serious loss. Much remains to be done: the desert locust, whose outbreak areas are in inaccessible desert areas of the Middle East, is still a grave menace to large areas of Asia and Africa, and is swarming as these lines are being written. But the fundamental knowledge needed for control is now available.

The example of locust control is one of many. Although there are serious pests which we are still quite unable to control, and much more research will have to be done, for many species the deficiency is not so much in knowledge as in application: there is, for instance, no locust control organization in South American comparable to that in Africa.

AGRICULTURE AND SOCIETY

Man's relationship with his environment, and especially with the food-producing part of it, is continually changing. Some of the changes are for the worse, but we have the knowledge to prevent them; the scope of possible change for the better is incalculably great. It follows that calculations, such as those which purport to deduce the amount of arable land per head necessary for a satisfactory standard of living, can have little validity. There is one much quoted statement, based on North American practice, that the area needed is 2·5 acres to each person; the actual amount of arable land in the world has been variously estimated at from just over one to nearly two acres per head. But since climate, crops, land, and farming methods vary enormously from time to time, from country to country, and even from farm to farm, such statements have little significance.

These calculations will have even less point if completely new methods of food production are introduced on a large scale. It has been possible to produce sugar from wood shavings by a method known as the Bergius process; other foodstuffs, including protein, could be made from coal; the cost is very high, though it is likely that it could be reduced with further research. Another possible source of food is the microscopic plants – the green algae – of sea or fresh water: the plants might be grown in shallow coastal basins with plenty of sun; another method, already successfully tried, would be to grow them in sewage. This could yield far higher quantities of foodstuffs per acre than any conventional agriculture. By controlling

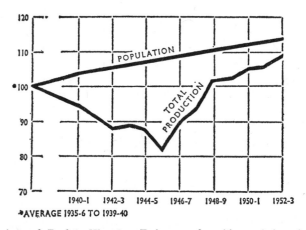

Population and Food in War-time. Estimates of world population showed a continuing slow rise during the Second World War, while food production declined. The post-war recovery could have been far steeper if greater effort had been diverted to scientific farming

the conditions in which they grow it is possible to influence the food substances manufactured by the plants: in some conditions certain species can produce a very high fat content; in others, large amounts of protein are produced. The final product might be used for animal feeding stuffs, and so release arable land for the growing of bread grains; fats might be used even for human food. The capital outlay required for an economically worthwhile installation might be very great; but not greater than that needed for the production of atomic bombs.

An alternative means of using the marine plankton (as it is called) would be atom-powered submarines designed to function as artificial whales; they would be vast processing factories, feeding in the most densely populated parts of the world's oceans. Yet a further proposal involves drawing on the enormous sources of food materials in the plant leaves which are ordinarily inedible. Leaves are potentially a rich source of both protein and sugar, and it is perfectly possible to extract these substances and make a nutritious, palatable soup.

The importance of these novel suggestions is that they illustrate the possibilities of technical advance. Given a practical problem, however vast, we are quite justified in turning confidently to the methods of science to solve it. The most formidable obstacles often arise only when the main technical difficulties have been overcome, and when the application of the new knowledge becomes a task for the whole community.

For scientific knowledge to be applied fully it is not enough to have a few scientists, however well endowed with money and ability, working on the problems. Large organizations have to be created, staffed in part by technically trained men and women, who can transmit the results of research to the public in general, or to particular sections such as the farming community. Nor is the relationship a simple one of the scientists telling the technicians, and the technicians telling the public. The flow of ideas is in both directions. Laboratory research is essential, but a great part of scientific agriculture has to be worked out in the fields or milking sheds. If it is to be done on an adequate scale the farmer must not only be ready to accept sound methods when they have been worked out: he must be prepared to make an actual contribution, by recording the results of applying new methods or by taking part himself in large-scale experiments.

It is not enough for action to be taken on a national scale. Mankind can be adequately fed only if the problem is faced as a single one for the whole world. The existence of the Food and Agriculture Organization reflects this fact. Before the Second World War, among the absurdities of world economic disorganization was the fact of mass starvation and malnutrition side by side with the deliberate destruction of food, such as wheat and oranges, in producing countries: the food destroyed could not be sold at a profit, and so it was considered by the producers better to let piles of oranges rot, under the eye of an armed guard, than to distribute them to those in need. That is what happened in times of glut. In a bad year even those who could afford to pay might be unable to get the food they wanted.

In a unified world economy a surplus of wheat would be stored against a bad year; surplus oranges would be canned, probably as juice. Similar treatment would be given to other surpluses. Much new organization and equipment would be required, perhaps on an even larger scale than that created during the war for military purposes. Up to the present, however, the pressure for a rational economy has failed to prevent complaints in North America of 'overproduction' of food. By 1949 plans for restricting the wheat harvest were once again being put forward. In 1950 the U.S. Government was destroying potatoes, and feeding millions of dollars' worth of raisins to pigs. There were vast accumulations of dried egg (of which some was used as fertilizer for arable land), of butter, and other foods. Even in the 1960s, the United Nations again reports unsaleable surpluses of cereals, dairy produce, and much else.

MALTHUS TODAY

In some people the world's food problem has induced a profound pessimism. Since the Second World War apparently authoritative predictions of disaster have been made, based on increases of populations and a declining or stationary food production. The history of such predictions is a long one, beginning with the *Essay on the Principle of Population* first published by Malthus in 1798. The core of the Malthusian view, in Malthus' own words, is that 'the power of population is indefinitely greater than the power in the earth to produce subsistence for man'. According to Malthus, where food is abundant men multiply rapidly until their numbers outrun the food supply; where food is already scarce, populations grow little, or not at all. These statements can perhaps sometimes be applied to animal populations in nature; the question is, to what extent do they apply to man?

We have already seen what scope there is for increasing food production, by both conventional and unconventional methods. There are many facts of recent history, overlooked by prophets of doom, which tell a very different story from the neo-Malthusian one. Sugar production in Java is an example. In the period 1910 to 1939, productivity per hectare doubled, as a result of improved strains and methods of cultivation. During this period the human population increased by only thirty per cent. This dramatic success for scientific agriculture so alarmed the producers, that an international agreement was made to restrict sugar production.

It is sometimes said that, whatever effort is put into food production, the 'law of diminishing returns' will eventually operate, and further improvement will become impossible. This argument rests on a misunderstanding: the law of diminishing returns, as applied to agriculture, states that returns per head in a densely populated agricultural country will be less than those in a less densely populated country (other things being equal) *if additional capital or improved farming methods cannot be used.* In practice, however, more capital or improved methods are continually being introduced. In these conditions, the law of *increasing* returns operates. This law states that in a modern industrial community the denser the population, and the larger the scale on which production is carried out, the greater the resulting economies. Indeed, modern industry, on which modern agriculture depends for its machines, its fertilizers and much else, depends wholly on a dense population.

The population, for efficiency as well as happiness, must also be healthy. Some pessimists have expressed the remarkable view that the endemic diseases of undeveloped lands – malaria, hookworm and the rest – should be encouraged, or at least should not be treated, since they help to keep human numbers down. But these diseases, most of them chronic infections, also help to lower productivity. Recently, in an area of eastern Bengal, only one season's work on a scheme of malaria control increased the rice yield of the area by fifteen per cent.

It is sometimes argued that, even if food supplies can be increased, population will nevertheless always outstrip them. This is what Malthus himself asserted. Yet in the past hundred years the effects of increased production in highly developed countries have usually been the opposite. Instead of a rise in fertility and a steeper population growth curve, there has been a dramatic fall in the birth-rate and the attainment of almost stationary population in many countries. In the 1930s it was fashionable to express alarm about the 'sterility' of Western nations and the grim prospect of a declining and ageing population. It seems to be a general rule that improved living standards are accompanied by a decline in births.

Today, faced with formidable difficulties, both biological and economic, we can adopt one of two attitudes. We can conclude that there is nothing to look forward to but widespread famine and tens of millions of deaths from starvation and disease, and that the Malthusian prospect of limited food and unchecked reproduction is all that can be foreseen; or we can admit the difficulties, agree that famine threatens in many parts of the world (as it has threatened for the past seven thousand years), yet nevertheless deny that this state of affairs need continue: the technical difficulties can be overcome; economic systems can be changed; populations can be regulated.

Unmitigated gloom is rarely found among those who are actually trying to produce more food. We have seen something of the biological advances already achieved, or possible. Of equal importance are the advances in social and economic organization. The great schemes of land development and conservation, described earlier, demand unified planning and administration which can be done only by governments. A fully mechanized agriculture, making use of every means to raise production, is impossible in a system of peasant farming, with small farms worked, as a rule, by primitive means under a heavy burden of debt.

Feeding the world adequately presents great difficulties, which can be overcome, on the most optimistic estimate, only after decades of effort. Nevertheless the effort has already begun; existing biological and economic knowledge can take us far if it is applied, and it can be rapidly increased. To the extent that we fail, the failure will be a social and political one, and not a consequence of something inherent in nature and unalterable.

12

FOOD AND NUTRITION

If every just man that now pines with want
Had but a moderate and beseeming share
Of that which lewdly-pampered Luxury
Now heaps upon some few with vast excess,
Natures full blessings would be well dispenc't
In unsuperfluous even proportion,
And she no whit encumber'd with her store.

JOHN MILTON

ONE of the scientific triumphs of the twentieth century has been the growth of our knowledge of nutrition. This knowledge made it possible, in the preceding chapter, to write of 'adequate' and 'inadequate' diets. Today a well-devised government can have a national food policy with a scientific basis, and a housewife can plan her family's meals scientifically.

THE QUESTION OF QUANTITY

The first problem is the total quantity of food required. A normal person needs no telling whether he is eating enough: hunger is the guide. There is some individual variation, especially in relation to weight, but the amount needed depends mainly on the type and quantity of the work done. In this respect our bodies can quite legitimately be compared with a railway locomotive burning coal, or an automobile petrol, in proportion to distance travelled or to speed. The energy value of food is measured in kilocalories. (A kilocalorie is the amount of heat needed to raise one kilogram of water from 15 to 16° C.) An adult man of average weight lying in bed, and taking no exercise at all, needs about 1600 kcal a day to prevent loss of weight. This is the basic quantity needed to keep us going at the lowest level of activity. An hour's light work, such as typing or sewing, adds about seventy-five kcal to the basic need. An hour's

232

housework or slow walking may add between seventy-five and 150. A man like a coal-miner, doing very hard physical work, requires 300 kcal or more for each hour, and in times of shortage men doing heavy work may receive extra rations of such foods as bread and cheese.

Most readers of this book consume between 2000 and 3000 kcal every day. This is the equivalent of 500 grams (just over one pound) of *dry* food such as sugar or flour. (Most foods contain a lot of water.) This disposes of the notion that a 'scientific' diet of the future might consist of a few unappetizing pills.

Chemically there are three types of foodstuff that supply us with energy. (A fourth, ethyl alcohol, contained in wine, has been reckoned to provide Frenchmen and Italians each with an average of about 100 kcal a day, but most nations are less fortunate.) First there are the *carbohydrates*, of which the most important are starch (the main constituent of cereals and potatoes), and sugar. In practice, whether most people have enough to eat depends on whether they have enough starch. Wheat, rye, and rice (the first two largely in the form of bread) supply, in an average year, enough kcal for more than half the population of the world. Barley, maize, oats, and millet are also eaten in large amounts.

The second type of foodstuff, *protein*, provides, weight for weight, roughly as much energy as carbohydrate, but it is much less important for most people as a source of energy. The main sources of animal protein are meat, fish, cheese, and eggs; milk too is important. Plant protein is eaten mainly in pulses and whole cereals. An adult can do with very little protein indeed, but he can, if necessary, manage on a diet of which almost all the solid is protein: this is what men such as Eskimo, who depend on hunting, have to do. We need, too, very little of the third main type of foodstuff, the *fats*, provided we have plenty of palatable carbohydrate. Fat, however, provides about twice as much energy per pound as protein or carbohydrate and is therefore a more concentrated form of energy food. Today there still remains a world shortage of fats. Fat shortage can affect us in two important ways: first, it may reduce our intake of the fat-soluble vitamins A and D, which we discuss below; second, it makes it more difficult to prepare palatable meals. The traditional sources of fat in the West are butter and cheese, and meat, but vegetable fats are becoming more important. They have long been in general use in, for instance, large parts of India, and in the South of Europe where olive oil is in every kitchen.

Carbohydrate, fat and protein are needed, not only as energy-givers, but for the growth and maintenance of the body tissues. In this respect protein is of especial importance. It is possible for children to suffer protein deficiency where there is no shortage of energy-producing food. The term 'protein deficiency' is, however, imprecise. There are many proteins and each has a different chemical composition and so a different nutritive value. It has, therefore, been customary to distinguish 'second-class' plant protein from 'first-class' animal protein. This is a very crude classification: some animal proteins, notably gelatin, hardly deserve to be called first-class on any scheme; and the value of plant proteins – which we get mainly from whole wheat, peas, beans, and lentils – depends partly on what other protein is being eaten.

There are two important practical points. First, growing children, and pregnant and nursing mothers, have a special need for protein, and so should have first call on proteinous foods of animal origin: milk, meat and fish, cheese and eggs. (Men doing heavy work have no special, physiological need for protein. They may however be dissatisfied with meatless meals in a country such as England, with a long tradition of a heavy consumption of beef, mutton, and pork or bacon. Moreover, meat contains substances which stimulate appetite, and so increase the amount of food eaten. The justification for extra cheese for heavy workers is that it provides, owing to its high fat content, a considerable amount of energy in a form easily put into a sandwich.)

Second, if children and mothers throughout the world are to have adequate diets, there must be an enormous increase in milk production. Milk is the most complete of single foods, and is an excellent source of animal protein. The importance of milk is most clear in the large populations of the tropics in which the childhood disease of kwashiorkor is prevalent. This condition usually occurs a few months after weaning, between the ages of one and four years. (In these communities final weaning from the breast often occurs very late.) The child is fed mainly on cereals – maize, rice and so on – and receives hardly any protein foods such as meat, fish, eggs or milk.

Growth slows down, and the muscles are small and weak. Sometimes there is excessive fat which may deceive the casual observer. Intellectual development is impaired, and the child is both apathetic and irritable. There is often a diseased condition of the skin and sparse hair. There is usually poor appetite, and vomiting and diarrhoea occur. Kwashiorkor itself, in many populations, merges into marasmus, in which there is no fat under the skin and in which the child is verging on starvation.

Only a small amount of protein is needed to cure kwashiorkor – at most five grams for every kilogram of body weight of the child daily. This can be obtained from 150 ml (5 oz.) of liquid milk per kilogram body weight. Once appetite has been restored, a mixed diet of solids is given. At this stage plant foods containing plenty of protein are useful.

'FAT'

Undernourishment and bad diets are the major food problems; but there is also over-eating. About ten per cent of the body weight of a typical healthy young Europiform man is made up of fat. The corresponding figure for his sister is about twenty-five per cent. In primitive conditions, an extra food reserve for the women is probably useful in preganancy and lactation; women lead more sedentary lives than the men who have to hunt. In the savage state, in which our human ancestors lived for perhaps a million years, the opportunities for putting on much fat are few, and chronic obesity must be almost impossible. In rich countries today, by contrast, middle-aged men probably average around twenty-five per cent fat, and women forty-five per cent.

These averages conceal immense variation even among the well fed. Half the total weight of a really gross man may be fat, but only two or three per cent of a very thin one. Moreover, some men and women remain skinny however much they eat, while the girth of others increases inexorably on what seems to them a light diet. Is this important? Many people, at least in western countries, try to remain slim for the sake of appearance; this is a matter of fashion. Less often they do so in the interests of athletic fitness. But obesity is also a danger to health. The word 'overweight' can be given a precise meaning in terms of the expectation of life: a man's weight (though not a woman's to the same extent) is an important factor in predicting how long he will live. The statisticians employed by insurance companies have published impressive figures on the hazards of fatness. Very few obese men live to draw an old-age pension.

Much has been published on how to become and to remain slim, though if one thinks only of physics and chemistry the problem may seem a simple one. All foods are sources of energy. The energy contained in food may be used by the body in movement or in heat production. Food materials not used in either of these ways are available for growth. In an adult human being, the only structure that grows substantially is adipose tissue: the tissue, under the skin, in the abdomen and elsewhere, lays down increasing stores of fats. It follows that to get fat a man or woman must eat more than is used for movement and heat. If *less* is eaten, existing fat stores are depleted. It is impossible for a starving person to remain fat: there can be no obesity in a population under prolonged famine, or among the prisoners in a concentration camp.

Hence to lose weight a fat person must either eat less than enough food to provide the energy he uses, or he must use more energy in exercise; and once slim, he must keep his intake and output balanced by weighing himself regularly and adjusting his eating or his exercise accordingly. Unfortunately, it is easier to say this than to do it. Some people, under special pressure, achieve a spare figure with notable success: fashion models and jockeys are obvious examples. But some people of vast size behave as though they were addicted to food, just as others are to nicotine or alcohol: they cannot keep off it. The essential for success is to eat very little carbohydrate, and this may be an intolerable privation.

Nevertheless, fat people are not necessarily, or even usually, heavy eaters. Often they are sluggards rather than gluttons. The daily activity of fat Americans has been compared with that of otherwise similar thin ones: twenty-five obese men aged thirty-six, and of sedentary occupation, walked 3·7 miles per day on the average, while the slender controls walked 6·0 miles; corresponding figures for women were 2·0 and 4·9. Such facts do not tell us why certain people are much less active than others; but inert people could certainly lose weight if they exercised more *and ate the same amount*. Again this change in habit is hard to achieve.

Exercise must not be confounded with sweating. Sweat is mostly water, but contains salts and traces of other substances. It is quickly replaced by drinking water; the salts are made up from food. A jockey can help to keep his weight down for a race by taking no fluids for some hours beforehand; he may then endure severe thirst. But slimming cannot be achieved by dehydration.

Vigorous exercise can not only keep one's weight within bounds, but be beneficial in other ways. The clearest example concerns one of the commonest causes of illness and death among the middle-aged in rich countries: this is a condition of the arteries, called atheroma, which is responsible for the alarming recent increase in coronary thrombosis. An atheromatous artery accumulates fatty substances in its inner lining, so that the flow of blood is reduced or, eventually, even stopped altogether. The process is a little like the 'furring' of a water pipe. Sometimes the blood supply to part of the heart muscle is suddenly interrupted as a result of complications of atheroma; there is severe pain, collapse and possibly rapid death. There have been suggestions that various foodstuffs help to cause atheroma, but they have not been unanimously accepted. If the reader wishes to protect himself against atheroma, it is doubtful whether he will achieve anything by avoiding animal fats or sugar; but he will make at least coronary thrombosis most unlikely if he takes regular exercise. (If the reader is a woman, she has less to fear.) If he is a post-office worker, but not a postman, he should imitate the postman's daily mileage; for postmen have far fewer coronaries than post-office clerks, telephonists and others. Similarly, bus conductors are less atheromatous than bus drivers. And within largely sedentary groups such as professional workers, those who take regular exercise, even golf, are in less danger than their immobile colleagues.

A physiologist, R. Passmore, has classified *Homo sapiens* in three sub-species, *laborans*, *sedentarius* and *sportivus*. The first covers all men before civilization allowed the second to appear in increasing numbers. The third represents the small minority who possibly represent civilized man of the future. Today we are ashamed to be dirty, verminous or stinking; this is a quite new-fangled phenomenon. Perhaps people will soon be equally ashamed to be paunchy, obese or unable to run upstairs without puffing.

'MINERALS' AND VITAMINS

We turn now to other essentials. Bones and teeth are made largely of calcium phosphate, and so calcium and phosphorus are both required. Milk and cheese are excellent sources of both. In Britain today calcium salts are added to the flour from which bread is made. Iron is another chemical element easily identifiable in the body, particularly in the blood: lack of it causes one kind of anaemia. Infants and young women are especially liable to be short of it, and today it is probably the dietary component of which people in rich countries are most likely to be deficient. Meat, fruit, vegetables and whole flour are important sources. Iodine, as we saw in chapter 2, is also an essential element. Even sodium chloride, the common salt of our tables, is a serious problem in many countries, particularly in the tropics where the heat causes much loss of salt in sweat. In the past it has been an expensive (and heavily taxed) commodity even in Western Europe.

Carbohydrates, fats and proteins, the inorganic salts mentioned in the last paragraph, and water: these are obvious necessities. However, if a diet consisting only of these materials in a pure form is given to animals such as young mice, the animals stop growing, sicken and die. On the other hand, if a small amount of milk is added the animals survive and grow. Milk makes this difference because it contains several further substances essential for life: these, the *vitamins*, are present, and are needed, only in very small amounts. Look at the table on page 240.

Many large human populations have a high incidence of vitamin deficiency. In some of the densely populated areas of Asia beri-beri is common because the principal food is rice without the husk: this supplies starch without B vitamins, and beri-beri is due mainly to extreme vitamin B_1 deficiency; the heart is affected, there are muscular spasms and weakness, and death results unless suitable food is given. Another disease with a high incidence in India is xerophthalmia, due to vitamin A deficiency: the eyes are affected, and the disease is a common cause of blindness; it is often fatal. A third disease, pellagra, has been common in the south of the U.S.A., especially among the Negroes, and in south-eastern Europe. It is due to lack of another of the B vitamins. The skin becomes scaly and sores develop; once again, it may be fatal.

The Main Types of Foodstuff

NEEDED IN LARGE AMOUNTS USED AS FUEL		
	MAIN SOURCES	SPECIAL FUNCTION IN BODY
PROTEIN	Meat, fish, eggs, milk, cheese; peas, beans, lentils, wheat	Especially important in growth; also a source of energy
CARBOHYDRATE	Cereals and cereal products; sugar; potatoes	Main source of energy for most of world's population
FAT	Meat, butter, cheese, margarine	Twice the fuel value per unit weight of carbohydrate or protein; contains fat-soluble vitamins
INORGANIC SUBSTANCES: NEEDED IN SMALLER AMOUNTS		
CALCIUM PHOSPHORUS (as phosphate)	Milk, cheese	Make up a large part of the constituents of bone and teeth
IRON	Vegetables, fruit, whole wheat	Contained in haemoglobin (the red pigment of blood)
IODINE	Most foods	Contained in the thyroid hormone
All these elements are found in every cell of the body, as well as in the tissues mentioned		

The Main Types of Foodstuff – continued

VITAMINS: NEEDED IN VERY SMALL AMOUNTS			
	MAIN SOURCES	GROSS LACK CAUSES:	MINOR LACK CAUSES:
A	Fish-liver; milk, butter, eggs; green vegetables	Keratomalacia; xerophthalmia	Night-blindness (one kind); less growth in young
D	Fish-liver; milk, butter, eggs; (sun on skin)	Rickets (children); osteomalacia (adults)	Inadequate bone growth
B₁ (THIAMIN)	Whole wheat; wheat germ; meat; eggs; yeast	Beri-beri	Nervous disorder; fatigue
RIBO-FLAVIN	As B₁	Degeneration of cornea of eye	Inflammation of lips and mouth
NICOTINIC ACID	As B₁	Pellagra	Nutritional diarrhoea
C (ASCORBIC ACID)	Citrus fruits, tomatoes; other fresh fruit and vegetables	Scurvy	Anaemia; slow healing of wounds

There are other vitamins, most of them of less practical importance

The two other outstanding deficiency diseases, scurvy (vitamin C deficiency), and rickets (vitamin D deficiency), are more likely to occur in northern climates. Vitamin C is found particularly in oranges and lemons, and in fresh vegetables. Scurvy has in the past been common in Western European towns in late winter. It can be fatal, especially among infants. At one time it was called 'the London disease'. England, in spite of its thriving agriculture, has a bad reputation for deficiency conditions. Rickets used to be called 'the English disease'; until well after the First World War gross rickets was widespread among the children of workers in the large towns throughout Britain. Even now, in the 1970s, one may still see in Glasgow, for example, elderly, bow-legged, pigeon-chested men and women, whose skeletons, distorted in childhood, have inevitably remained so throughout life.

Today the value of fish liver oils has become generally known, and serious rickets has diminished, though some calcium deficiency is still general among our children. Moreover, in the 1950s and 1960s gross rickets reappeared, notably again in Glasgow. Among its victims were the children of Indian immigrants whose food habits, originating in the tropics, are ill-adapted to the sunless existence of a dark, northern industrial city. Rickets is rare in sunny climates, because vitamin D is formed in the skin by the action of sunlight.

Among the other important vitamins, those of the B group, which are water-soluble, occur particularly in whole wheat, whole rice, oatmeal and potatoes, and emphasis has come to be placed rather on these than on the more purified forms of carbohydrate such as white flour and sugar. This is of especial importance because the amount of B vitamins required varies with the amount of carbohydrate eaten.

As for the fat-soluble vitamins, vitamin A (or a substance that becomes vitamin A in the body) is fairly easily obtained from green vegetables and from carrots, although this has not prevented a good deal of mild vitamin A deficiency among the poor in England and elsewhere. Both A and D are found in liver, the fat of meat, fat fish such as herrings, and eggs and butter. They are also now added in small quantities to margarine in the United Kingdom.

WHAT PEOPLE EAT

For the whole world, the primary food problem is one of quantity, not quality. The problem is not new. The novelty is in the fact that, for the first time in history, it can be defined and action can be taken to solve it. In the 1930s Europe, with a population just over one-third that of Asia, consumed more cereals and more than six times as much meat as the whole of the people in Asia. This is a measure of the inadequacy of the food available to more than half the world's population. In dairy products the disparity was, no doubt, even greater. The people in Central America and large parts of South

America and Africa were similarly short of food. This situation has not changed substantially. After the Second World War there was famine in Bengal, in which vast numbers of people died of starvation. In 1968 there was famine in Bihar.

Even where there is enough food such as rice, there is a high incidence of vitamin deficiency diseases. The complaint used to be made by Europeans that 'natives' in Asian and African countries were idle and bad workers. But nobody can work hard if they are chronically underfed. (Nor, as we shall see in the next chapter, can they do so if they are chronically infected.) In the words of a report from the Food and Agriculture Organization: 'The whole manner of life is adapted to an insufficient supply of calories, with results that are socially undesirable: lack of drive and initiative; avoidance of physical and mental effort; excessive rest.'

The richer countries of the west might be thought to have no difficulty in getting enough good food. But even in Britain and the United States this was and is far from true. Until the beginning of the nineteenth century the problem in England was to produce enough food. Most people grew their own, and if the harvest was good all was well. This had been the position for centuries among the peasantry. Chaucer's widow in the *Nonnes Preestes Tale* did not have much variety:

> No winne dranke she, neyther white ne red:
> Hire bord was served most with white and black.
> Milk and broun bread, in which she found no lack,
> Seinde bacon, and sometime an ey or twey.

But a diet based on milk, rye or wholemeal bread, bacon, and eggs is not likely to lead to serious deficiency, except perhaps of vitamin C. Little sugar was eaten, but there was a good supply of vegetables, at least in summer. The only serious hazard was famine.

Industrialism led to a great change. The industrialists wanted cheap food for the working people in the towns, since without it they could not get hands for the factories. The landowners, on whose estates food was produced, wanted food prices kept up. At the beginning of the nineteenth century there was a duty on imported wheat, and the 4-lb. loaf cost fourteen pence. Wages were one or two shillings a day. In 1846 the factory workers and industrialists achieved the repeal of the Corn Laws: the import duty came off, and by 1900 the 4-lb. loaf cost sixpence. During the nineteenth century the population of England and Wales doubled, and from being agricultural became predominantly urban and industrial, living largely on cheap imported cereal foods, sugar, and potatoes. Wheat was eaten mainly as white flour, and the annual consumption of sugar rose from a few pounds per head to nearly one hundredweight. Agriculture declined, and the consumption of dairy products, vegetables, fruit and oatmeal fell. Rickets and scurvy became common. At the beginning of the century the minimum recruiting height for the army was five feet six inches; by the end it had to be reduced to five feet. The high proportion of recruits rejected as unfit for service in the Boer War eventually led to the introduction of school meals.

> When will they notice us? When will they
>   flatter us? When will they help us? When there's a war!
> Then they will ask for our children and kill them:
>   sympathise deeply and ask for some more.

But it was not until the 1930s that it became possible, by investigation of the diets of large numbers of families, to determine the extent and character of the still prevailing malnutrition. Admittedly, standards vary, and there is even now no agreement on the necessary amounts of certain essentials: nobody can do without vitamin C, for instance, but we cannot lay down precisely, with reasonable certainty, the minimum any person, or even any class of persons, must have in order to avoid all ill effects. It is easy to see the effects of gross deficiencies, but far from easy to relate less obvious symptoms, such as an apparently excessive susceptibility to some infections, to shortage of a particular vitamin.

One difficulty is that individuals almost certainly vary genetically in their vitamin needs. Tooth decay is unquestionably influenced by diet; but one child may have excellent teeth, while another on the same diet may have extensive decay. And complexities do not end there. In one investigation it was found impossible to induce certain volunteers to show signs of vitamin B_1 deficiency: although deprived of the vitamin they continued to excrete it in their urine, as if they were synthesizing it in their bodies. A drug was then given to kill most of the bacteria in their intestines. (Our intestines always contain harmless bacteria.) The excretion of B_1 at once stopped; it was the bacteria which had been producing it. Hence our liability to vitamin B_1 deficiency depends in part on the bacteria we harbour.

Despite these difficulties, nutrition surveys have given valuable information. Those carried out before the Second World War illustrate the state of nutrition attained in a period of relative

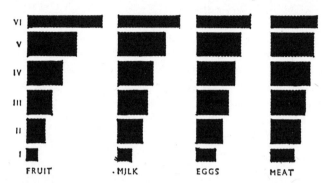

Food and Income. Relative consumption of certain nutritionally important (and expensive) foods from Orr's survey of nutrition in England in 1935. They illustrate the relationship between income and nutrition, and help to account for the lower average height and inferior physique of the children of the poor. Group I is the poorest 10 per cent, group VI the richest 10 per cent; each other group represents 20 per cent of the population

stability. The effect of poverty was clearly shown in Orr's famous report, *Food, Health and Income*, published in 1935. The diagram above is based on it. The food of at least half of the population of England and Wales was seriously deficient. The malnourished fifty per cent belonged to the poor, and since the poor had, on the average, larger families than the rich, about seventy-five per cent of the children of England and Wales were inadequately fed. Later surveys confirmed Orr's findings. Within each income group there is wide variation from the average: some individuals or families do much better, and others correspondingly worse. But this does not invalidate the conclusions drawn from the surveys.

Orr's results, and those of later workers, show what, in fact, people do eat. If every housewife were a skilled dietician, had unlimited time and patience, access to the cheapest markets, and adequate skill and cooking facilities, nutrition would doubtless be better. This, however, is academic, except that it suggests the need for a long-term policy of education and of improvement in kitchen equipment. But the malnutrition of the poor cannot be attributed to ignorance; Orr's figures show that, even with the maximum of knowledge and skill, twenty per cent of the population, with then existing wages and prices, could not have afforded a satisfactory diet. His comment was as follows:

It has been suggested that the standard adopted, [namely] what is needed to enable people to attain their inherited capacity for health and physical fitness, is so high that it is impracticable. One writer terms it 'utopian'. In animal husbandry, an optimum standard, far from being utopian, is regarded as good practice. Every intelligent stock farmer in rearing animals tries to get a minimum diet for maximum health and physical fitness. A suggestion that he should use a lower standard would be regarded as absurd. If children of the three lower groups were reared for profit like young farm stock, giving them a diet below the requirements for health would be financially unsound. Unfortunately, the health and physical fitness of the rising generation are not marketable commodities which can be assessed in terms of money.

The position in the United States, the wealthiest country of all, was probably slightly better than that of England. But it was not good. The United States Department of Agriculture Yearbook for 1939 contains the following passage:

If the total quantities of food produced in this country were distributed in proportion to need, a fairly satisfactory diet would be provided for every individual. As it is, the national dietary level appears high because of the high consumption of certain foods by some families. Urban families with limited funds for food and rural families with limited opportunities for home production tend to lay emphasis on the kind of foods that satisfy obvious hunger cheaply and to neglect those that satisfy also the 'hidden nutritional hunger' – for vitamins and minerals – described by science.

To raise consumption of all groups to the level of the most favoured it would have been necessary to increase the production of milk by twenty per cent, of butter by fifteen, tomatoes and citrus fruits seventy, leafy and yellow vegetables one hundred, and eggs thirty-five per cent. The similarity to England holds too in the relationship between poverty and malnutrition. In 1936 about thirty-two per cent of families and single individuals in the U.S. had incomes under 750 dollars a year, and none of these could afford satisfactory diets at the prices then prevailing. Extensive studies made since the Second World War show that malnutrition and even deficiency diseases remain common. Children and pregnant women suffer most.

Reports of widespread malnutrition in advanced countries were at first received with a good deal of scepticism, but they were confirmed by the effects of improving diets. These are most clearly seen in children and in women before and after childbirth. In a study of an English village colony for boys, some of the boys were allowed an extra ration of milk each day, while others remained on the usual diet. The average annual gain in weight of boys in the milk group was 6·98 lb.; that of the boys receiving the normal diet, 3·83 lb. Other experiments have had similar results in both Britain and the U.S.A. These observations are paralleled in both countries by two well established facts: that the children of the poor are smaller, weaker, and suffer more disease than those of the rich; and that there has been a steady improvement during the twentieth century in all classes.

The clearest index of improvement is the increase in average weight and height of children of all ages. This has been accompanied by progressively earlier achievement of maturity. In Europe, U.S.S.R., North America, Japan and elsewhere, during this century, the average age of girls at first menstruation (the menarche) has declined: around 1900, in some populations, it was about seventeen years, while by mid-century it was thirteen. Another index of maturity is the age at which growth stops. During recent decades, in advanced countries, not only has average stature gone up, but also – more recently – the age at which it is attained. When people are living in bad conditions, as in the slums of big cities, they may go on growing to the age of twenty or more; in better conditions, growth may cease at sixteen.

The improvement is probably not due only to better nutrition. Infectious disease has been much reduced, and this is only partly due to better food and consequent higher resistence. Smaller families and child-welfare clinics have both led to better care of children. Nevertheless, food has certainly played a major part. In Britain even during the Second World War the improvement continued. This was probably a result of three things: the rationing of most important foods, controlled prices, and full employment (which abolished most of the worst poverty).

Growth in height and weight is generally used in assessing physical condition. This is primarily because both height and weight can be measured accurately and quickly. But it is further justified by the fact that other qualities vary with physical growth. Children who grow most rapidly have, on the average, higher resistance to infection and are better at all kinds of school activity, both physical and intellectual. This does not signify that small people are inferior, but only that, on the whole, growth in the ordinary sense goes with the growth of intellect and ability.

For the effect of diet on pregnant women the simplest criteria to use are the proportions of deaths in childbirth, stillbirths, and deaths of the children in the first month of life. In South Wales in 1934, when there was much unemployment among the miners, over 27,000 women were studied, some of whom were given extra food. Here are figures obtained in one year:

		Attended clinic only	Clinic + food
Maternal death rate	per 1,000	11·3	4·8
Stillbirth rate + neonatal mortality	live births	84·0	59·0

The extra food included a small amount of protein, together with calcium, phosphorus, vitamin A, and B vitamins. This supplement, although it markedly influenced death rates, still left the total diet of the women far below any recommended standard.

Many of these figures may seem to have only an historical interest; but even in the rich countries not everyone yet has enough good food. In Britain, malnutrition had still not been wholly overcome a decade after the Second World War; and in the 1960s the situation worsened in certain ways. As usual there was a marked effect of poverty: the lower the family income, and the larger the family, the slower (on the average) was the growth of the children in it. This is almost certainly due largely to differences in nutrition between the economic classes. In 1964 severe rickets was reported in the Glasgow slums. But not all the bad feeding of children is due to poverty, for surveys of the buying habits of parents have revealed a new factor. Commodities such as biscuits, of low nutritional value, are so skilfully advertised on television that they are excessively eaten. Equally ingenious advertising of products (useful in themselves) which contain vitamin C has evidently misled some conscientious mothers into believing that this is the only vitamin their children need.

Most of the world's population is nutritionally in a far more precarious state than the city poor of western countries. A very rough classification divides the world into three nutritional regions. First, the rich areas are North America, Europe, the U.S.S.R., Australasia and Japan. Second is China, which is in a process of rapid change from profound poverty. Third come the two thousand million poor of Asia, Africa and Latin America. This majority of mankind has so far received virtually no benefit from modern science or technology. A peon in South America, a villager in India or a herdsman or farmer in Africa lives much the same life as that of a peasant of four thousand years ago – all too often 'nasty, brutish, and short'. A small minority of landlords and merchants are wealthy and accordingly resist proposals for change.

Moreover, the gap between the rich and poor nations is widening. In the rich world, in the 1960s, in each year there has been an increase in wealth per head of more than three per cent; in the poor world the figure was less than half that. Yet of course it is the poor nations which most need a rapid increase. It is sometimes said that poverty is a result of the unremitting growth of populations. But the population of the U.S.A. is increasing at a rate similar to that of India; and, although there is a large minority of very poor people in the United States, on the whole Americans are still becoming richer. The crucial need in the poor countries is implied in the commonly used adjective, 'underdeveloped': industry must be vastly increased in parallel with improvements in food production. The experience of the U.S.S.R. since 1918 has illustrated both the possibilities and the hazards of such a programme. In the second half of the twentieth century the pacemaker for the poor world is China.

The seven hundred million people in China are increasing, probably, at a rate of at least fourteen million a year. By the end of the century there may be twelve hundred million Chinese. To cope with this situation agricultural improvement is proceeding on an unprecedented scale. Freedom from starvation depends still on rice, and rice growing has been extended from its original area south of the Hwai River far to the north. The scope of cotton growing has been similarly enlarged. The change in the face of the Chinese earth depends on the control of floods, irrigation and a revolution in land management. There are no longer landlords taking a large and regular percentage of the peasants' crops. Instead, the farms are grouped in co-operatives; and these in turn are organized in communes which have an average membership of about twenty thousand people. These large units allow the economic use of modern methods and equipment. The peasants retain private plots of land on which they produce food for their families. At the same time, the Chinese are contriving to train geologists, agricultural experts and others, and are consequently beginning to make use of the enormous resources in metals, oil and other minerals, of which the existence was hardly suspected until the middle of this century. Consequently, China is rapidly becoming a major industrial nation.

Today, in the west, the usual notion of China among people who read the newspapers is a political one. But in the long term it is these economic changes which promise to be important. Eventually, they will be copied elsewhere; and indeed, they are being copied now, though not yet very successfully as a rule. The bitter struggle entailed in wrenching a nation of peasants into the twentieth century can be much relieved if help is given by the rich countries. The average income in Western Europe is something like ten times that of an Indian, African or South American peasant. The rich, in fact, could spare a good deal and yet suffer no more than a temporary slowing of their increase in wealth. The poor countries need knowledge and equipment. There are international bodies, such as the Food and Agriculture Organization, through which they could be efficiently supplied. Throughout the advanced countries there is immense goodwill and an increasing feeling of responsibility towards even remote countries which need help. A major task for the rest of this century is to make this feeling effective.

13

LIFE AND DEATH

Death be not proud, though some have called thee
Mighty and dreadfull; for, thou art not soe.
JOHN DONNE

THROUGHOUT human history the two great causes of premature death have been famine and infectious disease. The casualties due directly to war have been trifling by comparison, at least until the middle of the twentieth century. Among the twentieth-century objectives of applied science, the conquest of infection remains second only to feeding people. What has already been accomplished represents one of humanity's major achievements.

The problem arises from the crowded populations of civilization. Primitive peoples untouched by advanced cultures seem to have few serious epidemics or endemic infections, though individuals rarely reach more than middle age. This is inferred from the study of their skeletons, and from the reports of the civilized men who first reached them. Regular contact with advanced communities is followed by a complete change: primitive groups not before exposed to the disease germs of civilization are highly susceptible; the first experience they have of them is often a sudden, heavy infection: there is little possibility of getting a mild or undetectable attack from a light infection, such as often occurs in other communities. In addition, since isolated groups have not been selected for resistance to these diseases, they are probably genetically more susceptible than larger communities. The inhabitants of Tierra del Fuego, in less than a century, were reduced from about 60,000 to 200, largely through infection with smallpox, measles and tuberculosis. The Pacific islands were similarly depopulated of their attractive inhabitants, after the European invasion.

These three diseases are mainly airborne, and so depend for their spread directly on the crowding of people together. But the density of civilized populations also gives opportunities for other noxious organisms. Water supplies may be infected; sewage and other household waste may harbour the germs of disease or the animals that carry them; food itself, in its journey from the farm to the consumer, may become infected, and is liable, like waste, to maintain populations of germ-bearing pests such as flies and rats, as well as the human population for which it is intended.

THE 'SANITARY IDEA'

None of this was properly understood anywhere until the middle of the nineteenth century, when the germ theory of disease was established. Although a relationship between disease and filth had long been suspected, the connexion was not proved. 'Foul airs' or miasmas were believed to be the agents of disease, and the name of *malaria* (bad air) remains a memorial to this view. Microscopists had demonstrated the presence of bacteria and other microbes in a variety of places, including decaying material, but these organisms were believed to grow directly from the stuff they lived on. The foundation of bacteriology was the demonstration that microbes do not appear 'spontaneously' in any medium, however suitable for their growth: they appear only if the medium has been exposed to infection from elsewhere: microbes, like larger organisms, grow only from other, similar bodies. Thus it came to be realized that filth caused disease on account of microbes which grow in it and which can also live in men's bodies.

Infection from these sources is far from being the cause of all disease. (In the last chapter we had examples of deficiency diseases which are in no way infectious; and in chapters 3 and 8 we encountered abnormal conditions which are fixed genetically.) But many of the worst killers of children and of men and women in their prime turned out to be infections preventible by sanitary measures.

The need for these measures had never been so great as in the new industrial towns of the nineteenth century. The squalor and degradation of the working population in English towns is fully described in a series of official reports published during the 1840s. Edwin Chadwick (1800–1890), the inventor of the expression the 'sanitary idea', wrote:

Such is the absence of civic economy in some of our towns that their condition in respect to cleanliness is almost as bad as that of an encamped horde, or an undisciplined soldiery.

He describes army standing orders for camp sanitation, and goes on:

The towns whose populations never change their encampment have no such care, and whilst the houses, streets, courts, lanes, and streams are polluted and rendered pestilential, the civic officers have generally contented themselves with the most barbarous expedients, or sit still amidst the pollution, with the resignation of Turkish fatalists, under the supposed destiny of the prevalent ignorance, sloth and filth.

Similarly the Frenchman, J. Blanqui, describes how in 1849, in the industrial town of Lille, 3000 families lived in unventilated, insanitary cellars. Conditions like these are still the fate of many millions in, for instance, India and the poor countries of South America.

Improvement required the setting up of a national public health organization in each country, and effective public health departments for each local government authority. This was a big task, both administratively and technically. Engineers, sanitary inspectors, dustmen and sewermen, as well as doctors, had to be recruited, trained, and paid. It is only recently that, even in Britain, all houses in towns have had a reliable piped water supply free from infection; (the poorer houses often have even now only one tap, and in the country much water still comes from wells, some quite shallow and easily infected); but today most urban areas have, not only enough water for drinking, cooking, washing, and cleaning, but also a bacteriological service to keep watch on the quality of the water supplied.

A necessary complement to a good water supply is an efficient system of drains and sewers. In 1840 household waste of all kinds was put in cesspools (Windsor Castle had 250 of them), or human excrement was collected in heaps for sale as manure; refuse collection was unorganized and sporadic, where it existed at all. The new working-class houses whose occupiers suffered these conditions were flimsy, airless, ill-lit, and commonly built in terraces back-to-back, with only a narrow alley in front. Some of these houses are still lived in.

Although the first attempts to improve the hygiene of cities were made even before the elements of bacteriology were understood, the squalor remained almost untouched for most of the century; the efforts of the wealthy taxpayers who did not wish to spend money on the poor, of the water companies, of some sections of the medical profession and of other vested interests prevented progress for several decades. Nevertheless, by the first decade of the twentieth century the application of the sanitary idea had wrought a vast change in mortality and morbidity from some major diseases, not only in Britain but also in the main countries of western Europe, and in the United States. The extent and limits of this advance can be shown if we consider the main epidemic diseases of human populations.

PESTILENCE

Throughout the world the worst *water-borne* diseases are cholera, typhoid and various forms of dysentery. Today cholera is called a 'tropical disease', but there were four major outbreaks in western Europe during the nineteenth century. Epidemics are nearly always due to infection of drinking water; in 1824 a single infected well near Piccadilly Circus, in London, caused 485 deaths in ten days. Cholera is no longer a disease of western Europe, but when this book was first written a serious epidemic was reported in Egypt, and it is continually present in India, especially Bengal.

Much the same applies to typhoid fever, or more generally to the enteric fevers of which typhoid is the worst, but they have not so completely disappeared from the western world. One of the most notorious epidemics was in Plymouth, Pennsylvania, in 1885. About 1200 persons in a population of 8000 had typhoid in the spring of that year, and one in ten died. During the winter a man living near a stream that flowed into the town's reservoir had had typhoid, and each night his wife had thrown his excreta on to the frozen ground. When the thaw came in the spring the accumulation was washed into the brook and infected the reservoir.

The last serious epidemic in England, at Croydon in 1937, was similarly traced to the individual who was the source of the infection. He was one of a party of men working on an unchlorinated well, who had been in the habit of urinating nearby; the man had

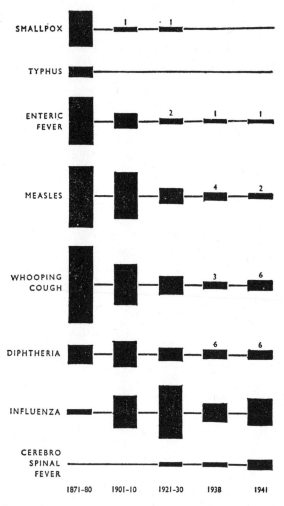

SMALLPOX

TYPHUS

ENTERIC FEVER

MEASLES

WHOOPING COUGH

DIPHTHERIA

INFLUENZA

CEREBRO SPINAL FEVER

1871-80   1901-10   1921-30   1938   1941

Mortality. Deaths from eight diseases, per 100,000 persons per year, in England and Wales. The first group of diseases has been almost wiped out, the second has become much less serious. The third represents new problems which have arisen in the twentieth century

had typhoid and was a carrier. There were 311 cases, with 42 deaths. A century earlier such an incident would have attracted little attention, but in 1937 it aroused great public interest for many weeks, and was the subject of an official inquiry. In this case the public health organization had failed at two points: the well had been unchlorinated, and a healthy typhoid carrier had not been detected by bacteriological tests and prevented from working where he might infect the water supply.

The last important outbreak in Britain was in Aberdeen, and was due to infected food. It, too, was due to a series of failures. The source was a can of corned beef. These cans are cooled in river water. The water usually contains large amounts of sewage, and can infect meat if there are minute flaws in the tins. Hence, in the 1950s, Argentinian producers began to chlorinate the cooling water. On 31 December 1962 a chlorinating plant broke down. It was not repaired for more than a year, but the factory concerned continued to can beef, since to stop would have entailed financial loss. A British government inspector discovered this situation in January 1964, and cabled London accordingly, but the Ministries concerned took no action. In May 1964 an infected tin was sold in Aberdeen. By July, when the outbreak ended, there had been over 400 cases of typhoid; but this time, owing to the use of antibiotic drugs, there were no deaths due solely to the infection.

Hence the diseases carried by water may also be food-borne. And food can be a source of other infections as well. There are several forms of 'food-poisoning' caused by bacteria or other organisms, and gastro-enteritis is a general term for the resulting conditions. They are especially serious in infants and young babies. Cleanliness in the handling and preparation of food at all stages; preventing infected persons from working in food establishments; and the use of effective preserving methods for canned and bottled foods: these are the principal preventive measures.

In general, food-borne disease is less likely to cause epidemics on a large scale than is disease carried by water. Milk, however, occupies a special place among foods: it is distributed in bulk to very large numbers of people in towns, and it is as good a food for some bacteria as it is for men. Infected milk can cause epidemics of typhoid, dysentery, tonsilitis, Q fever, and undulant fever. It is also the source of one type of tuberculosis. The heat treatment of milk,

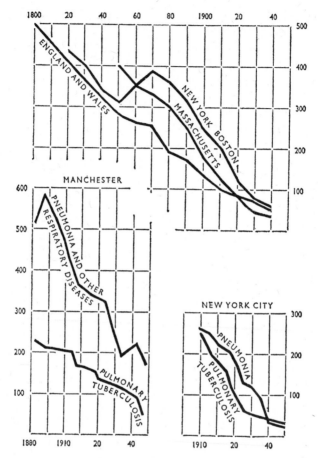

Mortality. Changes in annual death rates from some respiratory infections, per 100,000 living, in advanced communities. The upper figure refers to tuberculosis alone

which is now compulsory in some communities, can prevent the transmission of all these infections. The name of the process, pasteurization, is a memorial to Louis Pasteur (1822–95), who did more than any other man to found the germ theory of disease.

Food may be infected, not only by man himself, but by various animals: flies provide the most familiar example, and are still a menace in the western world as carriers of germs of enteritis and food poisoning. However, the discovery of specific insecticides, of which DDT is the best known, promises the elimination of flies in communities in which they are used on a large enough scale.

But fleas, lice and mosquitoes take pride of place among animal carriers of disease. All these infect man directly and not through food or water. Rat fleas are the source of plague, the Black Death of the Middle Ages. The plague bacillus is primarily a parasite in the bodies of various species of wild mammals, from ground squirrels in central Asia to rabbits in California. In these animals it causes little harm, and it certainly does not give rise to epidemics with a high mortality. It is transmitted from one individual to another by fleas, and rats become infected in the same way. Rat populations too may maintain a comparatively mild plague infection.

Human infection occurs – though not invariably – where there are many infected rats, and the rats have many fleas. These conditions hold today in large parts of India and have held until very recently in China; and there are plague reservoirs also in North and South Africa, and in North America. In India, where there are vast populations of rats closely associated with man, plague is a continual source of anxiety even when there are no human outbreaks. Today, in the 1970s, there is concern because a species of rodent, the bandicoot rat, which is exceptionally susceptible to plague, is multiplying in several major centres of population, such as Calcutta. Hence an outbreak is possible at any time. Nor are the most advanced countries free: there are large populations of plague-infected rodents in California; and there have recently been cases of plague in San Francisco.

However, present dangers are probably not comparable to those of the past. We know for certain of three world outbreaks, or pandemics, of plague, though others probably occurred before them. A pandemic begins suddenly, and spreads over a large area, such as Europe, within a few years; initially the proportion of people dangerously infected is high – perhaps ten per cent. Death rates vary with the exact character of the disease. In the common form, bubonic plague, lymph nodes ('glands') in the groin, the armpit or, occasionally, the neck become swollen and form a bubo. The death rate may then be only fifty per cent, even without modern treatment. The highest mortality – usually one hundred per cent –

occurs when the bubonic form gives place to pneumonic plague: the lungs are involved and bacilli are coughed into the air. For a century or more after the first outbreak plague continues intermittently and with diminishing intensity. Finally in large areas it disappears completely.

We cannot explain this sequence. The first fully authenticated pandemic, the 'plague of Justinian', began in the sixth century, and we have no detailed knowledge of what happened. The second was the Black Death which began in the fourteenth century, and reached France and England in 1349. The initial mortality, though high, was probably less disastrous than the steady drain of lives and health that followed during the next hundred years. This was a period of falling population and collapsing economy in western Europe, and plague made a major contribution to that state of affairs. The last flare-up of the Black Death in England was the 'great plague of London' of 1664. The third pandemic is still going on as this book is written. It began in China, probably in the 1870s, spread rapidly to India, and then to the main ports of Africa and Asia Minor. Europe largely escaped. England had a few cases during the period 1910–21, when rodents in an area of East Anglia were infected.

Plague is far from being a simple problem of public health, and we cannot attribute Europe's escape simply to improved hygiene and precautions against rats at the ports, though they doubtless played some part. With our present knowledge the remedy for plague is prevention by killing rats and their fleas, and by reducing filth that encourages them; protection can also be given by inoculation. We have still to get full understanding of the complex relationships between the plague-ridden rodent populations, their fleas and ourselves.

While plague is a problem of the rats that live in our houses, and of public cleanliness, epidemic typhus fever is a problem of the lice that live on our bodies and of personal cleanliness. This, the worst form of typhus, has destroyed armies and altered the course of wars. The great outbreaks occur when unwashed people are crowded together, and the lice can move rapidly from one to another. In earlier times alternative names for typhus were jail fever and hospital fever. The habit of washing which has become so widespread in the western world in modern times has made perhaps a contribution to disease prevention comparable with the control of the water supply. A Lancashire miner, in 1842, was asked how often the coal-drawers washed their bodies. He is reported to have replied:

None of the drawers ever wash their bodies. I never wash my body; I let my shirt rub the dirt off. I wash my neck and ears and face, of course.

Even more to the point is the cheerful mention in the diary of Samuel Pepys (1633–1703), a First Lord of the Admiralty, of the presence of twenty lice in his hair one evening – 'more than I have had this many a long day. And so with great content to bed'.

The diseases so far discussed are often called 'tropical' by medical men in temperate lands, because they have been largely banished from the temperate zone. The main mosquito-borne infections have a more permanent right to the name, since they are almost confined to the tropics and sub-tropics. Malaria can occur as far north as Archangel, and one form of it turned up regularly in the London hospitals and even in the south of Scotland as recently as the 1860s; but ague, as it was called, was never such a menace in the north as it has been, and still is, in hotter climates.

In large parts of the most densely populated countries malaria is almost universal, and it is the world's leading infectious illness and cause of death. A conservative estimate of its total incidence suggests that a quarter of the world's population suffered from it until at least the second half of the twentieth century. In India the number of people treated for malaria each year is of the order of ten million, but this is only a small proportion of the total infected. Malaria differs from the acute infections (such as plague and typhus) in being, very often, a chronic disease. An acute disease either kills in a few days or weeks, or subsides; a chronic infection may persist for years, perhaps for a lifetime. People with chronic malaria are weak and lethargic, as well as subject to fever every few days; and uninformed and uninfected Europeans, seeing them, have been led to believe that all 'natives' are naturally lazy. We have seen that the effects of chronic undernutrition may encourage them in this mistaken view.

The principal means of preventing endemic malaria is destruction of mosquitoes of the genus *Anopheles*. This is a formidable task requiring a large organization of trained persons. Methods include the draining of marshes and streams, where the mosquitoes breed; poison in the water; and the introduction of plants or fish that prevent breeding. What is done depends partly on the species of *Anopheles*. Mosquito teams applying these methods have already had considerable success in countries as diverse as India, Italy, Panama, and Brazil.

In Central and South America, and in West Africa, they are called on to operate also against *Aëdes aegypti*, the mosquito that carries yellow fever, or *vomito negro* – the black vomit. This terrifying disease has been known only since 1648. It was common along the coasts of the Americas and of West Africa. One of the best recorded outbreaks occurred in Philadelphia in 1793, and killed 4000 out of a population of 50,000. Many fled the city. The doctors advised the burning of gunpowder and the smoking of tobacco as preventives. The cause, a mosquito-borne virus, was established at the beginning of this century. It was the destruction both of *Anopheles* and *Aëdes* that finally made possible the completion of the Panama Canal in 1914. Today, epidemic yellow fever has been eliminated, but endemic yellow fever remains; like plague, it depends on a complex set of animal vectors, including mosquitoes (not *Aëdes*) and various species of monkey. As such, both in tropical Africa and in South America, it is still a potential threat. However, immunization is possible, and is compulsory under international law for travellers in certain regions.

All these diseases can be prevented, and in some places have been prevented, by applying a rather wide interpretation of the sanitary idea. They represent the easiest targets for public health authorities. This is because they depend on other animals besides ourselves, whereas most infectious diseases are carried from man to man. This is the case with the group of *air-borne* infections, which are – in principle at least – a more difficult problem. The worst of them, smallpox, however, had been shown, by an astonishing feat of empirical medicine, to be preventible more than half a century before the germ theory of disease was established; the technique of vaccination was invented before the end of the eighteenth century. At that period few people in Europe escaped having smallpox at some time in their lives, and about one in twelve of infected persons died. Most survivors were disfigured for life by the pockmarks, and some were blinded. Today deaths from smallpox are rare in the West, partly as a result of vaccination.

The other outstanding success against air-borne infection is that of immunization against diphtheria: in the countries where it has been carried out on a majority of children it has been reduced to an almost negligible danger. In England and Wales at the beginning of the century sixty-five in every 100,000 children under fifteen died of diphtheria. Between the wars, when the numbers of children immunized were still low, the figure was steady at about twenty-nine. During the 1940s the proportion of children immunized was greatly increased as a result of publicity campaigns by the government and local health authorities, and in 1947 the death-rate was

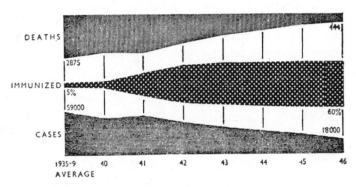

Diphtheria in England and Wales. Widespread immunization of children in the first year has gone far to defeat this disease

down to two per 100,000. Even this could be improved on, given a sustained effort to get every child immunized at the age of one year.

The almost complete disappearance of diseases such as typhus, typhoid, and smallpox in some countries is a triumph of applied science. It has involved the use not only of biology, but also of engineering, chemistry, and other disciplines. Just as with food production, so with the control of disease we find it necessary to consider an intricate nexus of living things; and, just as with food production, the task is one for the whole community as well as for specialists.

This knowledge is applicable, not only in the areas with good public health services, most of which are in the temperate zone, but also in the tropical lands, with their immense populations, where the great epidemic diseases remain as potent as ever. There is a notion that the tropics must be unhealthy, both to people unaccustomed to them and also to the native inhabitants, but there is no valid evidence to support this view. The temperate zone too was 'unhealthy' until public health measures brought improvement. The 'white man's grave' of West Africa was so called for reasons that need no longer apply today: in particular it is a home of malaria, which is now preventible. Certain diseases occur mainly or solely in hot countries, just as others, such as rickets, belong mainly to the lands in which there is little sunlight for part of the year. Perhaps, if Africans had colonized large areas of the temperate zone, northern Europe would have been called 'the black man's grave', although it is in fact possible for Africans to live there in good health.

The tropical countries remain graveyards by comparison with advanced countries, at least for their native inhabitants, mainly because the known principles of public health have not yet been generally applied in them. Throughout the tropics the vitality of the people is sapped, not only by malaria and other diseases already mentioned, but by many others, of which hookworm is probably the most widespread. There are two types of hookworm: both are passed out of the bowel with the faeces, and re-enter a human being through the skin. The people among whom there is a high incidence of infection are those who live in communities with inadequate sanitation and who do not wear shoes. Hookworm is rarely fatal, but it is chronically enfeebling. We do not know how many millions of people are infected with hookworm, but we do know that there are whole communities, for instance in the West Indies, living a depressed existence on account of it. Prevention requires sanitation; educating people to use latrines instead of the ground; and a standard of living which permits the purchase of shoes.

RESISTANCE

The great epidemic diseases can be avoided by rather simple and easily understood methods designed to block the routes by which the disease germs enter the body. For public health the question is: are people liable to be infected, say, with the cholera germ? If so, we must expect them to get cholera; if not, all is well. But, in general, infectious disease is not merely a result of the entry of a disease germ into the body: the body itself must be susceptible to the germ. An attack of a particular disease may confer immunity, at least for a time, to that disease. The immunity is a result of a change in the composition of the blood, and for some diseases such a change can be induced by 'inoculation' which gives rise to little or no discomfort. But the problem of resistance is far wider than this: we have already seen that *nutrition* is an important factor; the *psychological state* of a person may affect his resistance to some infections; and a number of other environmental features, including *housing* and, in some trades, *working conditions*, may be of vital importance. Once again, we see that disease is a social problem, influenced by all the conditions in which people live.

All these effects can be illustrated from one disease, tuberculosis. In each year after the Second World War nearly 2000 English and Welsh children died of tuberculosis, but the worst sufferers were young adults: about one in twenty of all deaths in England and Wales were due to tubercle, and the majority occurred between the ages of fifteen and forty-five; in a quarter of all cases the disease is first diagnosed between fifteen and twenty-five. However, there is now rapid improvement, owing to early diagnosis and the use of new drugs and new kinds of surgery. But even in the United States tuberculosis is still third on the list of causes of death, coming after diseases of heart and blood vessels, and cancer. Apart from the principal diseases of infancy and childhood, tubercle has a special importance compared with the other main causes of death: it kills people in their prime, whereas cancer and the disorders of the vascular system, scourges though they are, are largely problems of the later years of life.

The history of tuberculosis in modern times shows how the disease is a product of economic circumstances.

Youth grows pale, and spectre thin, and dies

wrote Keats in the spring of 1819. This was an accurate description of what was happening at that time, not only to poets and their friends, but to the enfeebled, disease-ridden young men and women of the new manufacturing towns. As early as 1796 a Manchester commission had reported:

Children and others who work in the large cotton factories are peculiarly disposed to be affected by the contagion of fever, and . . . it is rapidly propagated, not only among those who are crowded together in the same apartments, but in the families and neighbourhoods to which they belong.

Such warnings were ignored. As René Dubos, the distinguished bacteriologist, has written:

The passion for financial gains made acquisitive men blind to the fact that they were part of the same social body as the unfortunates who operated their machines. Tuberculosis was, in effect, the social disease of the nineteenth century, perhaps the first penalty that capitalistic society had to pay for the ruthless exploitation of labor.

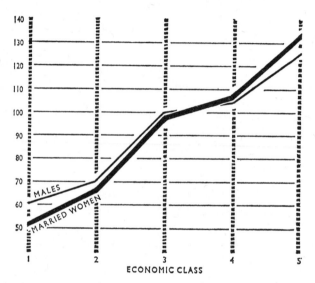

Tuberculosis: The Influence of Income. Relative death rates from tuberculosis in five economic classes. Class 5, the poorest, comes off worst

As we saw in chapter 2, there is genetical variation in the liability to tuberculosis, but there are several environmental factors which have a far more important influence in practice. Of these, working conditions that promote the development of tubercle are notorious: miners and others working where there is much silica dust in the air. are especially liable to the disease, and prevention takes the form of various measures to reduce the amount of dust. There is, too, ample evidence that poor ventilation, in factories for example, increases the amount of tuberculosis. The same applies in the home, but over-crowding there is also likely to cause a greater amount of air-borne infection from one member of a family to another. The connexion between nutritional deficiency and resistance to tubercle has not been fully worked out, and remains uncertain. As for mental state, it is well enough known that some illness, not caused by germs, such as gastric ulcer, is associated with anxiety and unexpressed emotion (acting in a susceptible person), and that such states can cause symptoms of illness in any part of the body. Sometimes the effect is to reduce the resistance of an organ of the body to disease germs. This certainly applies to some tubercular patients, and for them psychological and physical treatment may have to be combined.

With the doubtful exception of psychological disturbance (such as 'worry') all the environmental factors which promote tuberculosis press more heavily on the poor than on the rich. The picture is not, however, even for the poor, uniformly black. Since 1875 in England and Wales there has been steady improvement, apart from two brief checks due to war, in all classes. Moreover there is now a means of inoculating people against tuberculosis, and so immunizing them. This is particularly valuable for workers, such as nurses, whose occupation exposes them to exceptional risks.

The problems of public health are therefore far more complex than might be supposed from a superficial study of the achievements against a few epidemic diseases. The prevention of disease involves not only bacteriology and sanitary engineering, but also a host of other branches of knowledge, from psychology to economics. The attack on tuberculosis alone calls for better housing and a rise in the general standard of life, and for better ventilation in factories, which is again in part an economic problem; for early diagnosis a greater development of mass radiography is required, and for adequate treatment, more beds in sanatoria and more nurses, doctors and other trained persons. And this does not exhaust the list.

Another example of the effects of housing and working conditions is measles. If the population of England and Wales is divided into five groups, according to income level, the proportion of children who contract measles is roughly the same in each group; but the proportion of children who *die* from measles in the poorest group is nineteen times that of the richest. Whooping cough – which has been the main killer of children between one and five years – shows a similar contrast. The difference between the social classes is, for these two diseases, entirely due to the bad housing of the poor and the difficulties that go with it. Crowding makes it more likely that very young babies will get these diseases; resistance is lower in the first year of life than later, hence many babies are killed. We have no such scientific standard for housing as we have for nutrition, but housing which makes it impossible for a baby to be put to sleep apart from the rest of the family is certainly inadequate.

Another condition affected by housing is rheumatic heart disease in children. In Britain between twenty and thirty thousand people probably die of this disease each year, and it is responsible for nearly all the deaths from heart disease before the age of forty; among youths and young adults its place is second to that of tuberculosis. In one investigation a number of working-class families were first classified by their economic position; this is not the same as classifying them by total income, since a couple with one child and £15 a week are much better off than a family of seven with the same income. An arbitrary 'poverty line' was then chosen, below which, it was assumed, a family could not maintain a standard of living adequate for health. Seventeen per cent of the families studied fell below this line, and among them the frequency of rheumatic heart disease was thirty-nine per cent above the average. On the other hand, twenty-two per cent had at least double the chosen minimum income, and among them the frequency of the disease was twenty-three per cent below the average. One immediate conclusion could be drawn from these results: to get a satisfactory reduction in the rate of heart disease in children a standard of life well above the chosen minimum would be necessary. It is by objective standards such as this that minimum wages, family allowances, and other aspects of the standard of living, should be judged. The higher incidence of the disease among the poorest families was due mainly to overcrowding: other consequences of poverty, such as inferior diet, could not be shown to have any effect in this instance.

PROBLEMATIC VIRUSES

Diseases such as tuberculosis and rheumatic heart disease can be overcome only by a general change in the way of life of the poor. The problem is not primarily one of finding specific remedies, even though such remedies can sometimes be of value once the disease is diagnosed and the patient got into a suitable hospital. Prevention is as much a social and economic task as it is medical or scientific. There remains, however, a group of common infectious diseases which are still a problem to the bacteriologist and epidemiologist. They are all caused by viruses, organisms smaller than bacteria and correspondingly more difficult to study.

Of this group acute *poliomyelitis* is the most dreaded, although if we consider its total incidence we find that its importance has perhaps been exaggerated: in Britain and North America, motor traffic presents at all times greater danger to life and limb than polio even in its worst epidemics. Its former common name, infantile paralysis, was based on the fact that when the disease first became important, in the late nineteenth century, most patients were children under five, and the most conspicuous sign was paralysis. More recently the main incidence has been among children of from five to ten years, and in epidemics today an appreciable proportion of adults become seriously infected; moreover, only a minority of those infected have any paralysis. The most remarkable feature of poliomyelitis is that it is a disease of advanced communities: epidemics occur in the countries with the best public health organizations and the highest level of hygiene. The virus is present in the undeveloped countries; during the Second World War soldiers from advanced countries suffered severely from poliomyelitis on being posted, for instance, to Asian countries. Yet the local inhabitants remained unaffected.

Probably, in lands where hygiene is poor nearly every child suffers a mild, non-paralytic infection at a very early age, while it is still being fed by its mother and partly protected by substances in the milk, and this sets up a natural resistance. Infected persons pass polio virus in their faeces. Most children with infected faeces present only minor signs such as slight fever, or symptoms such as backache. In Western countries, presumably, a proportion of children escape early infection, and so are susceptible, later on, to a more severe form of the disease. Even then, it is believed, most of those infected show no serious effects: only a minority, in whom the virus invades a particular part of the nervous system, show any paralysis. In Britain more than fifty per cent of adults contain substances in their blood which indicate a previous infection by the virus, though they give no record of the actual disease.

The great problems are how the infection is spread, and how to prevent it. The virus is passed out with the faeces, and there are detectable amounts of the virus in the sewage of a city during an epidemic, though not at other times. This suggests the desirability of ordinary hygienic precautions. But the virus is also almost certainly air-borne; it follows that crowds, especially in badly ventilated places, are to be avoided – another commonplace principle. Fatigue increases the likelihood of severe infection, and so parents are recommended to avoid over-tiredness in their children during epidemics. Finally, the operation of removing the tonsils greatly

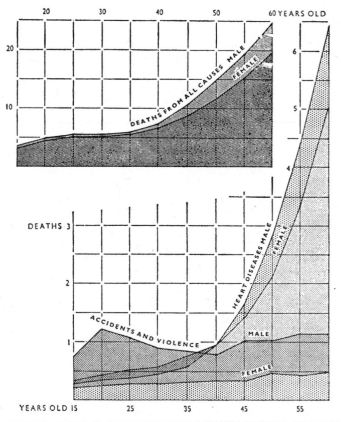

Mortality. The principal causes of death in England and Wales, expressed as deaths per 1000 living (continued on the next page)

increases the danger of infection, and as far as possible surgeons avoid carrying it out if there is a poliomyelitis epidemic.

None of these precautions can prevent epidemics, though personal hygiene of a high standard can probably be valuable. Prevention is now possibly by the use of vaccines, made from virus grown in tissue culture. Owing to the small number of people who ever develop severe poliomyelitis, tests of such vaccines have to be made on vast numbers. In one American inquiry nearly a million children were inoculated. Today, millions of children are being immunized as a routine, since the value of this protection is now fully proved.

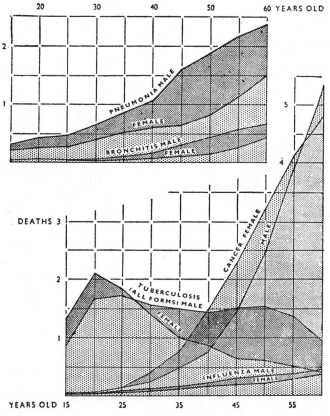

Mortality. The principal causes of death in England and Wales, expressed as deaths per 1000 living (continued from previous page)

The other virus diseases to be mentioned here are so common-place as to be quite unfrightening; yet they cause far more ill health and inconvenience, even suffering, than poliomyelitis. They include the common cold, a number of more severe infections without a definite name, and epidemic influenza. In one investigation of the work of general medical practitioners it was found that about one-third of all ailments treated in patients over sixteen belonged to this group. All are primarily due to infection with viruses, but how many different viruses are involved, and what decides the degree of illness in each infected person, are still unsolved problems.

Colds themselves may be due to more than one microbe, but research has been hampered by the fact that the common laboratory animals do not get colds. Chimpanzees do, but they are very expensive to keep. Today research is done on human volunteers. In the United States the average number of colds a year for an adult is about 2·5, most of them in the colder half of the year. During each winter there are epidemic periods when the incidence of colds is particularly high. The susceptibility of individuals to colds varies very greatly and, what is less well known, any one person may vary in this a great deal from year to year. Psychological state is an important factor in a person's response to infection, and this may be the explanation of the apparently favourable effect of some anti-cold vaccines: none of the vaccines so far used has proved effective under rigorous test, but anything can act as a faith cure if the patient believes in it. Low temperatures are not important in causing colds, but variation of temperature is: in one experiment medical students were kept for a fortnight in conditions of constant temperature and humidity; every effort was made to give them colds by contact with infected persons or material, but all failed.

Efforts have been made by manufacturers to persuade physicians and the public that certain drugs, called 'anti-histamines', cure colds. These drugs do relieve the symptoms of hay-fever, and similar conditions. In an experiment, large numbers of people with colds (but no hay-fever) were given anti-histamines, and a control group, also with colds, were given a dummy medicine, without being told that it was a dummy. Many members of *both* groups reported that their colds were cured, but not more in one group than the other. The anti-histamines were concluded not to be cold cures. This investigation illustrates well the nature of the scientific tests required to assess statements about cure or prevention. The procedure used is called the double blind.

Rather more serious than colds are the infections commonly called influenza but different from true epidemic influenza. There is no accepted name for this group: the U.S. army name is curd (common undifferentiated respiratory disease), but the U.S. navy talks of cat fever (acute catarrhal fever). Some of these fevers may be due to the same viruses as colds, others to one of the true influenza viruses, but most are evidently due to neither. Some may be due to mild infection with the poliomyelitis virus.

Finally we come to *epidemic influenza*. This differs from colds and curd in producing mainly general toxic symptoms, such as headache and muscular pains; there is less local effect on the nose, and less coughing. In a typical epidemic, from ten to twenty per cent of the population in a particular area develop the disease, during a period of four to six weeks. Deaths due to influenza are confined to infants and old people. There are two viruses involved, called A and B, but epidemics due to virus B are rare. Serious outbreaks of influenza A occur at intervals of two to four years: an epidemic seems to confer general immunity on a population for at least the following winter, sometimes for longer. What happens to the virus between epidemics is unknown, but a few people can perhaps remain carriers for many months. There is no specific treatment for influenza.

In 1918–19 there was a pandemic, or world epidemic, of influenza, which is generally supposed to have been due to virus A, although no direct evidence exists on this point. The most remarkable feature of the outbreak was the high mortality, especially among young adults. It is believed that the world mortality was 25m. There was another, less lethal, pandemic of 'Asian' influenza in the late 1950s.

All these diseases are transmitted through the air, probably by 'droplet infection' of which the fine spray given out with each cough or sneeze is the main source. Research on air sprays, which might kill the viruses in crowded buildings and vehicles, promises to give useful results. Dust particles may play a part in spreading infection, and the application of a light mineral oil, spindle oil, to the floors of public buildings reduces the amount of dust in the air and may have a preventive effect.

A potentially important line of study is provided by the very difficult problem of immunity to these diseases. Newcomers to an established community, for instance recruits entering an army camp, have much more respiratory disease than those who have been there six months or more. Similarly, isolated groups, such as the crews of ships exploring remote waters, or small island communities, may be quite free from colds, curd, and influenza, yet develop an explosive epidemic as soon as contact with members of other communities is made. In most groups there is probably constant interchange of the local viruses and a consequent setting up of a temporary immunity; so long as this immunity is regularly reinforced by repeated infection, there will be freedom from the various diseases the viruses may cause. This does not, however, account for the fact that people do get respiratory diseases: no doubt the factors involved in the failure of immunity include the appearance of a new strain of virus in the neighbourhood, and a lowering of resistance in particular individuals.

True influenza confers a high degree of immunity to the virus which caused it, but this lasts only two or three months. Vaccines which confer a similar immunity artificially have been made, and are now being used among people, such as doctors and nurses, for whom immunity is especially important. Whether they will finally prevent influenza epidemics altogether, as diphtheria immunization can prevent diphtheria, is uncertain.

The story of these virus infections is therefore incomplete and unsatisfying. It would have been easier to omit it altogether, and to have restricted this chapter to the diseases of which the scientific account is fairly complete. But to do so would have been misleading: although the most obviously urgent need in the field of public health is the application of existing knowledge, especially in the backward lands, there is still work for the research microbiologist. The public are called upon to support this research in various ways, notably by paying for it, and they need to know something of the problems which face the scientists.

HEALTH IS PURCHASABLE

The special health problems of the advanced countries can be studied from another point of view. Today, in the West, most people die when they are either very young, or over fifty: the great reduction in mortality has most affected the intermediate ages. This is why diseases which occur mainly in elderly people, in particular cancer and disorders of the heart and blood vessels, now loom so large in medical practice: the proportion of men and women over fifty is far higher than ever before. The study of the problems of ageing, or gerontology, is only in its earliest stages. There is, however, much to be said about the health of young children – a current problem which deserves just as much attention.

The health and physical and mental development of each individual is strongly influenced by the economic position of his parents. Nutritional level depends, in most countries, largely on income; and nutrition affects, not only growth directly, but also susceptibility to many diseases. At the same time poverty involves bad housing, and so evokes a further group of diseases.

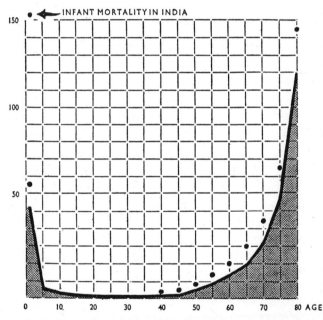

Mortality at Different Ages in England and Wales. The dangerous ages in the Western World today are the first year and after sixty; female mortality is shown by the shaded area; male mortality is higher than female. Where the difference is significant the male mortality is indicated by dots. The infant mortality in India is shown for comparison. The figures show deaths per thousand living per year

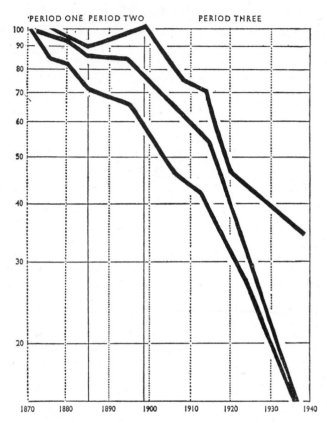

Mortality. Changes in infant mortality (top line) in England and Wales, compared with death rates at ages 1–2 and 2–3 (bottom line). Infant mortality lags behind. There has, however, been further improvement in the post-war 'welfare state'. Mortality is expressed as numbers dying per thousand

The combined effects of the various consequences of poverty in the advanced countries are clearly shown in the figures for diseases of children. The figure on page 273 shows that, of all ages below seventy, the first year of life has the highest death rate. The death rate in the first year is called the infant mortality, or IM. It does not include still-births. The IM for England and Wales in 1938 was fifty-three, signifying that fifty-three infants died out of every 1000 born alive. For the whole world this was rather low. The highest accurately recorded in peacetime was that of Malta, where it was 243 in 1937; during the decade immediately before the Second World War almost one in every four Maltese babies died in the first year of life. (Since then the Maltese IM has been reduced to about 116.) The highest figure for a large country was 241 for Chile; the lowest, thirty-one, was for New Zealand, though the Maori section of the population was less well off than the whites in this respect. In Europe, Iceland with thirty-three and Holland with thirty-eight did best, Rumania with 178 had the highest figure.

Until about 1900 the IM for England and Wales was like that of Indonesia or India today, but in the first forty years of the twentieth century it fell by sixty-six per cent. However, there remains, even within Britain, much variation in IM between different towns. A few small towns have an IM of less than thirty, while in some larger ones, such as Liverpool and Edinburgh, it approaches one hundred. The differences between places are quite independent of latitude: the fact that the south of England does better than the north is evidently not because it is warmer or drier, but because a smaller proportion of the inhabitants is poor. The figure below illustrates the difference between the economic classes: the child of an unskilled labourer is more than twice as likely to die in the first year, as the child of a professional man. In later years the differences between the classes become still greater; no doubt this is because the inferior

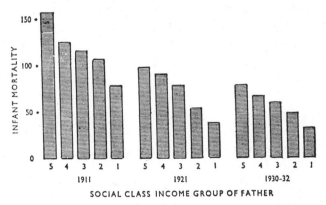

Infant Mortality. IM by social class of father in England and Wales. Class 1, the 'professional and managerial' group, is the richest, class 5 is the poorest

environment of the poor has a cumulative effect on the health of the growing child.

Improvement in the survival rate of working-class children has been opposed by a few; they say that large numbers of the 'unfit' – of weaklings – are consequently kept alive; there are then many who are unable to make an adequate contribution to maintaining themselves as useful members of society. This view is held in particular by those who believe the working-class to be genetically inferior. If this belief were true a fall in IM would be followed by a corresponding rise in mortality at later ages: relatively many of the weaklings would show their unfitness by dying before they reached old age. But no such effect is found. A lowered IM is always accompanied by lowered mortality in later years. Moreover, as death rates fall, so do sickness rates: that is indeed one reason why death rates are so much studied, since they provide a convenient index of health in general. Further evidence against the genetical inferiority of the poor is the fact that *congenital* malformations causing death in infancy are of roughly equal frequency in all classes; and these conditions are largely of genetical origin and little affected by environment.

The decline in IM in the Western countries undoubtedly reflects the better nutrition, housing, sanitation, and medical care, and not genetical change. It occurs in all classes, and it might be thought

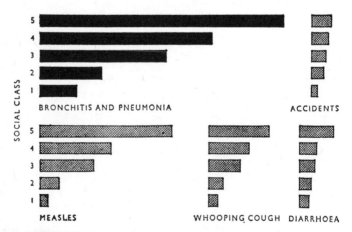

Infant Mortality. IM from five causes, by social group. Class 5 is the poorest

that differences between the different economic levels are of secondary importance. After all, the IM of the lowest income group in 1931, in England and Wales, was the same as that of the highest group in 1911. But a statistical study of IM by social class in England and Wales has shown that class differences are not only not diminishing: they are increasing. In 1911 a child in the lowest income group was three times as likely to die between the ages of six and twelve months as a child in the highest group; in 1931 it was *five times as likely to die* as a child in the highest group. The same point can be illustrated for the period since 1931. In 1931–2 the ten English county boroughs with the highest IM had an IM twenty-two per cent higher than the average for the whole country; in 1944–5 their IM was thirty per cent higher than the average. Since 1945, however, improvement has continued: the national IM is now, in the 1970s, well below thirty; and in the most favoured English towns it is below twenty.

Death rates, though still the most important, are not the only measures of national health. This is well shown by recent studies of death and sickness rates in the U.S.A. In 1900 there were about seventeen deaths for every 1000 people each year. By 1950 the rate was between nine and ten; since then it has been steady. This low mortality, for the whole country, conceals much variation in sickness among different classes. In a sample survey, members of families with an income of less than 2000 dollars a year lost on average about twenty-nine days every year from illness; at the other extreme, those with more than 7000 dollars a year lost about thirteen days. Some of this difference is no doubt due to low earnings *resulting* from sickness. But, more important, the amount of medical attention is lowest among the poor – who need it most. Better health services would not only relieve much suffering but would also be an economic asset by increasing productivity.

'MENTAL' HEALTH

Preventing infection is mainly a matter of applying existing knowledge. The same cannot be said of preventing (or curing) disorders of behaviour. Yet no survey of public health, however brief, is adequate if it ignores the psychological aspect. In Britain, at least one in three of doctors' surgery patients have conditions largely or entirely of nervous origin. These conditions often need as much attention, and sympathy, as those due to microbes or to a fractured bone, but unfortunately psychological medicine is still far behind bacteriology or orthopaedics.

One general advance, however, has been the recognition of the nervous or emotional influences which act on *all* parts of the body. In the past it has been usual to speak of human beings as if they

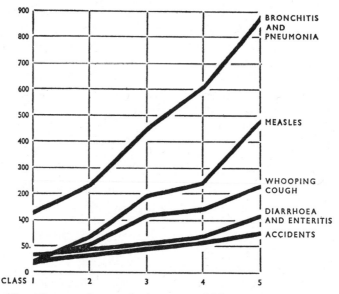

Mortality. The second year: deaths among children aged 1–2, per 100,000 legitimate live births in England and Wales, in relation to social class

consisted of two separate entities, a 'mind' and a 'body'; whereas in scientific psychology today it is commonly found convenient to speak of each individual as a single whole, in whom all parts interact. The same attitude is beginning to influence medicine. Hence we have the 'psychosomatic' approach to medicine, in which emphasis is put on the emotional or nervous causes of certain illnesses, such as ulcers, asthma, and many others, in which quite specific failures of certain organs (stomach, lungs, and so on) are evident. Unfortunately, the term 'psychosomatic' in itself perpetuates the mind-body distinction, since it is derived from Greek words meaning 'soul' or 'spirit', and 'body', respectively. Hence more strictly, the modern trend might be described as simply 'somatic'. Emotional changes, which we know in ourselves as feelings, are regarded as a function of the nervous system, influenced both by the internal state of the rest of the body and by what we see or hear.

There is no sharp division between the so-called psychosomatic conditions and the psychoneuroses which have been so much discussed ever since Sigmund Freud (1856–1939) published his theories on their causes. The psychoneuroses cover a vast field of abnormal behaviour, from a failure of function such as the hysterical paralysis of a limb, to a compulsion to wash the hands every half-hour. (Lady Macbeth is a portrayal of a disorder, due perhaps to repressed feelings of guilt, of this sort.) Owing, no doubt, to the publicity which psychoanalysis has received, they are generally thought of as illnesses which have to be dealt with by prolonged treatment of the individual sufferer. But, while treatment by psycho-analysis has perhaps thrown light on the causes of neurosis, its curative value is still not rigorously assessed; and in any case, the number of people who can be analysed, even by the shortest methods, is small compared with the numbers of sufferers. The only way of dealing effectively with many common conditions, such as chronic severe anxiety, sexual inadequacy and other emotional difficulties, is to prevent them. This makes psychological medicine a vital part of public health.

On how to prevent these disorders there is much to learn. One method of investigation is the social survey. A notable example is a recent study of the newly created English town of Harlow. The number of the unequivocally mad was low – less than one in a thousand. But about 330 people in every thousand had at least some neurotic symptoms. These people fell into two groups. About eighty out of a thousand had 'neurosis proper', defined as neurotic conditions which lead to consulting a doctor. This group includes a substantial number of severely incapacitated people, often with the serious illness called anxiety state. The second group is of those with an ill-defined, but very real condition, which includes 'nerves', depression, excessive irritability and sleeplessness. The authors of the survey are pessimistic about the prospects of treating neurosis proper when this is mainly due to adverse conditions of childhood. It is dismaying to realize that about one in twenty of their readers in Britain, America, and other countries belong in this group. Such people, though they may be living useful lives, require exceptional support from their family and friends.

How can we hope to prevent neurosis? This question cannot be answered with scientific rigour. Nevertheless, the current emphasis on the quality of relationships between people deserves thoughtful discussion. Many people feel, or seem to feel, that they are of little account. They lack self-confidence and a sense of belonging to a community or family. Such people may be excessively unassertive, or disagreeably aggressive. In either case the lack of self-love is accompanied by difficulty in loving others. Others are instead used, as sources of domination or as targets of sadistic humiliation. All such people, whether crushed or arrogant, are in fact excessively dependent on others. This feature has emerged most clearly in studies of what is misleadingly called the 'authoritarian personality'. During the Second World War research was done in England on German prisoners-of-war. Among them was a substantial minority of bullies. Their past histories and present attitudes were carefully investigated; an important finding was that they usually came from families in which the father was a tyrant and the mother submerged. By contrast, the sociable, 'civilized' individuals came rather from families in which the mother had been treated with greater respect and played a more positive part. Later this sort of investigation was carried out on a much larger scale in the United States, with similar results.

An important feature of the authoritarian personality is that the bully is also a lickspittle: he treats the weaker with brutality, but worships a dominant figure. This desire to be dominated by a powerful and admirable personality is to some extent present in all of us; only in some is it excessive; it then leads to the worship of a Hitler or some lesser tyrant.

The lack of ordinary affection and friendliness for others has been called alienation. A common feature is an apparent difficulty in seeing people as persons: a bureaucrat sees them in terms of man-hours, housing units and so on; a physician or nurse sees a patient as a case of diabetes or hysteria. This attitude is most serious when parents cannot treat their children as persons in their own right and deserving of respect.

On the ancient Greeks, Maurice Bowra has written: 'The city-state . . . fostered a freedom of intercourse, a sense of personality, and a social frame in which men were exposed to the full observation of their fellows but not prevented from being themselves.' The The conditions of a modern, urban, acquisitive society provide the opposite. A man feels at the mercy of impersonal forces which he is powerless to influence. The letters he receives are often not from persons but from organizations. The writers of these letters, when themselves human and not 'computers', are obliged to follow mechanical procedures which, too, have been laid down impersonally. Some people in this kind of society find security only in some such work. Men come to influence and distinction in such a state through wealth and the power it confers. Many people, accordingly, come to think that the proper aim of a man's existence is accumulating property or money, if necessary at the expense of others. This fundamentally anti-social attitude helps to alienate the individual from others. The majority live by selling their labour to an organization: they are units of production, not people; they are valuable as 'hands', not as individuals. Correspondingly, the value of education or of a health service comes to be assessed in terms of money and not of its effects on human beings.

The most widespread of our 'mental' ills are the least clearly defined – the minor neurotic traits and other sources of maladjusted behaviour. But true madness, or psychosis, is not rare. In the United States and Britain about one half of all hospital beds in use are occupied by patients under psychiatric care; and about two fifths of all beds by sufferers from the commonest sort of madness, schizophrenia. This and other psychoses are certainly influenced by the conditions in which people live. In the enquiry into Harlow, quoted above, much less psychosis was found in this new town than in a dormitory suburb with little social life or local employment; a 'decaying London borough', too, had more mad people.

Social environment similarly affects suicide – itself often an indication of psychosis. People are more likely to kill themselves in socially disorganized city centres than in stable communities. Economic disruption can probably have a similar effect. When the English cotton industry declined, the suicide rate among the people affected rose. In 1957 the cotton town of Burnley had twenty-seven suicides per 100,000 people, when the average for all England was twelve.

It would be wrong to dwell only on these depressing statistics. For reasons given in the previous sections, city populations in the advanced countries are becoming increasingly healthy and vigorous. The rate of growth of technology and populations is putting a heavy, if temporary, strain on human adaptability; but our increasing awareness of our problems is the guarantee that they will be solved.

PEOPLE AND 'STATISTICS'

This chapter, more than most, is full of numbers and percentages. It is therefore perhaps appropriate to quote a passage from a recent publication of the British Ministry of Health. 'Statistics may be dull things and are much abused by cynics, but they have provided the starting point for many of the advances in preventive and curative medicine and they will continue to do so.'

A topical example is primary carcinoma of the lung. In wealthy countries this form of lung cancer has been increasing so dramatically that it has been correctly called the greatest menace to public health of our time: in the period 1911 to 1919 the annual death rate due to lung cancer in England and Wales was about 250: in 1952, 11,981 men and 2,237 women died of it. In 1965 the total for both sexes was 26,000. Other countries have had similar increases. This is not merely due to better diagnosis. Research in Britain, the United States and elsewhere has established a statistical correlation between smoking, especially the heavy smoking of cigarettes, and lung cancer. The more a person smokes, the more likely he is to develop lung cancer; if he stops smoking, the danger is correspondingly reduced. Since this type of cancer is responsible for one in four of all cancer deaths in men, and for one in twenty of *all* male deaths in Britain, the matter is one of serious concern for large numbers of people, in fact for the whole community. According to a recent report by the United States Public Health Serivce, smoking also increases the chances of developing cancer of the mouth, larynx and oesophagus. Many men die of these hideous diseases when they are still in vigorous middle age. Smoking can also lead to an increase in respiratory infections, shortness of wind and chronic pharyngitis; and it is accompanied by an increased incidence of coronary artery disease and of defects of the blood vessels of the brain. In an American experiment, dogs were induced to inhale cigarette smoke.

Like men, they learned to like it. And like men, they developed emphysema. This diseased condition of the lungs kills about seventeen thousand people in the U.S.A. in every year, and is thirteen times more common among smokers than non-smokers. Finally, smoking by a pregnant woman can influence her unborn child: mothers who smoke have a higher proportion of still-born children than non-smokers, and their living newborn infants weigh less.

At least three governments, those of Britain, U.S.A. and the U.S.S.R., have issued warnings against the habit of heavy smoking among young people, though in Britain at least there is little evidence that the warnings have been heeded, except by doctors. A chief medical officer of the British Ministry of Health has said that, in the face of all the evidence, no rational person would go on indulging in the habit. Unfortunately, nicotine is a drug of addiction; smoking is also a social ritual; and the tobacco companies are wealthy and can maintain expensive advertising campaigns, regardless of the effects of their products on consumers.

The tar produced by burning tobacco can induce skin cancers in mice, and the research now going on, stimulated by the original statistical observations, will no doubt reveal much of interest and importance. The main fact, that smoking is causing emphysema, cancer and other diseases – and shortage of money – in increasing numbers of people, is, however, fully established. A few eccentrics have tried to obscure this fact, but most smokers merely do their best to forget it. It behoves all governments, all responsible persons, and above all broadcasters and other public figures, to discourage the young from developing the habit of smoking.

Lung cancer does not wholly depend on smoking for its development: some, though very few, non-smokers develop it. Further, there are proportionally higher numbers of lung cancers among town-dwellers than country-folk. Atmospheric pollution by smoke or petrol fumes is evidently responsible. (The occasional disastrous mortality, due to 'smog', in large cities, is of course nothing to do with cancer.)

Since nobody is addicted to fog or smog, and nobody makes a profit by selling it (though some save money by failing to abate it), it might be expected that strenuous efforts would be made to get rid of it, without the additional incentive of cancer prevention. A principal obstacle today is the automobile industry. Cars give off carbon monoxide, and in big cities, of which Los Angeles is only the most notorious, this and other products accumulate in injurious amounts. The only evident remedy is the replacement of our present poisonous vehicles by electric cars.

Other examples of the importance of 'statistics' have been given earlier in this chapter. To determine some of the main causes of rheumatic heart disease it was necessary to study sample groups of families, and to relate the incidence of the disease to various factors, including economic status and overcrowding. The techniques of sampling, and of correlating one group of facts with another, come under a particular branch of mathematics, statistical analysis. A statistician, when he uses his special methods, is taking the results of counting or measuring something – perhaps the number of persons suffering from a particular disease – and working out the significance of the results of the counting.

There is no more justification for criticizing the statistician for doing this than there would be for criticizing a farmer who reported that he owned forty dairy cows, and that thirty of them (or seventy-five per cent) were in milk. A possible reason why many nevertheless feel a distrust of 'statistics' – which generally means a distrust of general statements about large numbers of people or things – is that they are necessarily impersonal. For the statistician as such the latest group of deaths from some disease are, so to speak, just another few bits of information for the computer. We need to relate the results of his calculations to individual experience. It is one thing to read of the tens of millions of sufferers from chronic malaria, quite another to appreciate the suffering of these many persons, condemned throughout their lives to a debilitated existence in poverty and squalor. In discussing a community with a high infant mortality it is necessary to understand what the figures mean for the individual mothers who have to watch their babies die after a few days of vomiting and diarrhoea.

A book of this sort can do little more than report the facts of starvation or disease in general: the task of conveying what the facts signify, in terms of individual suffering or the relief of suffering, must be left to the journalist or the novelist writing of particular persons and incidents.

One lesson of this chapter is the immense power of modern bacteriology to prevent a great number of the worst diseases.

Although there are some serious gaps, our knowledge of the causes and means of prevention of infectious disease is remarkably complete. Cholera, the dysenteries, typhoid, typhus and smallpox not only can be, but in many countries have been, almost completely wiped out. Even malaria and yellow fever have been brought under control in some areas, and infected regions are, in the 1970s, diminishing steadily. Full application of existing knowledge could reduce tuberculosis and the main causes of death in infancy to a small fraction of the present total.

But the knowledge cannot be applied simply by the passage of laws or by government regulations. Just as food production and nutritional standards can be raised only as part of a general process of economic improvement, so the prevention of infectious disease requires vast expenditure on public health services, and education of the whole community to take advantage of them. In the long run such expenditure justifies itself not only by an increase in health and happiness, but also by the release for productive purposes of human energy which would otherwise be drained away by disease.

14

POPULATION

Be fruitful, and multiply, and replenish the earth, and subdue it: and have dominion over the fish of the sea, and over the fowl of the air, and over every living thing that moveth upon the earth.

GENESIS

AMONG animals our species is rather infertile: women bear as a rule only one child at a time, and the interval between children is seldom less than a year; often it is much more even in the absence of contraception. Nevertheless, in the most favourable conditions a large human population can double itself in about seventeen years. This rate of growth hardly ever occurs; but, for every four persons

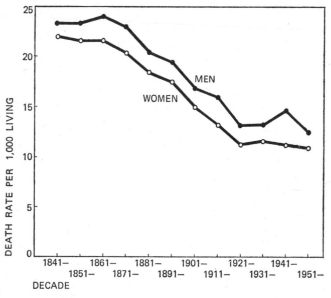

Mortality. The decline, during 110 years, in the mean annual death rate in England and Wales

alive in 1950, there were five in 1965; and, at the rates prevailing in the 1960s, there will be ten in the year 2000.

The first great increase in human numbers, as we saw in chapter 10, arose from the invention of agriculture: before that, food scarcity had evidently severely limited human populations. During the past seven thousand years food has still often been a limiting factor, but epidemic disease has also played a part in restraining population growth. Today, some populations are still increasing, while others remain roughly stationary. They may be facing, in the first place, famine and a greater incidence of infection; in the second, economic difficulties due to an increasing proportion of old people.

DEATH RATES

The death rate is the number of persons dying in one year, in each 1000 of population. Three kinds of influence affect it. First, the direct causes of death may become more, or less, effective: measles, for instance, seems to have become more virulent in the past fifty years, and scarlet fever less; also the incidence of crimes of violence, riot and war varies. But changes of this sort have, as a rule, only a minor importance. Second, death rates are influenced by changes in resistance to the causes of death: resistance may be within the individual, as when a poor diet impairs it, or outside – for example sanitary measures which prevent infection. The third factor is the age-composition of a population. If a population has many old people its death rate will be correspondingly high: some English south-coast towns, with favourable climates and excellent hygiene, have high death rates because many of their inhabitants have come to them on retirement.

The death rates referred to above are called *crude* death rates, but when the rates of two countries are compared we use *standardized* death rates: that is, we allow for differences in age composition. Recently the crude death rate in Sweden was twelve per thousand, while that of Australia was between eight and nine, but the standardized rates were almost identical. So, insofar as the death rate is a measure of health, Sweden and Australia had equally good health. The reason for the lower crude rate for Australia was the presence of immigrants in the prime of life, among whom the death rate is lower than that for other age groups.

In large parts of the world, but especially in the west, death rates have fallen strikingly since 1800. The most obvious cause has been improvement in the health services. Recently the rise in nutritional standards also has contributed. Other social changes have played a part: since about 1750 the availability of cheap cotton clothing, which can be washed, has made cleanliness easier and so has reduced infection. There are also political influences: wars and internal disorder tend to increase death rates, not only directly but even more by the social disruption they bring about.

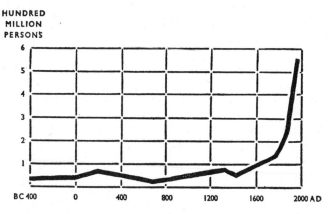

European Population. Estimates showing the recent striking increase in numbers, compared with the relatively steady state during the previous millennium

One way in which mortalities can be compared is by taking the *expectation of life at birth* for different places and different times. In England and Wales in 1841 it was just over forty years for men; in 1891 it was forty-four, and in 1931 nearly fifty-nine; today, in the 1970s, it is over sixty-eight years for men; for women it is over seventy-four. In India, between the two world wars, it was about twenty-five. In colonial Africa it was very low, and even fell during this century. In underdeveloped countries mortality is still much as it was in the ancient world: the mummy cases of Roman Egypt suggest that the upper-class Egyptians two thousand years ago had an expectation of life at birth of between twenty-five and thirty years; in Rome it may have been only twenty, but in some Roman provinces it was probably about thirty-five. The last figure is close to some of those computed for the Middle Ages: in Breslau in 1690, for instance, it is believed to have been about thirty-four.

These figures do not signify that most Indians, for example, die at about twenty-five: very many die in their first few months, and most of the remainder pass the age of thirty: the expectation of life is, in fact, only an average, and can be misleading unless the death rates at

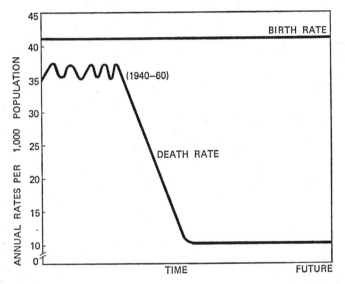

Scheme Representing Birth and Death Rates in Countries whose Living Standards are now Rising

different ages are kept in mind. This is illustrated in the figure on page 273.

This is illustrated in the figure on page 273.

BIRTH RATES

The decline in death rates has been followed in some countries by a decline in birth rates. For much of the world's population, however, birth rates are near the maximum. In Japan, China, India and Indonesia early marriage is almost universal and, except in Japan, family limitation is hardly attempted. The decline in birth rates has occurred on the whole in the countries where death rates have fallen most, and in particular where child mortality has been much reduced. Had there been no decline, the populations in these countries would have increased enormously in the past century, and most parents would be faced with the upbringing of between five and twenty children. In Britain in the mid-Victorian period each couple had on an average about six children born alive. The corresponding figure by 1925–9 was 2·2.

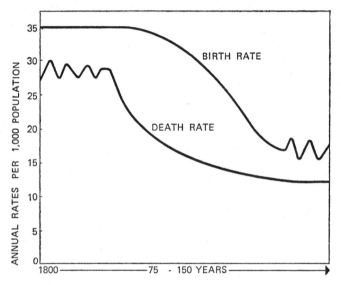

Scheme Representing Birth and Death Rates in Western Europe since 1800

The crude birth rate is affected by three main factors. First, as with death rates, it is influenced by the age distribution: births are almost confined to women between the ages of fifteen and fifty, and the birth rate depends on the proportion of such women in the population. The age distribution within the child-bearing range can also have some effect, since women are most fertile in their twenties. A second factor is marriage: there are fewer births the more women remain unmarried, or the more marriage is delayed. This has probably been important both in Europe and in the United States. In the U.S.A. the birth rate is reckoned to have fallen from fifty-five in 1800 to twenty in 1930; yet the proportion of women of child-bearing age rose during that period. Part of the explanation is an increase in the proportion of single persons, which was particularly marked in the census of 1890. Similarly, in Britain, age of marriage rose after 1871. By 1911 more people were marrying at ages twenty-five to twenty-nine than at twenty to twenty-four. (Recently, however, this trend has been reversed, and now the commonest age of marriage for women is about twenty-one.)

But the decline of fertility in the West cannot be attributed only, or even mainly, to less marriage. The decline has been so great that the obvious explanations have seemed to be inadequate, and some fancy ones have been put forward. For example, vitamin E deficiency reduces the reproductive capacity of some mammals, and it has been suggested that if we ate more vitamin E we might have more babies; but there is no evidence that we lack vitamin E: it is present in most foods. Then cleanliness has been accused of some responsibility in two ways. First, soap tends to kill human sperm and is indeed a good deal more spermicidal than some of the chemical contraceptives that have been widely used; perhaps soap in the vagina reduces fertility. But again there is no evidence. On the other hand there is some experimental basis for the second theory. Human sperm are killed at temperatures only a little above that of the scrotum in which the testes are suspended, and the application of hot water to the scrotum reduces the number of live sperm produced in subsequent ejaculations. Hence hot baths before retiring might reduce male fertility. An entirely different suggestion attributes lowered fertility to less coitus resulting from an increase in alternative sources of enjoyment. However, it is difficult to measure the extent to which people are enjoying life, and there is no evidence that enjoyment does lessen sexual activity.

The most obvious and probably the principal cause of the falling birth rates is the increasing use of contraception. The decline of the birth rate in most countries coincided with outbursts of birth-control propaganda. In most countries the rich set the fashion of small families, presumably because they were the first people who could afford contraceptive devices.

Further evidence comes from the fertility of groups of different religious faiths. In Holland and Canada, Protestant groups can be compared with Catholic, among whom birth control (except by means of the 'safe' period) is forbidden. Catholics have a much higher fertility. The low fertility of the nominally Catholic populations of France and Austria is held to be due to the decline of religious belief in those countries: certainly in Austria the birth rate in the country districts, where the Church is powerful, is higher than among the more sophisticated townsfolk.

An American investigation gives direct evidence on family planning in one group. White Protestant couples of good education were studied in Indianapolis; all had been married for twelve to fifteen years. Thirty per cent of these couples had planned every pregnancy: that is, pregnancy occurred only when contraception was stopped with the object of having a child. Among another fourteen per cent, at least the last child had been planned, and so the total number of children had been deliberately chosen. A further thirty per cent had the wanted number of children, but had not planned the last child and would have preferred to have it later. Hence in this inquiry seventy-four per cent of the couples had the number of children they wanted; and it was further found that most of the remainder had only one more than the desired number.

The evidence leaves little doubt about the part played by birth control in reducing fertility. In Britain, U.S.A. and other countries, in the 1970s, it is, however, no longer leading to a decline in birth rates. In Britain there has been a steady rise in the birth rate since 1955, although before that it had not changed for some years. In 1954, in England and Wales, rather fewer than 700,000 babies were born, but in 1961 nearly 900,000 – an increase of over twenty per cent. By 1963 the population of England and Wales was 47m., instead of the 45m. which had been expected in 1953.

GROWING POPULATIONS

Despite modern contraception, the main feature of the world population is its rapid increase. If present trends continue there will be over 4000m. people by 1980 – an increase of more than fifty per cent in thirty years. It was already 3220m. by 1964. Though we do not know, even now, exactly what the world population is, we have estimates of tolerable accuracy covering the last three centuries. In this period there has been what is now sometimes called the population explosion. The number of human beings has increased nearly four times. The increase has taken place in all continents, though it has been greatest among Europeans, who have increased seven times; only they have overflowed in large numbers, especially to

North America, and there are now more than 200m. outside Europe.

The 3000m. human beings are very unevenly distributed throughout the world. Europe, with 520m., is densely populated, and parts of Asia, with its total of more than half that of the world,

ESTIMATED WORLD POPULATION AND DISTRIBUTION BY CONTINENTS: 1800-1955

	1800	1850	1900	1913	1955
POPULATION IN MILLIONS					
WORLD	919	1091	1527	1723	2700
Asia	600	664	839	923	1680
Europe	188	266	390	468	588
Africa	100	100	141	135	223
N. and Central America .	15	39	110	134	245
South America . .	14	20	41	56	125
Oceania	2	2	6	8	15
PERCENTAGE DISTRIBUTION					
WORLD	100·0	100·0	100·0	100·0	100·0
Asia	65·3	60·9	54·9	53·6	52·7
Europe	20·5	24·4	25·5	27·2	26·1
Africa	10·9	9·2	9·2	7·8	7·5
N. and Central America .	1·6	3·6	7·2	7·8	8·8
South America . .	1·5	1·8	2·7	3·2	4·3
Oceania	0·2	0·2	0·4	0·5	0·5

Many of the figures in this table are only approximations, especially the earlier ones. China in particular, which now probably accounts for one-fifth to one-fourth of the world's population, had not had any adequate census during this period. The present (1970) population of China is probably about 700m.

Although the total increase in the population of Asia in the past 150 years has been about 1000m., its relative increase has been less than that of any other continent except Africa. Potential increase in both these continents has been checked by famine and pestilence. The enormous relative expansion in North and Central America, and to a less extent in South America, has been due to the emigration of Europeans who have subsequently rapidly increased in numbers. Correspondingly, the percentage of Asians and Africans in the world total has diminished. There is no question of 'whites' being swamped by other groups

also have dense populations. The Americas are more thinly occupied: North America has 187m. (1962) and Central and South America about 58m. and 125m. respectively. The population of Africa is estimated to be 223m., a small figure for a large continent. (These figures will, of course, soon have to be revised again.) The densely settled areas are southern China, India, Europe, and eastern North America. These all have fertile soil, adequate rainfall, navigable rivers, and coal and iron, and are well placed for trade.

The current increase in world population is not due to a uniform increase going on in all countries, but largely to the growth of the populations of India and Indonesia. Some smaller nations, such as Egypt and Ceylon, are also growing rapidly, and even Europe had 130m. more people in 1955 than in 1940; this was due mainly to increases in S.E. Europe. The United States, strangely enough, also has a quite rapidly increasing population. Of all these, India has the largest numbers. Since the First World War mortality in India and Pakistan has steadily declined, and will fall still more steeply if the health services proposed since the Second World War are made to work. During the twenty years from 1921 the population of India increased by 83m., and this rate of increase could, according to an official report published in 1946, easily be doubled if the health services were improved without a corresponding reduction in fertility. Today there is the possibility of a decline in fertility. As early as 1924 the birth rate among the Brahmins living in Madras was no higher than that of the Europeans, but Brahmins belong to a very small, privileged section of the community, and drastic social changes will be required in India and Pakistan before their example can be widely followed. The following estimated birth and death rates for India illustrate the position.

	birth rate	death rate
1881–91	49	41
1891–1901	46	44
1901–11	49	43
1911–21	48	47
1921–31	46	36
1931–41	45	31

If these trends continue we may expect the population of India and Pakistan to become 730m. by about 1980. For the whole of this

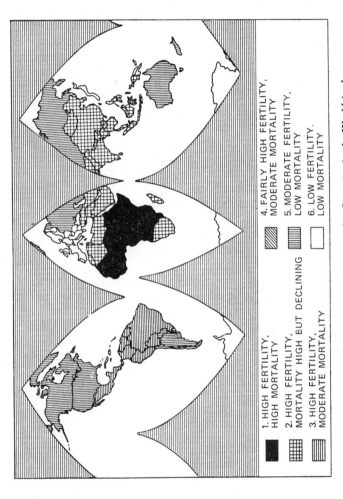

1. HIGH FERTILITY,
   HIGH MORTALITY

2. HIGH FERTILITY,
   MORTALITY HIGH BUT DECLINING

3. HIGH FERTILITY,
   MODERATE MORTALITY

4. FAIRLY HIGH FERTILITY,
   MODERATE MORTALITY

5. MODERATE FERTILITY,
   LOW MORTALITY

6. LOW FERTILITY,
   LOW MORTALITY

The Distribution of Various Types of Demographic Situation in the World in the 1950s

number to be adequately fed, food production in India will have to be nearly three times as great as it is now.

There is a similar situation in Indonesia. In Java, for instance, the population was about 4·5m. in 1815, 28·4m. in 1928, and about 50m. in 1945.

These are countries in which neither birth nor death rates have come under secure control. The same applied to China until recently, though now conditions are changing very rapidly; and it still applied to many of the South American countries. But in these, as far as we know, death rates are not falling as in India and Indonesia: they remain high, and in step with the high birth rates. Consequently the tendency to increase in numbers remains only latent. The Chinese population, by 1960 about 650m., may grow rapidly for a time, when health services, such as were introduced into Western Europe in the nineteenth century, become widespread. Until recently the Chinese population fluctuated violently owing to famines and epidemics, without any steady trend.

One further large population is still increasing, that of the U.S.S.R. It differs from all those so far mentioned, except that of the United States, in that both death and birth rates are declining. The birth rate in 1927 was probably about 45·0, whereas by 1959 it had fallen to 25·0. The death rate had, however, fallen further, from 26·0 to 9·0 – the same as that for the U.S.A.

DECLINING POPULATIONS?

Although their death rates are low, western Europe and the British Dominions have nearly stationary populations. In these countries birth rates have fallen enough at least to balance the much lowered death rates; if this were not the case their populations would have a standard of living more like that in the underdeveloped lands. The decline of fertility in the West, and among European populations generally, has led to a good deal of discussion of what has been called 'race suicide', the 'invention of sterility' and so on. Since about 1930 the main population problem has been represented as the 'twilight of parenthood' or the 'parents' revolt'. It might be. thought that the attainment of a stationary population when the death rate had been so much reduced would be a source of satisfaction. That it has been instead a source of alarm is due to the fear that the populations of some countries would fall rapidly: the apparent stability was thought to be illusory.

The prediction that European populations must decline depended on the study of the *net reproduction rates* of these populations. The net reproduction rate measures the extent to which a population is replacing itself. The need for a special means of measuring replacement can be illustrated by an example. Suppose an area, say, an island, were newly settled entirely by men and women of between twenty and thirty-five. The number of births per hundred persons would be exceptionally high, since every individual would be in the reproductive phase. There would also be a very low death rate, and so the population would increase rapidly. The rate of increase would, however, fall off as some of the original population grew old, and as the proportion of children increased. It might indeed turn out that, despite the initially high increase, the birth rate had not been high enough to maintain the population indefinitely at a steady level. For stability each mother must be replaced by another mother. This does not signify that each family should, on the average, consist of one daughter and one son: there is mortality to be allowed for, and the fact that some women never have any children. It is calculated that, in western Europe, for replacement to be assured, each couple who produce children should have, on the average, about 2·2. Given this, the net reproduction rate would be about 1·0 – the figure that represents a fertility rate just high enough to keep the population constant.

A number of countries have or had net reproduction rates of less than one. The indigenous population of France, indeed, where the net reproduction rate had until recently been below unity since the beginning of the century, began to decline, but now French fertility has been partly restored. An important question is whether there will be a decline elsewhere. Certainly, if the trends of the 1930s had continued for long the depopulation of some countries would have been startling. The population of the United Kingdom, if we ignore the effects of emigration and immigration, would have fallen to about 4·5m. in 2035.

Figures such as these must never be regarded as prophecies: they show only what would happen if the rates of a particular period continued unchanged. The likelihood of the maintenance of particular trends cannot be accurately assessed, because of the many

influences which affect the birth rate. The way in which net reproduction rates may mislead can be illustrated by a calculation made
in 1935, that the population of England and Wales would be 40·14m.
in 1947 if the prevailing trends continued. The actual population in
1947 was 43·02m. Moreover, the calculations made in 1935 suggested that by 1945 the population would be decreasing at the rate
of 125,000 a year; but in fact, the excess of births over deaths in the
first half of 1947 alone was 176,000. And, as already mentioned, since
1955 the birth rate in the United Kingdom has again risen.

The rise in fertility during the 1940s was common to a number of
very diverse European countries, including Eire, Czechoslovakia,
France, and the Scandinavian nations. Various explanations have
been suggested, including full employment, and better health
among the young men and women who became mature during this
period. There is little direct evidence on what factors have actually
been most important.

Although we cannot predict future populations with any precision, we have some idea of the motives which have led people to
limit their families. We saw that birth control, rather than any
increase in sterility, has been the probable means of family limitation, and it might be thought that the decline in fertility has been
simply due to the spread of knowledge of contraceptive methods.
But many inquiries have shown that the most used method even today is *coitus interruptus*, in which the semen is not discharged until the
penis is withdrawn; and this method (frowned on by psychologists)
must have been known for as long as the connexion between coitus
and conception has been understood. The spread of knowledge of
contraceptive methods has probably contributed, as we saw earlier,
but it seems unlikely that it was the primary cause.

The most obvious motive for family limitation is the burden
imposed on women by a large family. J. S. Mill wrote:

> The family is rarely a large one by the woman's desire, because upon
> her weighs, besides all the physical suffering and a full share in all
> privations, the unbearable domestic toil which grows from a large number
> of children.

But this was written at a time when, nevertheless, families remained
large. Children were, until very recently, an economic asset to their
parents. Apart from their ability to work when still very young, they

would probably be their parents' only support in old age. This seems to have been an origin of the practice, still kept up in some places, of a young couple awaiting the pregnancy of the woman before marrying.

Some Net Reproduction Rates

Country	Year	NRR
New Zealand	1937	1·00
	1960	1·90
U.S.A.	1959	1·74
Thailand	1954	1·70
Australia	1937	0·98
	1960	1·61
Netherlands	1960	1·46
Norway	1939	0·86
	1959	1·34
France	1939	0·90
	1960	1·28
England and Wales	1958	1·18
Yugoslavia	1959	1·08
Sweden	1941	0·84
	1959	1·04
Japan	1959	0·93
Hungary	1938	1·00
	1958	0·91

Today the economic motive for having a large family is much reduced: the lowered death rate makes it unnecessary to ensure the survival of one or two by having a large number; and old-age pensions and other social services reduce the likelihood of complete destitution even for the childless. Most parents reduce the size of their families but few voluntarily remain completely childless: the aim seems to be to have perhaps two or three children, but not more. (This disposes of such explanations as 'fear of war' for family limitation.) The important factor is probably the higher standard of child care now expected, and the heavy cost of maintaining it. In a survey in Britain after the Second World War the average age of mothers at the birth of a first child was found to be twenty-six in the most fertile income group, and even higher in other groups. The delay was evidently due to waiting until a certain income level or degree of security had been achieved.

It may seem anomalous that the decline of the birth rate begins among those who could presumably best afford a large family. Perhaps family limitation was at first not so much a function of wealth as of freedom from convention. This explanation, though speculative, fits the fact that the reproductive decline has recently spread to all economic classes. In fact, in Sweden, the tendency has for some time been for the richer families to have the larger numbers of children; and the same trend is beginning to be seen in the U.K. and U.S.A.

Probably, then, in the countries with net reproduction rates at about unity, family size is becoming stable in all classes at a fairly low level. When this seemed to threaten a decline in national populations, various attempts were made to prevent or arrest the decline in fertility. In France, the country with at one time the lowest net reproduction rate, a much-discussed system of family allowances was introduced during the First World War, and made the subject of a law in 1932. The allowances have been estimated to cover about half of the cost of each child. They did not prevent the continued decline in fertility, though they may have reduced it. Much the same applies to Italy, where there were a bachelor tax, and a higher income tax rate on bachelors and the childless, as well as family allowances. In Germany under the Nazis a number of minor measures were introduced, including marriage loans: there was a temporary increase in births, but no evidence of any long-term effect. In the United Kingdom small allowances for second and subsequent children were introduced in 1945. (A grant is not yet given for the first child.) Two years later a report on child-bearing in Britain, based on a nation-wide inquiry, commented as follows:

The costs of childbearing are so high that they are likely to deter many mothers, of all classes, from having children. It is not unlikely that, in many working-class families, this expenditure has to be met by borrowing or drawing upon savings. A substantial reduction in the costs of having a child is only likely to be achieved by lowering the price of baby clothes and equipment.

We may ask whether it is not necessary also to reduce the rents of larger houses and to increase their number, and to make the rearing of children, at a high standard of care, easier, by increasing services such as home helps and nursery schools. Security of employment may also turn out to be important. In 1949 the Report of the Royal Commission on Population commented on the 'economic and other handicaps of parenthood' of the period from 1910 onwards:

It remained true throughout the period that for most families the addition of children involved a substantial reduction of the family's standard of living, that the greater the number of children the smaller the chances of each child (and of the parents) of advancing in the competitive struggle and the greater the chances of falling back, and that some of the non-monetary costs of parenthood – the discomforts and risks of pregnancy and childbirth, additions to domestic work, restrictions on freedom, demands on nervous energy – increased more than proportionately with the size of the family. This is true despite the solid gains in human welfare that were achieved since the middle of the 19th century. Indeed, in the process of social advance, the position of parents and of members of larger families relative to others grew worse. The standard of living of the mass of the people rose, leisure increased . . . but the gap between parents and non-parents widened.

The attitude of governments and people towards the family has varied with time and still varies much between nations. Western European writers and publicists have sometimes simultaneously bewailed the lowered fertility of their own countrymen and the high fertility of the inhabitants of undeveloped lands. In the principal socialist countries, by contrast, the anxieties expressed in the 'west' were at first received with indifference or even derision. After socialist governments had come to power in the U.S.S.R. and China, little interest was taken in family planning. There was and is no unemployment; and there is plenty of space.

Today, however, the outlook on contraception has changed in both countries, and encouragement is being given to the use of sound methods. It is no longer held that populations can be left to

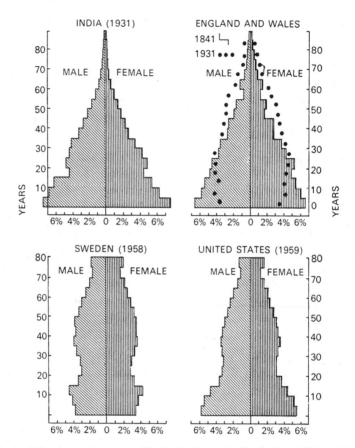

Age and Population. Age pyramids for India (1931), England and Wales (1841 and 1931), Sweden (1958) and the United States (1959). Each population is shown as a series of slabs one on top of the other: each slab represents an age group of five years, for example all the people between 30 and 35 years; the oldest are at the top. The width of each slab shows the percentage of the population made up by that age group. In 1841 England and Wales had an age distribution rather like that of India in recent times, with a high proportion of very young people; the 'pyramid' for England and Wales in 1931 shows the temporary effect of a heavy decline in birth rate. The eventual expected shape is an approximate rectangle (indicating few deaths in early or middle life) with a tapering top representing death among those over 60

themselves. In China it has been suggested that numbers might level off eventually at about 800m., that is, about thirty per cent more than in 1960. In India, too, (also on its way to socialism) efforts are being made to spread knowledge of and access to contraceptives. The new oral contraceptives, and perhaps still more the use of intra-uterine devices, may make these policies more quickly effective than could have been hoped until recently. The result, eventually, will be more than the regulation of numbers, for the health of both mothers and children will greatly improve.

FUTURE POPULATIONS

Every population may be regarded as having a place in a sequence of changes in which the ratio of births to deaths alters in an orderly manner. A country's population policy must depend on its position in the sequence.

The *demographic sequence* has three main phases. In the first both birth and death rates are high: in times of peace and abundance the population rises; famine, pestilence and war at other times bring numbers down. In 1950 about three-fifths of all people were in this phase of high potential growth; but, in this phase, the growth is repeatedly checked. In the second phase better social organization leads to a fall in the death rate, while the birth rate remains high; the population increases rapidly. This applied to about one-fifth of the world in 1950, but the proportion promises to rise. In the third phase approximate stability is reached, with both birth and death rates low. The net reproduction rate is about one; the population does not increase or decline steeply and, unlike that of the first phase, it also escapes severe fluctuations. The richest countries, such as those of Western and Central Europe, U.S.A., U.S.S.R., Australia and New Zealand, have nearly achieved this stability, though the population of U.S.A. has recently resumed quite rapid growth. This change in the U.S.A. is a result, not of a return to old-fashioned large families, but of a slight increase in the average size of small ones; instead of having two or three children, people are having three or four.

The occurrence of a sequence of changes in many countries does not signify that the sequence is inevitable. On the contrary, once described and understood it can be altered. The first, hesitant attempts at national control of populations are represented by the family allowances designed to increase fertility and to raise the living standards of the poor, and by campaigns on behalf of contraception designed to limit the size of families.

National policies apart, in countries with low fertility, the birth rate at least is much influenced by what is going on in the world. To establish this, the conception rate has to be studied; birth ráes

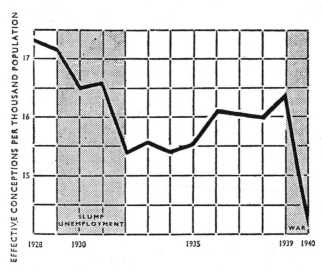

World Affairs and Fertility. Influence of world events on effective conception rate in England and Wales. The diagram is based on the number of live births

are affected by what was going on rather more than nine months earlier. In Britain the slump and unemployment of 1929–33 were accompanied by a steep decline in the conception rate in 1931–3; after this there was a rise which ended in 1939. During the first four months of war there was a steep decline, followed by a much smaller fall in the period of military inactivity. There was another steep decline after the fall of France. In the United States the economic depression of the 1930s was accompanied by a substantial fall in marriage rates, and in the births of children to couples already married. Facts of this sort suggest that reproduction could be rapidly influenced also by a policy designed to change fertility.

If this is so there is no reason to regard the fall in the birth rate in the western countries as anything but fortunate. Certainly a return to the large families of earlier times would not be regarded as tolerable. The most formidable population problem remains that of countries in which fertility is still uncontrolled, and where numbers are increasing rapidly or are likely to increase with improved conditions. Part of the answer to this, as we saw in chapter 11, must be a tremendous effort to increase food production. Another part of the answer is suggested by F. W. Notestein, an American authority:

The matter cannot be rigidly proved, but the writer is profoundly convinced that only a society in which the individual (child or adult) has a reasonable chance for survival in healthy life will develop that interest in the dignity and material well-being of the individual essential to the reduction of fertility. He therefore firmly believes in directly fostering public health *as part of the program required to reduce growth potential.*

To sum up, in the past famine and epidemic disease have limited populations, and in times of plenty man was at the mercy of his own fecundity. Today we know how to produce much more food and to prevent much disease; we are also beginning to learn how to control reproduction. For most of the world the question is, when will the knowledge be put to use?

15

PRIMITIVE MAN AND HIS FUTURE

The philosophers have only *interpreted* the world in various ways; the point however is to *change* it.

KARL MARX

THIS book describes some of the contributions that biological knowledge can make to modern problems. It has been written, and will be read, at a time of social upheaval, and it has not been designed as a detached, disinterested account of man, such as a biologist might give of a dung beetle or an earthworm. It therefore presents science as a product of society, and as belonging to it. This will seem to contradict the perhaps more usual image of science as a product of a few inspired persons studying truth for its own sake. But there need be no conflict. The search for truth is a part of the good life, and so is the attempt to apply knowledge to practical ends.

Scientific advance does depend to an important extent on the work of a few people with a special talent for discovery and interpretation; but the work of such people is related to the needs of their own time and country. Pasteur was one of the greatest of experimental biologists; all his major contributions to knowledge had an immediate application, though at the same time he and his colleagues made an advance in theoretical biology that was of the first importance. Pasteur helped to found the science of bacteriology, and showed the way to prevent a good deal of human disease; moreover a great part of his work was inspired, directly or indirectly, by the needs of French agriculture and the wine industry, and he gave them valuable help.

Not all scientific work is related so obviously to immediate needs. The other leading figure of nineteenth-century biology was Charles Darwin, and his theory of evolution had at first sight nothing to do with his social environment. But he was not functioning in an intellectual vacuum. The theory of the origin of species by natural selection was arrived at, not only by Darwin, but also simultaneously by Alfred Russel Wallace working independently. Simultaneous discovery by independent workers is common in the development of science, and a major advance is almost invariably a product of the work of a number of scientists, working on similar lines. Scientific advance is part of a general historical process, and is not due solely to the fortuitous appearance of isolated geniuses.

The idea of organic evolution – which had been put forward by various biologists for a century before Darwin – came to be accepted at a time of especially rapid social change. Both Darwin and Wallace were led to the theory of natural selection by reading the work of Malthus on human populations. Malthus' theories implied that it was useless to try to raise the living standards of the poor, since they would then only breed more rapidly and so exhaust the food supply. This outlook fitted well with the objects of the rising capitalists of the nineteenth century. Their attitude was: every man for himself, and the most enterprising will come to the top and rightly earn the greatest power and wealth. There is an analogy between this theory of how human society should work and the theory of natural selection.

Natural selection has indeed been invoked as a support for the policy of 'devil take the hindmost' among human beings, although the fallacy in the argument is obvious enough: even if natural selection operates throughout the organic world, it does not at all follow that it operates in human society; and, even if it did, we need not acquiesce in its doing so. A cut-throat struggle between individuals is unlikely to be anything but destructive of society.

One further fact illustrates the way in which Darwin reflected the ideas of his times: some years before Darwin's major work, *On the Origin of Species*, was published, Herbert Spencer put forward a theory of the survival of the fittest, as he called it, to support the prevailing views on human social relations. Thus a theory similar to Darwin's had already been advanced in sociology.

To say that Darwin's work reflected the contemporary state of society, or was influenced by it, is not to detract from Darwin's great achievements. Scientists are not remote and isolated individuals: they grow up in an environment like anybody else, they have parents who usually hold views which belong to their own times, and teachers who give conventional instruction. They are part of the society in which they live. Darwin and Pasteur exemplify a general rule in the relations of science to society.

Progress in the application of technical knowledge depends on the use made of the abilities of especially gifted persons, such as Pasteur and Darwin, together with those of many less able men and women. These abilities include the passion for inquiry which is sometimes represented as the main source of scientific advance. It is one source, but its scope is limited by the extent to which people are allowed to apply it. Today this depends on two things. First, a child with potential scientific ability can use it only if government or parents pay for a lengthy education. Second, if his particular gifts are directed towards one line of inquiry, say, the study of moulds, he will still be unable to apply them fully, unless it is thought by the government (or by some other body with funds) that the study of moulds deserves support. This example is taken because penicillin, one of the most valuable of chemical agents for preventing or curing infections, is produced by a mould; and in Britain the study of moulds and other fungi has been, and is, seriously neglected. But for this, use might have been made of penicillin soon after it was discovered in London in 1929, instead of more than a decade later. This would have involved the employment of a number of botanists, chemists, and medical scientists whose talents during that period were perhaps less well used.

Biological science today is still, as it was in earlier times, largely a product of the efforts of men to get what they want. This is true even though there are a few men and women who study it without any practical end in view, and unconscious of being influenced by the society in which they live.

Whatever the motivation of scientists, most people wish to know what use their work is. The most fundamental contribution of biology to the study of man is a general law which has been exemplified in almost every chapter. Every individual is the product of a complex development, in which the effects of the genes and of outside influences are continually interacting: neither heredity nor environment can properly be said to be the more important, though one may have more influence than the other in causing variation in particular features. If we are considering differences – physical or behavioural – between 'races', classes, or the sexes, this interaction has to be allowed for.

We then find that 'human nature' is much more varied and changeable than has commonly been supposed. Every 'race' is both exceedingly heterogeneous genetically, and also capable of rapid changes from generation to generation: that is, each includes people with all sorts of potentialities, and the expression of these potentialities varies with social organization. In palaeolithic society there was little opportunity for the expression of many of the qualities we most admire today, except courage, some manual dexterity, and, in certain periods, skill in the visual arts, although the appropriate genes must have been available. But any human group, in an appropriate environment, can produce individuals with a high level of technical skill, artistic ability, and social sense.

Just as there is no monopoly of virtue among races, so economic or social classes are of mixed heredity; they are indeed even less permanent and less distinct than racial groups, and ability is lost if the children of any group are forbidden access to education, or to particular trades or professions, on account of the poverty or social status of their parents. In most societies, moreover, the female sex as a whole occupies, quite unjustly, an inferior social position.

Although heredity and environment are equivalent in individual development, they are not equally important when we come to action. There is at present little to be done to alter human genetical constitutions (though it is a different matter with domestic animals): if we find a group of persons of poor physique, low intellect or criminal tendencies we must alter the environment in which it has developed.

The emphasis on environment as alterable, while heredity is regarded as practically fixed, may seem to conflict with a second great biological principle. Just as each individual is a product of heredity and environment, so mankind as a whole is a product of evolution. Evolution depends on the survival of some genetical constitutions and the disappearance of others. But the genetical changes in populations occur on a quite different time scale from that of the changes in human society. *Homo sapiens* has barely had time to undergo even slight evolutionary change in 70,000 years. Yet in less than ten thousand years he has moved from savagery to civilization, and civilization has taken on progressively more complex forms. Today social change has become even more intense. This is because science has transformed, not only food and sanitation, but also power, transport and communications, and the mass production of goods, such as clothes, which had formerly been made individually by craftsmen or in the home.

But now scientific methods have a much wider range. For instance, we no longer need take for granted traditional building methods: in the words of one report, 'At present, . . . we drag more than 100 tons of material to the site of every house, when less than 5 tons would produce a house that would be much warmer and take less coal to heat it.' Inside the house the kitchen can be designed so that it fully meets the convenience of those who work in it, cooking can be done with little or no destruction of food content, and food can be kept without suffering decay or infection with disease germs. Similarly, in the factory, operational research can minimize fatigue, danger of injury, and loss of time; and this is not only a matter of such obvious things as ventilation and lighting, but may extend to the colour of the paint and whether workers should listen to music while they work.

Advances of this sort often depend on research requiring the help of laymen in large numbers. And once the research has been done the intelligent collaboration of the public is even more necessary. Diphtheria immunization is a notable example of what has already been achieved. Science is still often regarded as something remote – the property of a select few whose knowledge the majority of people cannot hope to share and whose outlook ordinary men would not think of adopting. The barriers are being broken down as the role and scope of scientific knowledge become more obvious to non-scientists, and as the scientists themselves become increasingly involved in the social and political turmoil.

The business of making the whole of society scientific has begun in a few countries with the acquisition of a general understanding of the nature of infectious disease; and, in the physical sciences, with the development of popular knowledge of, for instance, electricity. But there is still nowhere a widespread understanding of scientific method, even among those with a superior education, and there will probably be none until children have the opportunity to practise it in school. At present, education remains in the pre-scientific phase: we are told what we ought to think, instead of having to discover things for ourselves and to exercise our powers of criticism.

Probably parents who have recently co-operated in the mass testing of vaccines have learnt more of scientific method in doing so than they did throughout their schooling. In one group of tests, in which the parents of seven English boroughs co-operated, new whooping-cough vaccines were on trial: some thousands of infants were injected, one half with a vaccine and the remainder, the 'control' group, with a mixture outwardly similar but not containing the material under test. Neither the parents nor the doctors who administered the vaccines knew which was which: all injections were numbered, and the key was kept by the Medical Research Council. Two years after injection each child was observed again, and a comparison made of the incidence of whooping-cough in the various groups: if there is much less whooping-cough in an experimental group than in the control, that is evidence for the effectiveness of the vaccine given. In this case one vaccine showed great promise. The investigation illustrates the need for working with large numbers, and for controls and other rigorous precautions. When this sort of thing is generally understood it will no longer be possible for a responsible adult to take a patent medicine for some complaint, and to attribute his eventual recovery to the medicine without any other evidence of its efficacy.

Just as scientific advance leads to questioning of conventions about, say, housing and food, so it may also prevent us from taking moral ideas for granted. In 1941 C. H. Waddington wrote:

The contribution which science has to make to ethics, . . . merely by revealing facts which were previously unknown or commonly overlooked, is very much greater than is usually admitted. The adoption of methods of thought which are commonplaces in science would bring before the bar of ethical judgement whole groups of phenomena which do not appear there now. For instance, our ethical notions are fundamentally based on a system of individual responsibility for individual acts. The principle of statistical correlation between two sets of events, although accepted in scientific practice, is not usually felt to be ethically completely valid. If a man hits a baby on the head with a hammer, we prosecute him for cruelty or murder; but if he sells dirty milk and the infant sickness or death rate goes up, we merely fine him for contravening the health laws. And the ethical point is taken even less seriously when the responsibility, as well as the results of the crime, falls on a statistical assemblage. The whole community of England and Wales kills 8000 babies a year by failing to bring its infant mortality rate down to the level reached by Oslo as early as 1931, which would be perfectly feasible; but few people seem to think this a crime.

While for many such ideas are quite new, for some they may already seem nothing but common sense. Science itself has indeed been defined as organized common sense. But getting general agreement on new attitudes is not simply a matter of the steady spread of knowledge, as education becomes more widespread and more fitted to current needs. There is no walk-over for common sense. It is not only ignorance or even conservatism that has to be overcome: there is also active opposition.

There are plenty of examples from the subject matter of this book. Lies about race differences are promulgated by those who wish to use subject groups as a source of cheap labour, or for a background for wars of conquest. Class differences are said to be inherited and fixed, by those who profit from the existence of a privileged class with economic and political power over the rest. Food and patent medicine manufacturers advertise their products with misleading statements about their chemical composition and lies about the working of the body and the causes of disease. This propaganda has full scope in at least the advertisement columns of the daily newspapers; moreover the newspaper proprietors depend financially on the advertisers and cannot as a rule afford to expose them even if they wish to do so. Education can provide an antidote only if teachers can transcend the prevailing propaganda and do much more than reflect the ideas of the community to which they belong.

The full application of the modern knowledge of human biology, as of science in general, is impossible while there remain powerful groups with vested interests in ignorance and unscientific ideas. Throughout human history there are instances of drastic changes in social organization accompanying technical advances. The transition from primitive communism to government by priest-kings over populations of slaves and peasants followed the development of agriculture. In the West, states based on slavery collapsed and gave place to serfdom in a feudal society at the same time as new techniques in agriculture and other production came to be used. Feudalism in turn was replaced by capitalism when the physical sciences were

applied to industrial production. In the same way, today, the application of science for human good demands further social change.
The need for change, however obvious, is always denied, not only by
those whose special interests might be upset, but also by those ruled
by the principle that 'nothing should ever be done for the first time'.
The latter are, perhaps, the more numerous.

The application of biology calls for changes in at least two ways.
First, food production by modern methods depends on large-scale
planning and organization; it cannot be done by peasants working
small plots independently, in a chronic state of indebtedness to
money-lenders or banks. Even in the United States, where farms are
large, the problems of soil erosion have obliged the farmers and
other producers in some large areas to accept communal enterprise.
The problem of food production today is a problem for society as a
whole, and not for the family or village or the individual landowner.
This is only one example of the need for a planned economy. There
are many others.

Secondly, applying science to food production and disease prevention requires an educated people in which all adults are capable
of taking an active part in these social enterprises. We could not hope
for such a population anywhere, if in each country there were many
people genetically ineducable. There is no evidence for the existence
of such inferior groups; yet even now, in the world as a whole, only
a minority have access to learning. (All the readers of this book
belong to the minority.) These facts lead to the third major social
implication of the application of biology, and indeed of science in
general: we cannot make use of science properly while small
privileged minorities have a monopoly of knowledge. We must
therefore be rid of the social or economic divisions into classes as
they exist in most countries today. We shall then free ourselves at
the same time of the smaller groups whose positive interest it is to
promote ignorance.

As an example, employers often have experts to advise them on
methods of reducing the labour of production, and they employ
methods such as 'time and motion study' which can have a sound
scientific basis. In Britain and the United States these methods are
often opposed by trade unions, on grounds such as the excessive
speed-up which they impose on the workers. Yet scientific methods
could be used to make it easier and pleasanter for workers to

perform their tasks, provided they were applied with regard to their interests.

We are far from applying science fully to humanitarian ends today. Lord Boyd Orr, on the eve of his retirement from the position of Director-General of the Food and Agriculture Organization, said:

If the food problem is not solved there will be chaos in the world in the next fifty years. The nations of the world are insane, they are spending one-third of their national incomes preparing for the next war. They are applying their energies to building up a war machine instead of applying the world's steel and industrial production to conserving the resources of the land. That is the only basis of civilization.

Two years after the end of the Second World War, of £110m. spent by Britain in a year on scientific research and development, £67m. was devoted to war science; and the proportion in the United States was almost exactly the same. Since then in both countries the proportion has risen. Until scientific work is planned for peace, and not for war, we can hardly hope to make much progress towards a prosperous, egalitarian world society.

It must not be thought that the society to which we look forward is a vision of a scientific utopia peopled by robots. It is the tedious, automatic tasks that can most easily be done by the machines, and the more this happens the greater will be the demand for individual enterprise and ability. A part of mankind has already been liberated from the toil from sunrise to sunset which has been the lot of most men and women since agriculture began; but many of those so freed have been forced to work as long hours in worse conditions in industry, and to live in conditions of unprecedented squalor in industrial towns. Today, however, we have the technical knowledge needed to free men from slavery to production.

To make the fullest use of the liberty so acquired men and women must first have the basic essentials of food, good health, and shelter. But they must also have access to the refinements of civilized life. The printing press promoted the spread of literacy and the production of written works for popular use. The development of various forms of democracy also depended on it. Today television, radio, and the cinema are at least capable of taking us several steps further.

The new means of communication are, however, only partly used for worthy ends. A popular press with a systematic policy of vulgarity and deception has long done its best to corrupt its readers and to conceal from them all that could improve their understanding of the world or inspire enthusiasm for solving its problems. Now, advertisers are using press and radio to distort still further both the intellect and the emotions of their vast numbers of victims. Concepts of psychology, arrived at by men of great ability devoted to the ends of healing or education, are being perverted in order to persuade people to buy *this* overpriced commodity rather than *that* (of equal worth); worse still, efforts are made to induce still more acquisitiveness and competitiveness than already exist in our money-worshipping society: hence anxiety is aroused lest some spurious standard of expenditure is not attained.

Fortunately, the idea of cars, television sets, and so on as 'status symbols' has soon become the object of derision, through the good sense of the many who have been able to discern the racketeering behind the advertisements. Nevertheless, much harm has been and is being done. And the advertisers, whose activities are at the best an instance of monstrous waste of materials, labour, and ability, have the impudence to state that their work helps in the creation of wealth.

Despite our technical skill, the ability to photograph the other side of the moon or to circumnavigate Tellus in 108 minutes, we are still in a substantial sense primitive man. And until the captains and the kings depart we shall remain so; with them must go both the publicity men and, more important, their masters whose social role is to create material wealth for a minority without regard to any other considerations whatever.

Only then shall we be free to apply scientific knowledge wholeheartedly to human wellbeing. It is in action that the full implications of human biology must be learnt. Many will grasp the fallacies of race theory more easily by working with men and women of different colour than by reading books about it. The facts of nutrition or infectious disease are brought home to many for the first time when they are faced with the upbringing of their children. Certainly the small families of the West are more readily understood when one has become a parent.

Use and understanding go together. The attempt to reach some limited objective, such as a piped water supply or adequate sanitation in a village, can make real the knowledge passively acquired in school or by reading; it may also create a demand for more knowledge, which can be satisfied only by further reading. But the reading, if it is to be more than the casual acquisition of knowledge by a dilettante, must be an adjunct to action. This book tells a number of unfinished stories. The stories are being continued by the men and women who are working to apply the knowledge that we have.

BIBLIOGRAPHY

BIBLIOGRAPHY

ANDREWES, C. *The Common Cold*, Weidenfeld, London, 1965. An authoritative review for laymen.

ASHLEY-MONTAGU, M. F. *An Introduction to Physical Anthropology*, Thomas, Springfield, Illinois, 1960. An excellent outline for students.

BARNETT, S. A. (editor). *A Century of Darwin*, Heinemann, London, 1958. A centenary volume of fifteen essays on many aspects of evolution.

BARNETT, S. A. *'Instinct' and 'Intelligence'*, Penguin Books, Harmondsworth, 1970. An outline of animal behaviour with some human implications.

BERNAL, J. D. *Science in History*, Penguin, Harmondsworth, 1968. The growth of science, in all its aspects, from the prehistoric to the present, and the relations of science and scientists to other aspects of social organization, including a critique of the social sciences.

BERNAL, J. D. *Social Function of Science*, Routledge, London, 1952. The outstanding work on this subject.

BIBBY, G. *Four Thousand Years Ago*, Collins, London, 1962. A superbly readable account of the second millennium B.C.

BURNET, F. M. *Viruses and Man*, Penguin Books, Harmondsworth, 1953. An admirably written account of the smallest organisms.

CARR, D. E. *The Breath of Life*, Gollancz, London, 1965. Lively, short account of the deadly effects of air pollution.

CHILDE, G. *What Happened in History*, Penguin Books, Harmondsworth, 1942. A stimulating review of the main developments in human history.

CLARKE, R. *We All Fall Down*, Penguin Books, Harmondsworth, 1969. On biological and chemical warfare. Unfortunately, essential reading for the informed citizen.

COMFORT, A. *Sex in Society*, Penguin Books, Harmondsworth, 1964. Refreshingly rational and independent.

DURNIN, J. V. G. A., and PASSMORE, R. *Energy, Work and Leisure*, Heinemann, London, 1967. Energy use and misuse in activities ranging from croquet to coal mining.

ELTON, C. *The Ecology of Invasions*, Methuen, London, 1958. A highly readable and authoritative review of disturbances of the 'balance of nature' brought about by man, and of the remedies.

FROMM, E. *The Fear of Freedom*, Routledge London, 1961. An absorbing essay on the psychology of authoritarianism and neurosis in modern society.

HARRISON, G. A., and others. *Human Biology*, London, Oxford University Press, 1964. A textbook.

HOBSON, W. *World Health and History*, Wright, Bristol, 1963. The story of the great infectious diseases and their defeat.

HUTCHINSON, J. (editor). *Population and Food Supply*, Cambridge University Press, Cambridge, 1969. Eight informative essays.

LERNER, I. M. *Heredity, Evolution and Society*, Freeman, San Francisco, 1968. An outstanding elementary textbook.

MACPHERSON, C. B. *The Real World of Democracy*, Clarendon, Oxford, 1966. Stimulating talks on the meanings of 'democracy'.

MATHER, K. *Human Diversity*, Oliver & Boyd, Edinburgh, 1964. Variation among men, and its social implications, for the layman.

MEDAWAR, P. B. *The Future of Man*, Methuen, 1960. The broadcast Reith lectures of 1959.

MELLANBY, K. *Pesticides and Pollution*, Collins, London, 1970. A notable contribution to human ecology.

ORR, J. B. *As I Recall*, MacGibbon & Kee, London, 1966. Autobiography of the first Director General of the Food and Agriculture Organization. Both inspiring and shocking.

PEEL, J., and POTTS, M. *Textbook of Contraceptive Practice*, Cambridge University Press, Cambridge, 1969.

PENROSE, L. S. *Outline of Human Genetics*, Heinemann, London, 1959. A short but authoritative introduction for a wide public.

PENROSE, L. S. *The Biology of Mental Defect*, Sidgwick & Jackson, London, 1963. An important book, with implications far beyond its title.

PIRIE, N. W. *Food Resources Conventional and Novel*, Penguin Books, Harmondsworth, 1969.

WADDINGTON, C. H. *The Scientific Attitude*, Hutchinson, London, 1968. The nature of scientific thought, and the relations of science to art and politics.

YOUNG, J. Z. *Doubt and Certainty in Science*, Clarendon Press, Oxford, 1950. Broadcast lectures with additions, mainly on the human brain.

INDEX

INDEX

Page numbers in bold type indicate line drawings in the text

Nose:
 evolution of, 112, **109**
 shape and 'race', 142–5, 148
Notestein, F. W., 305
Nucleus, 21, 57, 80, 58, 73
Nutrition, 19, 201, 217–29, chapter 12
 passim
 class and, 247
 during pregnancy, 48–9
 in China, 248–9
 in India, 242
 in Thailand, pls. 17–18
 in UK, 241–5, 247–8
 in USA, 245–6
 in USSR, 246
 in world population, 193, 228–31,
  241, 247–8, 314
 national income and, 245–6
 of foetus, 63
 personal income and, 244–8, 273
 'race' and, 151–2
 work and, 152, 242

Obesity, 118, 235–6
Oestrogen, *see* Oestrogenic hormone
Oestrogenic hormone, 29, 31
Oestrous cycle, 27
On the Origin of Species, 307
Oreopithecus, 107
Orgasm, 39
Orr, J. B., 244–5, 314
Osteomalacia, 240
Osborn, F., 211–12
Ovary, 24 ff., 32 ff., 23–4, 27, 30
'Over-production of food, 228–9
Ovum, *see* Egg-cell

Palaeolithic age, 197, 309, **102**
 art of, 198
Panama Canal, 260
Panama disease of bananas, 214
Paranthropus, 98, 100
Passmore, R., 237
Pasteur, L.2, 256, 306, 308
Pasteurization of milk, 256
Patent medicines, 311–12

Pathans, 151
Peking man, 102 ff., 196, **114**
Pellagra, 238, 240
Pelvic organs, female, 45
Penicillin, 308
Penis, 39, **22**, 38
Pepys, S., 259
Perceptual generalization, 127
Pernicious vomiting in pregnancy,
 49–50
Pesticides, 216–17, 226
Pests, 213–17, 225–6, 251
Pharaohs and inbreeding, 85
Phosphorus in food, 238
Pill, contraceptive, *see* Birth Control
Piltdown man, 108
'Pining' disease, 224
Pithecanthropus, 101–2, **103**, 113
Pituitary gland, 28–32, 118
Placenta, 46–51, **41**, 47–8
Plague, 177, 257–8, pl. 19
Plankton, 227–8
Plant growth hormone, 225
Plasmodium falciparum, 177
Plato, 170
Plesianthropus, 98, **98**
Plough, 202
Pneumonia, 256, **256**, **269**
Poliomyelitis, 267–9, 271
Pollution, atmospheric, 283–4
 radiation, 81–2, 208
Polymorphism, 174
Polynesians, 155, 177, pls. 10–11
Polytypy, 142, 174
Population, 218, 220, 286–305
 age distribution of, **302**
 ageing of, 230
 cycle, 303–5
 decline, supposed, 296–303
 densities, 136, 199, 209, 230
 growth, 202, 303–5
  agriculture and, 199–201, 210,
   230, 287, **227**
 of China, 248, 293, 296, 303
 of France, 297
 of India, 242, 294, **302**